DATE DUE

HIGHSMITH 45-220

FUTUREWORK

FUTUREWORK

The Revolution Reshaping American Business

Edward E. Gordon
Ronald R. Morgan
Judith A. Ponticell

PRAEGER

Westport, Connecticut
London

Library of Congress Cataloging-in-Publication Data

Gordon, Edward E.
    FutureWork : the revolution reshaping American business / Edward
E. Gordon, Ronald R. Morgan, Judith A. Ponticell.
       p. cm.
    Includes bibliographical references and index.
    ISBN 0–275–94848–X
    1. Employees—Training of—United States. 2. Employer-supported
education—United States. I. Morgan, Ronald R. II. Ponticell,
Judith A. III. Title.
HF5549.5.T7G547   1994
658.3′124—dc20   93–39380

British Library Cataloguing in Publication Data is available.

Library of Congress Catalog Card Number: 93–39380
ISBN: 0–275–94848–X

First published in 1994

Praeger Publishers, 88 Post Road West, Westport, CT 06881
An imprint of Greenwood Publishing Group, Inc.

Printed in the United States of America

The paper used in this book complies with the
Permanent Paper Standard issued by the National
Information Standards Organization (Z39.48–1984).

10 9 8 7 6 5 4 3 2

Copyright Acknowledgments

The authors and publisher gratefully acknowledge permission for use of the following material:

Figure 2.3 and Figure 2.4, reprinted from J. W. Pfeiffer (Ed.), *The Encyclopedia of Team-Building Activities*, San Diego, CA: Pfeiffer & Company, 1991. Used with permission.

Figure 8.6, Figure 8.7, and Figure 8.8, reprinted from Richard A. Swanson and Deane B. Gradous, *Forecasting Financial Benefits of Human Resource Development* (San Francisco: Jossey-Bass, 1988). Copyright © 1988 by Jossey-Bass Inc., Publishers. Used with permission.

The following trademarked terms have been used by permission of Imperial Corporate Training & Development: FutureWork™ , Work Force Education™ , Work Force Education Triad™ , Individualized Instructional Programs™ , and Management Insight Development Programs™ .

Figures 4.2, 4.3, 4.4, 4.5, 4.6, 6.7, 8.2, 8.4, 8.5, 8.9, 9.4, and 10.4, used with permission of Imperial Corporate Training & Development.

Figure 10.3, from Clarke Goward Fitts Matteson Advertising Inc. Reprinted with permission.

This book is dedicated to the goal
that every person will achieve
his or her maximum human potential
through lifelong education.

Contents

Figures

Preface

How can the typical American business better educate more of its people to survive the relentless pressures of galloping technology, the demand for ever higher quality, and international competition? We answer with this formula for an effective 1990s business strategic plan:

> Employee Education = Competitiveness

FutureWork is our second collaborative effort. The first, *Closing the Literacy Gap in American Business,* already has found many interested readers both inside and outside the business community. In this current work, we have expanded the range of our research and findings to include a number of the areas now offered in the corporate classroom. However, many of these suggestions are just as applicable to students in school or to adult learners anywhere.

We remain very concerned that not enough small, midsize, or even large American companies include employee training and education as a serious part of their overall strategic business plan. The U.S. economy is increasingly lagging behind the rest of the world because we have too many people at work who need more appropriate education. School reform is coming. But the average business cannot wait any longer for it to "breakout" in its local community.

We have talked with too many corporate presidents who lament that their TQM, ISO-9000, business re-engineering or team programs are languishing because "the people don't comprehend what we're saying." However, many in management still believe that it takes a four-year college degree for an employee to be able to develop meaningful abstract reasoning and problem-solving abilities. Others may believe in their people's potential to find workplace solutions but refuse to act because they "haven't found the right training program."

This book contains our pragmatic business applications for employee development. These offer not just skills and training but also education that develops the individual thinking needed for TQM, ISO 9000, or other quality-team business programs. Our goal is to enable trainers to increase the power and scope of educational programs for the workplace.

This book presents compelling arguments and applications for a more cognitive training approach in every workplace. We believe that these ideas offer many more useful opportunities for trainers and educators to better satisfy individual learners' work needs. These include the increasing demand for training, skills, and education programs that develop the employee thinking, problem-solving, and comprehension abilities required by all service or production businesses. This Work Force Education Triad of training, skills and education encompasses our vision of FutureWork (see Figure P.1). It may very well establish the educational parameters for America's international economic success as business enters the twenty-first century.

We begin by discussing the leadership challenge throughout American business, and how training has evolved since the early nineteenth century to meet workplace needs. FutureWork is introduced as the next developmental step for modern business.

A brief overview is then given of behavioral- and cognitive-based training. There is great potential in using cognitive learning concepts to empower more people for quality and workplace leadership, and to move beyond behavior-based training techniques. We know how to better develop most workers' learning abilities to comprehend information, solve problems, and increase personal motivation.

The next two chapters explore the skills component of the Work Force Education Triad: how a business can train people to "learn how to learn" and give them the necessary basic educational skills (reading, writing, mathematics, etc.) required to participate in the team management of a modern workplace.

We then tackle the issue of what behavior-based training (the second component of the triad) can and cannot do in the development of employee creative thinking. Most businesses are rapidly moving away from controlling behavior and in the direction of developing insight for more people throughout the organization.

This leads to the examination of the last component of our triad — education, built on a cognitive training approach that better supports teams and quality issues. We discover effective ways that may increase the thinking abilities of most people in the workplace.

We then address the belief that an adult's personal intelligence (IQ) is rigid and cannot be altered through company training. Most adults are not necessarily limited by their lack of prior education or poor teaching-learning experiences. They can expand their knowledge and intelligence well beyond what has been popularly accepted, if cognitive learning practices are built into workplace learning.

In our chapter on assessment we offer trainers specific guidelines for "proving it works!" Training has long been criticized as the "fifth wheel" of business. It makes you feel good but has no direct economic bearing on the bottomline.

Figure P.1
FutureWork: The Revolution Reshaping American Business

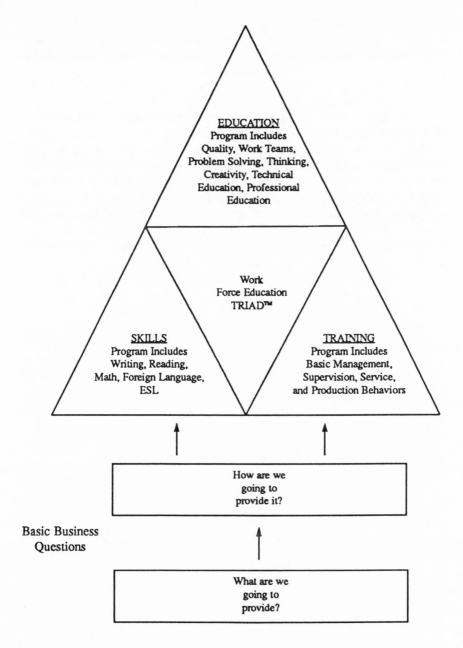

We examine realistic bottomline ideas to measure training results based on participant reaction, adult learning, behavior changes, and return-on-investment models.

We then consider the "how to" concepts for cognitive-based training programs. From our own work and the research of many others, we offer trainers specific, concrete ideas on using cognitive learning principles in the preparation of their own instructional courses.

Finally, we look to how FutureWork will meet the developing needs of American business well into the twenty-first century. We outline our recommendations as the strong medicine for American business that will help build people's leadership throughout the organization.

The message of FutureWork is very clear. If we choose, America now has the knowledge and tools to "reinvent" a far more competitive business environment for the next millennium. Those businesses that get serious and adopt substantive, lifelong education for all their people have a far better opportunity to survive, grow, and prosper. However, the United States has run out of "disposable" people. Those businesses that decide they cannot afford to invest in their human capital, increase the likelihood of someday appearing as an "obituary" in the *Wall Street Journal*.

Acknowledgments

Joint collaboration is indeed more of a practiced art than a precise science. Judy Ponticell, Ron Morgan, and I have worked diligently together to make what we hope are important, and at times complex ideas, more understandable to a wider reading audience. This has not been an easy task.

To whatever extent we have failed in our mission, we fully take the blame. However, for readers who find this book provocative or even useful, we wish to acknowledge the many other people who helped us better craft our ideas or contributed new information.

Above all others we are extremely grateful to Elaine H. Gordon, a research fellow at the North American Institute for Training and Educational Research. Her expert editing, research, and pertinent criticism of this entire manuscript greatly improved the final product. We also wish to thank the Institute for its general support of our ongoing field research that has made the publication of this book possible. Contributions were also made by Jill Sheehan of EHS Health Care, Nicole Lascola of Hinckley & Schmitt, and Ann Zimmerman of Xerox. Their ideas helped to clarify our training concepts.

Many companies are mentioned in this book that are representative of our ongoing field research. These training programs were conducted by Imperial Corporate Training and Development, Oak Lawn, Illinois, whose managers and staff closely collaborated with us during both program implementation and assessment. We wish particularly to acknowledge Ann Campagna, Imperial's Manager of Training and Development, who offered numerous useful suggestions. She helped with many training examples that added flesh and bone to our theoretical explanations of adult learning.

Finally, we wish to thank Sandra Gula Gleason, who prepared the final manuscript for publication. Our endless chapter revisions might have driven the most patient saint to despair. This book owes its accuracy and clarity to her superb word-processing and formatting talents. For whatever errors or shortcomings the reader finds in the text, the authors take sole responsibility.

Chapter 1

The Evolution of Management Development

THE LEADERSHIP CHALLENGE

Rapidity of change has become the central issue facing management development. Why? Look at the historic record of human technological progress. Between 1750 and 1900 human knowledge doubled. In the first fifty years of the twentieth century, it doubled again. Each decade since 1960 has seen a further acceleration in the pace of change (Steinmetz, 1976).

The challenge for training is to teach the principle of managing others during today's "future shock" period of rapid change and intense international economic competition. In order to perform the elastic, evolutionary jobs of the future, more employees than ever before must develop leadership abilities that require higher-level thinking and problem-solving skills. Static jobs for life have become a relic of the historic past.

We predict that the need for developing these leadership abilities will reach deeper and deeper into all businesses both large and small. This is symptomatic of fundamental changes taking place throughout the U.S. and worldwide marketplace (Conner et al. 1992).

As the economy becomes increasingly high-tech, existing jobs are being permanently wiped out through computerization, improved machinery, and new ways of organizing work. These are not all blue-collar jobs. Government data show that between 1982 and 1993 the country's 500 largest manufacturers slashed nearly 4 million jobs. Seventy percent of these lost jobs were white-collar jobs. During the 1980s new technology enabled U.S. policymakers to increase output by 30 percent and reduce labor rolls by 4 percent. In 1993 this trend is extending into service industries, affecting skilled professionals such as computer designers and programmers. Lifelong education for all American workers who will continuously experience job obsolescence is one of the realities of advancing technology (Myers, 1992; Zachary & Ortega, 1993).

This environment hardly encourages employee productivity and high personal motivation unless business adopts "lifelong education" thinking. Otherwise, America is faced with the prospect of hordes of educated people either underemployed or unemployed. If we factor in the up to 84 million currently undereducated employees, many of whom are incapable of handling almost any job in a high-tech twenty-first century workplace, the entire nation can anticipate serious social-economic displacement. Many of these Americans face the prospect of becoming the "new peasants of the information age."

Competition for goods and services is now driven by two main forces. How well does any business manage its "information content" of sophisticated technology and management design? How cheaply can it mass-produce goods or provide a service?

In 1992 U.S. business invested over $40 billion in employee training and development, trying to become more competitive (Lee, 1992). However, Henry Conn, coauthor with J. H. Boyett of *Workplace 2000* (1991), estimates that only 10 to 15 percent of all training was retained and used on the job. He sees a more realistic target in the 80 percent range, if America hopes to beat its global competition.

At issue for most companies are two questions. To what extent will more extensive and effective management development retool the work force? Will corporate decision makers adjust their strategic thinking to include lifelong education for all employees? To begin finding answers to these questions, we will review the evolution of training in the United States.

TRAINING'S EVOLUTION

Early Craft Training System (Before 1820)

Before 1820, America adapted an apprenticeship system from Europe. Trade guilds, which ensured that products met standards of workmanship, had developed in Europe during the Middle Ages (twelfth to fifteenth centuries). This guild system was a forerunner of today's unions. It strictly regulated members' hours, tools, wages, and, most importantly, training (Sonnenfeld & Ingols, 1986).

At the top of this work hierarchy was the fully trained master. He had many years of experience. Through the local guild he enforced professional craft quality standards and regulated the training of new workers. He supplied the tools and materials, and managed his shop. Apprentices, who lived with the master, learned their trade by passing through prescribed stages of training. If successful, they became journeymen traveling from town to town, receiving a fixed wage for their labors. Some remained in their master's shop to gain the requisite knowledge and take their final craft examination. If the journeyman passed the guild's examination, he became a master craftsman and was entitled to set up his own shop. A variant of this guild system was the organization of the medieval European university faculty system that awarded bachelor's, master's, and doctoral degrees. Modern Germany continues to use a formal craft training program as part of its dual educational system (Federal Republic of Germany, 1987; Miller, 1987; Nothdurft, 1989).

The apprenticeship system never worked well in early America because of a severe shortage of skilled labor. Colonial America was largely an agrarian economy based on small farms. There were few large cities. Most manufactured goods were imported from Europe. As a result, the majority of potential workers were never employed as tradesmen but were either farmers or associated with the shipping trade (Eurich, 1985).

The characteristics of the master-apprentice-journeyman craft system made it a very close-knit work team (see Figure 1.1). Apprentices were often viewed by masters as sons. Though the technologies employed were meager and simple, this working by doing learning approach required a very long-term commitment. The training program was geared to the individual artisan's craft needs and expectations. Employee motivation was critical to the success or failure of the entire training system (Sonnenfeld & Ingols, 1986).

Early Industrial Revolution (1820–1914)

By 1820 the Industrial Revolution was well under way in America. An average of 77 patents was issued each year prior to 1810. By 1860 Yankee ingenuity had raised the annual average to over 4,500.

Industrialization required training for specific tasks. The pattern of stable, lifelong occupations began to change. Work was not home-based but became focused on larger, depersonalized organizations, usually established in growing urban areas (Steinmetz, 1976).

Between 1820 and the outbreak of World War I (1914), factory schools were established to supplant the apprenticeship system. Hoe and Company, a manufacturer of printing presses, founded in 1872, established one of the first factory schools to train machinists. As the nineteenth century advanced, available machinists often proved incapable of operating more complex technology. Most machinists until then had relied on rule-of-thumb methods and had neither the mathematical nor the technical knowledge required to make precision parts (Stevens, 1990).

Factory schools were established by Westinghouse (1888), General Electric (1901), International Harvester (1907), Western Electric (then part of AT&T), Ford, National Cash Register, and many other manufacturers. They provided specific task education within the emerging modern business organization (Miller, 1987).

This early industrial period was driven by a work force of largely unskilled machine operators (see Figure 1.1). Both unskilled and skilled workers were viewed as a variable cost. Worker employment fluctuated with market demands.

Figure 1.1
Evolution of Training and Development in America

	Craft Training Before 1820	Early Industrial Revolution 1820-1914	Mass Production Era 1915-1945	Cold War Era 1946-1992	Work Force 2000 1992-2000
Work Force	Master, journeyman, apprentice	Unskilled machine operators	Interchangeable division of unskilled labor driven by machine pacing	Groups of workers under a supervisor	Self-directed work teams
People	Apprentices often seen as sons	Unskilled and skilled workers considered a variable cost	Workers may be substituted anywhere on the assembly line	Workers long-term, career-oriented community members	A human resource that needs constant development
Employment Time Frame	Long-term	Determined by market fluctuations	Some market fluctuations, seniority governs layoffs	Employment stability	Very changeable, intermittent
Technology	Meager and simple	New machines evolve with new energy sources	Machines dominate	Complex technology	Rapidly changing, interactive, high-tech
Training and Development Offered	Organized for individual employee needs	Less skills training for fewer people	Functional expertise and administrative efficiency expertise	Team building, technical skills, retraining	Lifelong learning that responds to change
Employee Motivation	Very important to craft system	Decreasing need	Decreasing need	Promotion, raises, benefits	Vested in job changes and job enrichment

Source: Adapted from Paul R. Lawrence, *HRM Trends and Challenges* (Cambridge, MA: Harvard Business School Press, 1985).

The technology of new machines was still evolving with the development of energy sources. Even though some technical training was offered, fewer skills were taught to fewer people in comparison with the prior craft system. The importance of individual employee motivation was replaced by the market forces of a unified national economy. By 1900 the United States had emerged as the world's largest industrial power (Sonnenfeld & Ingols, 1986).

Mass Production Triumphs (1915–1945)

In 1910 Henry Ford introduced assembly-line manufacturing based on Frederick Taylor's principles of scientific management. The assembly-line system consisted of small divisions of labor and machine work, further reducing the need for skilled workers. An individual tightened a specific bolt rather than assembling a complete product. Workers were not required to think, learn, adapt, or solve problems, but only to endlessly perform mechanically simple tasks.

World War I (1914–1918) provided a major stimulus for mass production. Charles R. Allen's "four-step method" (show, tell, do, and check) became a standard method for on-the-job training (OJT) adopted by burgeoning assembly-line war industries (Miller, 1987).

The ending of the Great Depression with America's entry into World War II (1941–1945) sparked a reformulation of the OTJ approach. America became the "arsenal of democracy" during World War II defeating the Axis powers (Germany, Japan, Italy) with mountains of assembly-line products. These tanks, guns, trucks, and jeeps all had mass-produced, interchangeable parts made by many different manufacturers, all of whom used assembly-line training systems.

A train-the-trainer system called Job Instructor Training (JIT) was designed for first-line and second-line supervisors to support the expansion of assembly-line production in the U.S. defense industry. Over 2 million supervisors received JIT or offshoot programs in job methods and human relations.

During the mass-production era (1915–1945) the work force was composed of large numbers of unskilled men (and, for the first time, women), who were largely interchangeable and driven by machine pacing (see Figure 1.1). Employment downturns occurred at the end of World War I and during the Great Depression. Layoffs were based on seniority. A machine technology clearly dominated. The training provided by business stressed functional expertise and administrative efficiency. Individual employee motivation was not considered an important factor in making this system successful (Miller, 1987; Sonnenfeld & Ingols, 1986; Steinmetz, 1976).

The Cold War Era (1946-1992)

The United States emerged from World War II the most powerful and prosperous nation on earth — a position it enjoyed until the 1990s. The technologies that had made America into a world power were now exported overseas. A postwar baby-boom helped ensure that the great industrial capacity built during the war years was retooled to support a large-scale, consumer-driven society. Management development was mobilized to meet these new complexities of production and distribution, using the military chain-of-command model with twelve layers of management.

By the early 1950s business training began to focus on supervisory development. This interest was directed, at least in part, by the rediscovery of Elton Mayo's Hawthorne studies, conducted in the late 1920s and early 1930s at the Hawthorne plant of Western Electric, near Chicago. This was the telephone manufacturing arm of AT&T then employing over 40,000 workers. The Hawthorne studies led to the recognition that managers trained in leadership can influence human relations, thereby improving employee morale and personal motivation (Roethlisberger & Dickson, 1941).

Later studies (Landsberger, 1956) debated whether the "Hawthorne effect" was behind the achievement of desirable productivity goals. Additional research conducted during the 1950s by James Worthy, Charles Walker, and Robert Guest documented the negative effects of repetitive, low-skilled, machine-paced work on employee morale and productivity.

For the first time in American history, the Engineering, Science and Management War Training Program (ESMWT) established during World War II, and the GI Bill after the war, exposed millions of adults to college courses on almost every aspect of management, technology, psychology, and education. These continuing education and management training programs provided the impetus to the formation of the American Society for Training and Development (1944) and fueled the vast expansion of the American Management Association (founded in 1923). These organizations helped increase the popularity of off-site management and executive development programs. By the mid-1950s, human resource development (HRD) had become a widely respected field. Training and development programs began to feature business games, "in-basket" exercises, simulations, and the extensive use of role-playing exercises.

The performance-based psychological theories of B. F. Skinner at Harvard University had a significant impact on training practices that were designed both to control human behavior and to bring about behavior change. Training laboratories of the 1960s used behavior modification techniques, programmed instruction, teaching machines, and training hardware designed to shape and control desirable work-related behaviors (Miller, 1987; Steinmetz, 1976).

The 1970s witnessed another behavioral application in HRD with the widespread growth of company assessment centers that "objectively" measured employee management potential. At the same time Malcolm Knowles (1987) stressed more humanistic-cognitive approaches to learning. He saw the role of the trainer as the facilitator of the learner's needs, rather than as the controller who sought to shape desired behaviors.

The concepts of organizational development (OD) also gained widespread support during the 1970s, interlocking all areas of business HRD. OD shifted the focus of concern from "people development" to one centered on the well-being and efficient operation of the entire organization.

Training and development in the 1980s witnessed the rapid growth of quality circles (based on Japanese models) throughout American business. Computer-based training and interactive video were introduced into many companies. They spread quickly with the increasing availability of personal computers (PCs) and appropriate software. However, entering the 1990s, their major limitation remained the lack of customized, inexpensive training and development software for specific company applications. Undoubtedly this issue will begin to fade as increasingly powerful PCs drastically reduce local software development costs.

Management development of the 1980s and early 1990s also saw the continued use of behavioral models of training. They were considered by many trainers and course designers as constituting the best practices for management development, technical, and educational training programs.

During the Cold War era (1945–1992), training and development programs characterized the work force as groups of employees under a supervisor (see Figure 1.1). Most workers were viewed as long term, career-oriented community members. Business emphasized employment stability. Because technology had become more complex and interactive, training began to stress teams and retraining, while still emphasizing technical skills. Employees were motivated through raises, promotions, and benefits (Knowles, 1987; Miller, 1976; Rush, 1987; Sonnenfeld & Ingols, 1986).

Preparing for Work Force 2000

By the early 1990s the training and development needs of American business had begun undergoing significant dynamic shifts. Many employees at all levels have discovered that much of what had been learned in school or on the job was now obsolete. They struggled to master high-tech skills or were forced to seek new employment. Many lamented that supple minds had become more important than supple joints. America won the Cold War by rebuilding and reequipping former adversaries. However, their new industrial base has produced complex technologies and an organizational versatility that place extreme competitive pressures on most U.S. business sectors (Gordon et al., 1991).

The 1990s reshaping of American business often will mean the elimination of many middle managers. But the success of this strategy will largely depend on how well newly empowered supervisors and line workers are educated to maximize their individual talents. Strategic manpower planning requires training programs that are designed to foster workers' abilities to perform complex jobs through the development of abstract thinking, problem-solving, and comprehension skills (cognitive abilities) (Boyett & Conn, 1991).

Future managers, supervisors, and workers must learn how to rethink new solutions to the old ways of doing business. These Total Quality Management (TQM), ISO 9000, business process re-engineering, team building programs feature problem-solving, creative-ability, cognitive-based learning. They are far more complex than past behavioral-based company training. They will challenge both manager and worker alike to develop leadership for tomorrow that maintains organizational competitiveness (Goldstein & Gillian, 1990; Greenwood et al., 1993).

The organizational structure of the work force for the year 2000 will most typically be smaller companies utilizing work teams (see Figure 1.1). An employee will be viewed as a human resource who needs constant development. Individual employment will be very changeable and intermittent, driven by rapidly changing technology and the need for extensive continuing education. The training and development offered will be committed to lifelong learning that copes with these frequent changes. Employee motivation will become vested in these job changes and in enrichment that broadens daily work assignments (Sonnenfeld & Ingols, 1986).

FUTUREWORK

Societal changes in the next decades will be enormous. The entire world is now in the midst of a second industrial/technology revolution. Over the next thirty years major scientific breakthroughs will significantly alter technology, the workplace, and daily life. International economic competitiveness will demand that America create and maintain a world-class, universal worker educational system. If both employees and organizations are to thrive, training and development must become a force in strategic planning that educates all people to their highest potential. However, too often in contemporary business, "wisdom" and "creativity" are seen as opposites. Many managers view creative people as "mavericks," not quite fitting into the corporate culture. They certainly are not the people who should be running the shop!

Yet many of these same managers have embraced quality as the competitive cure-all of the 1990s. A comparison of Crosby's fourteen steps, Deming's fourteen points and Juran's seven points finds a common call to expand training that promotes employee problem solving on the job. All three call for empowered work teams that can integrate a range of complex thinking tasks into their daily work activities. The quality "continuous improvement process" requires that people make decisions, analyze systems, investigate, invent new processes, classify, compare, and generally manipulate information. Increasing personal creativity has become the name of the game for American business (Hunt, 1992).

We believe that most companies need to encourage employee education at all levels. A business that cannot bridge the "business wisdom" versus "employee creativity" culture gap will soon experience serious trouble. The worldwide competitive marketplace has already begun this winnowing-out process.

The foundation of America's national wealth is really its human capital— people. Their knowledge, skills, and motivation remain the primary assets of any business. In 1987 William Wiggenhorn, director of training at Motorola, noted, "We've documented the savings for the statistical process-control methods and problem-solving methods we've trained our people in. We're running a rate-of-return of about 30 times the dollar invested" (Peters, 1987).

The $40-billion-a-year corporate training budget of U.S. companies sounds impressive. But it is only a fraction of America's annual corporate capital hardware bill, which runs about $400 billion each year. Motorola is not a nationwide industrial leader by accident. Employee education is at the heart of its short-term/long-term planning.

As part of your company's strategic business plan, you need to reconsider training by assessing your total work force's skills. What are your employees' educational skill levels in relation to your domestic and foreign competition? Is this educational skill gap increasing or decreasing versus key competitors? In many instances individual businesses will find that they are far behind in the education and training they will need to offer all their employees for the ultra modern, post twentieth-century marketplace (Peters, 1987).

However, the experience of too many managers is that for the most part training is "not worth what I've paid." People go and listen and say it was wonderful, and they do it for a while, only to forget it and go back to their old habits. Training is useless unless change results, and it is part of a process that awakens people to their own strengths and weaknesses (Harte, 1990).

In the 1980s many new adult learning strategies were discovered for stimulating thinking and intelligence. Frederick Goodwin, director of the National Institute of Mental Health, believes that educational programs cannot make a 70 IQ person into a 120 IQ person. "But you can change their IQ in different ways, perhaps as much as 20 points up or down, based on their environment" (Kotulak, 1993). There are many untapped abstract reasoning capabilities that currently are not being developed by traditional business training/educational programs.

We propose FutureWork as part of this human development revolution reshaping American business (see Figure 1.2). Companies will continue to offer training such as basic management, supervision, service, and assembly behaviors. They will add a component for employee skill requirements that increase overall personal comprehension: writing, math, reading, foreign language, and English as a second language. Only after addressing these two employee development areas will a business be able to successfully address the

Figure 1.2
FutureWork: The Work Force Education Triad

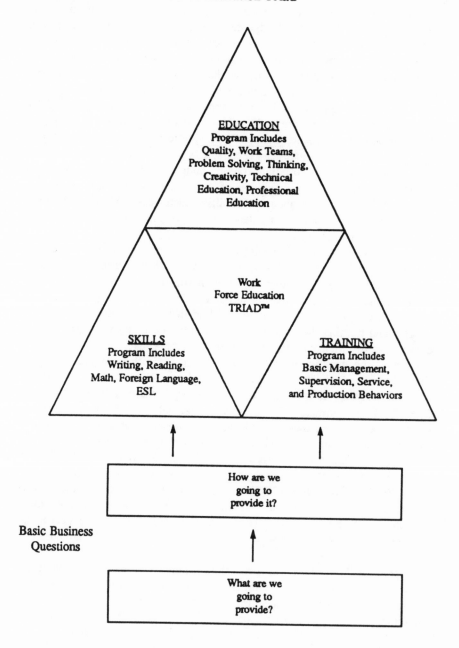

EDUCATION
Program Includes
Quality, Work Teams,
Problem Solving, Thinking,
Creativity, Technical
Education, Professional
Education

Work
Force Education
TRIAD™

SKILLS
Program Includes
Writing, Reading,
Math, Foreign Language,
ESL

TRAINING
Program Includes
Basic Management,
Supervision, Service,
and Production Behaviors

How are we
going to
provide it?

Basic Business
Questions

What are we
going to
provide?

education issues of building higher thinking skills for TQM, ISO 9000, business process re-engineering, work teams, problem solving, personal creativity, and advanced technical or professional education.

We see FutureWork as being based on the Work Force Education Triad of training, skills, and education. For the rest of the 1990s, maximizing the talents of all people is emerging as a major business goal. How America will reach these objectives will be presented in the following chapters.

REFERENCES

Boyett, J. H., & Conn, H. P. 1991. *Workplace 2000*. New York: Penguin Books.

Conner, D.; Bramer, W.; Kiefer, C.; Carnevale, A.; Mellander, K. 1992. Five views of change. *Training & Development*, 46 (3):34–37.

Eurich, N. P. 1985. *Corporate Classrooms*. Princeton, NJ: Carnegie Foundation.

Federal Republic of Germany, 1987. Public Information Document #28. Bonn: Press and Information Office of the Federal Government.

Goldstein, I. L., & Gilliam, P. 1990. Training system issues in the year 2000. *American Psychologist* 45 (2):134–43.

Gordon, E. E.; Ponticell, J. A.; and Morgan, Ronald R. 1991. *Closing the Literacy Gap in American Business: A Guide for Trainers and Human Resource Specialists*. New York: Quorum Books.

Greenwood, T.; Wasson, A.; and Giles, R. 1993. The learning organization: Concepts, processes, and questions. *Performance & Instruction* 32 (4):7–11.

Harte, S. 1990. Results, not good feelings, are seminar's test. *Chicago Tribune*, 1 April, sec. 7, 4.

Hunt, V. D. 1992. *Quality in America*. Homewood, IL: Business One Irwin.

Johnston, W. B., & Packer, A. H. 1987. *Workforce 2000: Work and Workers for the Twenty-first Century*. Indianapolis, IN: Hudson Institute.

Knowles, M. S. 1987. Adult learning. In R. Craig, ed., *Training and Development Handbook*. New York: McGraw-Hill.

Kotulak, R. 1993. Unraveling hidden mysteries of the brain. *Chicago Tribune*, 11 April, sec. 1, 1, 10.

Landsberger, H. A. 1956. *Hawthorne Revisited*. Ithaca, NY: Cornell University Press.

Lee, C. 1992. Industry report. *Training* 29 (10):25–65.

Miller, V. A. 1987. The history of training. In R. Craig, ed., *Training and Development Handbook*. New York: McGraw-Hill.

Myers, H. F. 1992. The outlook, some economic ills defy federal medicine. *Wall Street Journal*, 14 September, A1.

Nothdurft, W. E. 1989. *School Works*. Washington, DC: Brookings Institution.

Peters, T. 1987. Hardware over humans: Firms spend on technology, scrimp on training. *Chicago Tribune*, 12 October, C6.

Roethlisberger, F. J., & Dickson, W. J. 1941. *Management and the Worker*. Cambridge, MA: Harvard University Press.

Rush, H. M. F. 1987. The behavioral sciences. In R. Craig, ed., *Training and Development Handbook*. New York: McGraw-Hill.

Sonnenfeld, J. A., & Ingols, C. A. 1986. Working knowledge: Charting a new course for training. *Organizational Dynamics* 15 (2):63–79.

Steinmetz, L. S. 1976. The history of training. In R. Craig, ed., *Training and Development Handbook*. New York: McGraw-Hill.

Stevens, E. W. 1990. Technology, literacy, and early industrial expansion in the United States. *History of Education Quarterly* 30 (4):524–44.

Zachary, G. P., & Ortega, B. 1993. Workplace revolution boosts productivity at cost of job security. *Wall Street Journal*, 10 March, A1.

Chapter 2

Cognition and Learning: The Potential of Melding Theory into Practice

LEARNING'S BOTTOM LINE

Do we really understand how adults learn? To what degree will a cognitive-based Work Force Education Triad foster higher-level thinking and problem-solving skills? Based on our field research and the work of many others, we are optimistic that much more can be done to foster employee learning by updating training "best practices" for the twenty-first century. We must empower all employees throughout the business world to cope with the onrush of change. Thus, there is an urgent need to reorganize adult learning in the workplace. We believe that the increased use of cognitive training practices will improve learning and development in the corporate classroom.

In our quest for answers we will begin with a brief historical overview that presents a compelling rationale for improving adult training through the use of cognitively based curricula. We will discuss how a person develops cognitive thinking structures (schemata) over a lifetime. We also will learn why it is important to relate new knowledge to ideas that the employee already knows and understands.

Cognitive instruction methods have considerable training value because they encourage the acquisition of new ideas. Several specific cognitive training applications and concepts are described in this chapter, including analogies, advance organizers, intelligence, motivation, information processing, and cognitive style. We conclude with a summary of how cognitive-based training will improve overall adult learning in the workplace.

FROM BEHAVIOR TO SOLVING PROBLEMS

It may startle some readers to discover that a comprehensive theory of adult learning (instructional psychology) does not exist! Early in the twentieth century, learning theorists attempted to develop general principles of learning. They studied the use of reinforcements and punishments to motivate learning and to explain how and why behavior changed. This early perspective on learning was known as behavioral learning. Behaviorists focused on using rewards or punishers to engineer desirable learning behaviors.

From 1920 to 1960, the behaviorist movement dominated adult learning. One of its basic assumptions was that psychology as a science studied and explained only observable behavior. Problem solving, creativity, and abstract reasoning (cognitive processes) were left unexplained by the behaviorists. A person either had or did not have these skills. Behaviorally based instruction was designed by manipulating rewards and punishments to bring about desired human behavioral changes. Adult training has long been dominated by these ideas.

In the late 1960s and early 1970s, a shift occurred in learning theory. Many behaviorists, trainers, and educators began to believe that it was no longer possible to ignore the internal cognitive processes related to learning. As a result, new interest arose in the structure and content of the human mind. This change of focus became known as the cognitive revolution. It has brought about the development of cognitive theory and the cognitive movement in instructional design.

A cognitive learning perspective assumes that learning occurs as a result of the active attempts by learners to understand their environment. Knowledge is an organized set of mental structures and problem-solving procedures. Learning occurs with a change in a person's mental structures.

The behaviorists explain learning by means of external, overt, stimulus-response laws. They believe learning can be seen and manipulated. In contrast, the cognitivists explain behavioral changes and learning by emphasizing the role of internal, covert mental processes, such as understanding, thinking, focusing attention, problem solving, and reasoning. The foundation of this cognitive learning approach is the need to understand *how* these initial mental processes occur in the adult learner.

One of the main questions addressed by cognitive training designers is how to encourage students to become active learners. The importance of active learner involvement in the instructional process represents one of the main contributions of cognitive theory to instructional psychology and training design.

In addition to active engagement, one of the main goals of cognitive-based instruction has been the development of adult understanding. What is understanding? Cognitive practitioners maintain that understanding (deriving meaning from instruction) occurs through interaction between a new message or idea or experience and a person's existing knowledge and experience.

Learners do not receive meaning in a passive manner. Instead, they construct meaning by interpreting new ideas and experiences on the basis of prior knowledge and experience. However, real understanding will not occur unless the learner has relevant knowledge that can be activated to construct a new idea. For example, it is difficult for employees to use new team-building skills until they have had an opportunity to try them out. Meaningful course simulations often help adult learners move quickly to a stage of personal understanding and then application of team-building skills on the job.

BUILDING THE "COMPUTER OF THE MIND"

Cognitive-based instruction provides the adult students with information that assists in the integration of new instructional material with their existing knowledge base. There are multiple methods to achieve these goals. There is no one best technique.

Many cognitive educators have attempted to describe the process of learning and knowledge acquisition by designing computer simulation models of the human mind. Knowledge is the content stored in this "computer" (the human mind). In order to be accessible, knowledge is organized into meaningful cognitive structures (schemata). A person beginning to learn the concept of simple division organizes a schema of the rules governing the concept. As new information is learned, (for example, long division), the division schema expands to assist in present and future division problem-solving situations.

A schema consists of a learner's knowledge structure for a specific concept. It provides a framework (a context) in which different elements of information about a topic are organized into one conceptual unit. The management development schema (see Figure 2.1) includes the important features of leadership and the functions of supervision. It also includes rules (time management and resolving conflict); principles (customer service and ethics); and problem-solving skills (team building and interpersonal relations). A schema is considered to be a dynamic, generative system that expands by the addition of new information.

Where does an adult store schematic knowledge? Memory, the "storehouse of the mind," is divided into different rooms (see Figure 2.2). They are long-term memory (where previously acquired knowledge is stored), short-term memory, and working memory (where incoming information makes contact with prior knowledge).

The adult's decision of what specific knowledge to activate in solving a problem is controlled by the perception of the problem when interpreting new information. The adult learner gives personal meaning to the new instruction. Most academic knowledge is represented by the symbols of letters, words, or numbers. For this reason most learners attach great importance to language.

As an individual learns to read, write, and perform math, long-term, short-term, and working memories act imperceptibly as a team to raise the personal level of basic literacy, language fluency, and abstract reasoning. Acquiring these skills was accomplished for most of us very gradually, over twelve to sixteen years

Figure 2.1
How Does a Schema Work?

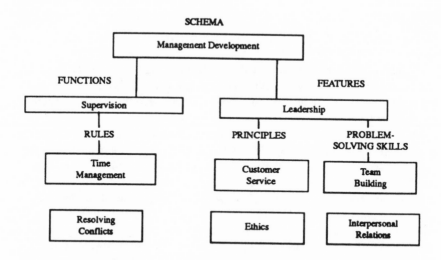

in school, or even longer. For this reason we tend to attach a "literate bias" to the number of years of school completed and the level of intellectual sophistication attained. Because of our education experiences, we tend to believe that the higher levels of education (abstract reasoning, problem solving, thinking) can be achieved only by a long schooling process. We will later discuss how to shorten this personal educational development process for many adult learners in the workplace.

Cognitive-based instruction is founded on the recognition of two different types of knowledge. Declarative knowledge refers to "knowing what," such as being able to talk about content (facts, figures, historical events, the steps to a successful sale). Procedural knowledge refers to "knowing how," such as being able to do something, or the strategies involved in solving a problem (applying math to a work need, or writing a sales proposal or the annual report).

Many problem-solving and thinking skills involve a nonspecific cognitive activity that can be generalized across many content areas. For example, team building is more effectively taught to adults if its elements are introduced gradually, are taught through course simulations that are self-critiqued, and are then practiced on the job. Spacing out team-building training experiences over months or even years may be far more productive in changing employee thinking and behaviors than compacting training over days or weeks. This long-term cognitive instructional approach isolates the sequence of steps an adult problem solver takes while solving a complex problem. The adult learner can be trained to perform these skills in a similar systematic order (Dillon & Sternberg, 1986).

Figure 2.2
Memory as the "Storehouse of the Mind"

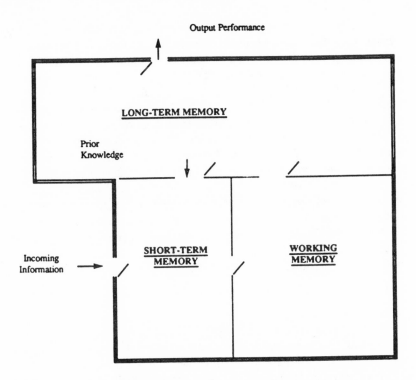

Another cognitive approach to instruction emphasizes the relationship between the cognitive activity of problem solving and knowledge acquisition within a specific content area. Teaching these skills can be done only within the boundaries of that specialized content area. Fostering team-building skills for a natural work team at a bank, insurance company, cellular phone manufacturer, or hospital means enhancing the specific content and procedural skills that are needed as they apply realistically to each of these work environments. This cognitive training method will enhance adult thinking skills for team building in a specialized context.

The cognitive view of learning believes that something is understood when it is meaningfully integrated into the learner's existing knowledge base. The following instructional techniques are designed to help the learner activate existing knowledge in order to foster understanding during the acquisition of new knowledge.

Analogies

Analogies often help adults integrate new information by relating it to familiar ideas.

In a train-the-trainer program that the authors helped conduct for the Illinois Department of Employee Security, the trainer activated the group's prior knowledge by getting the participants to identify the qualities of a good trainer. They were asked to remember the four or five best training programs or college courses they ever attended. Participants then recalled the instructors of these classes and listed on a flip chart some of the trainer's qualities they did *not* like. Then a list was made of things they liked from these classes. From both these lists the trainees developed a set of characteristics that make a good trainer. All this information came from the adult learners and not the course's trainer. The course trainer then proceeded to build upon these characteristics as starting points for delivering new concepts in train-the-trainer models.

We used another training analogy in our team-building program at Interstate National Insurance. In this exercise participants attempt to assess their personal contributions or roles as team members. By studying each part of the "team car" (see figures 2.3 and 2.4) and its function/work/role, each team member can identify the role he or she plays, whether positive or negative.

Advance Organizers

In an introductory discussion for a training methods course, the facilitator presents to the class a "chart of methods" (see Figure 2.5). This is filled in as members of the group discuss each method, and share their positive and negative personal experiences. Course instruction follows this exercise.

In a similar manner, an evaluation training course might use an "evaluation matrix" (see Figure 2.6). In both of these instances a concrete model, a chart, helps facilitate learning. In other instances an illustration, graph, map, or training video may act as a bridge between what adult learners already know and what they need to understand before the trainer introduces new material. Such advanced organizers provide context to adult learners, increase meaning and personal comfort, and heighten attention (Ausubel, 1980).

THE POWER OF COGNITIVE CONSTRUCTS

The cognitive view of learning also features the concept of constructs or ideas. These include intelligence, personality, the mind, motivation, information processing, and cognitive style. These constructs help us explain the behavior

Figure 2.3
Training Analogy: The "Team Car"

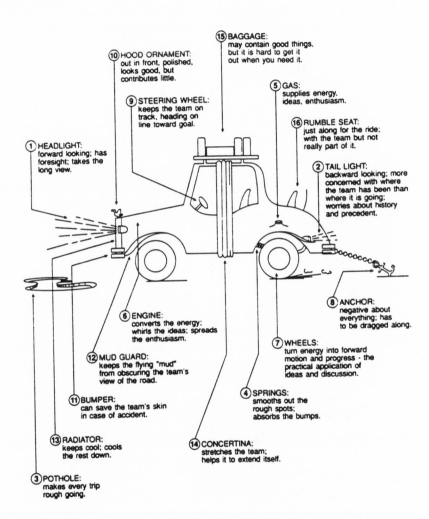

15 BAGGAGE:
may contain good things,
but it is hard to get it
out when you need it.

10 HOOD ORNAMENT:
out in front, polished,
looks good, but
contributes little.

5 GAS:
supplies energy,
ideas, enthusiasm.

9 STEERING WHEEL:
keeps the team on
track, heading on
line toward goal.

16 RUMBLE SEAT:
just along for the ride;
with the team but not
really part of it.

1 HEADLIGHT:
forward looking; has
foresight; takes the
long view.

2 TAIL LIGHT:
backward looking; more
concerned with where
the team has been than
where it is going;
worries about history
and precedent.

8 ANCHOR:
negative about
everything; has
to be dragged along.

6 ENGINE:
converts the energy;
whirls the ideas; spreads
the enthusiasm.

7 WHEELS:
turn energy into forward
motion and progress - the
practical application of
ideas and discussion.

12 MUD GUARD:
keeps the flying "mud"
from obscuring the team's
view of the road.

11 BUMPER:
can save the team's skin
in case of accident.

4 SPRINGS:
smooths out the
rough spots;
absorbs the bumps.

13 RADIATOR:
keeps cool; cools
the rest down.

14 CONCERTINA:
stretches the team;
helps it to extend itself.

3 POTHOLE:
makes every trip
rough going.

Reprinted from J. W. Pfeiffer, ed. *The Encyclopedia of Team Building Activities* (San Diego: Pfeiffer & Company, 1991). Used with permission.

Figure 2.4
Training Analogy: The "Team Car" Worksheet

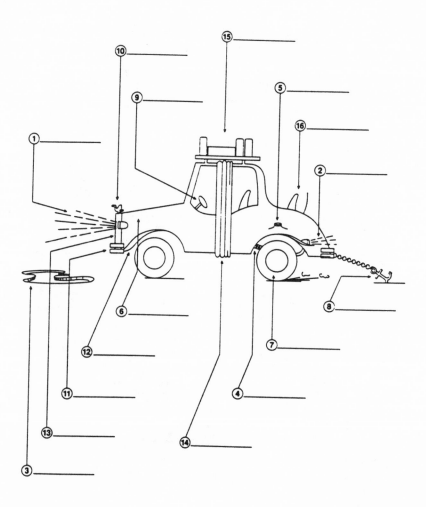

Reprinted from J. W. Pfeiffer, ed. *The Encyclopedia of Team Building Activities* (San Diego: Pfeiffer & Company, 1991). Used with permission.

Figure 2.5
Training Advance Organizer: Chart of Training Methods

METHODS	ADVANTAGES	DISADVANTAGES
Lecture		

Discussions:
   Small group
   Large group		

Handouts		
Case Study		
Demonstrations		
Role-Play/Rehearsal		
Exercises		
Games/Puzzles		

Visuals: Overheads
        Videos
        Flip Charts		

Figure 2.6
Training Advance Organizer: Evaluation Matrix

Levels	What Might be Measured	What Are Sources of Data?	How Should Data Be Collected?	What Are Potential Problems?
1. Trainee Reactions to Presentation				
2. Trainee Learning: Knowledge Skills Attitude				
3. Trainee Behavior after Presentation				

of persons in different situations. Intelligence often allows us to predict what an individual will do in the future. How the mind functions is a very flexible construct. Constructs have some social value. In other words, people invest some value in the construct as a sense-making mental tool. The personal motivation constructs are rooted deep within the personal conscience. A review of these cognitive constructs will help us establish stronger relationships between adult learning, work, and daily life.

Intelligence

In the past, society has overrated the significance of the personal IQ. Even though intelligence still helps us explain and predict an adult learner's performance, it is often unable to predict job success or success in interpersonal relationships. Intelligence's explanatory role has considerably diminished as a determination of an employee's overall success or failure on the job.

Intelligence as a construct certainly is not rigid. It also is invested with great social value. Most persons tend to use the construct of intelligence to compare themselves with others, deciding who is the most brilliant, and therefore worthy of attention. Most assessments of intelligence take place outside the psychologist's office. People are always sizing up each other and assigning a crude rating of intelligence. Trainers need to resist this tendency to subjectively rate their students (Weinberg, 1989).

Motivation

"Motivation" is a broad term covering personal needs, interests, values, attitudes, aspirations, and incentives. It is a regulatory process that directs and guides human behavior and learning. Trainers are increasingly aware that the amount of learning depends upon how enthusiastically a learner approaches a task.

Maslow's (1954) hierarchial notion of motivation claims that trainers cannot meet adult learners' higher needs either intellectually or aesthetically if their lower needs, such as job security or personal recognition, are not met. Unless trainers define and address sensitive local company productivity issues, such as employee basic skills, how will they successfully raise personal educational abilities to the higher levels of thinking required by quality, empowerment, and team building?

To what factors do we attribute the motivation of the employee to achieve success? (Murray, 1938). When they enter the classroom, most adult learners are concerned with what determines success. Some attribute success to their internal efforts of study and achievement (intrinsic). Others see only external factors as predetermining success, such as luck or who else is in the class (extrinsic). Adults who fail to see their internal control of the learning process often have experienced problems throughout their schooling experiences and may need extensive retraining (Weiner, 1986; Bar-Tal, 1978).

Intrinsically motivated adults learn best with cognitively based instruction, and extrinsically motivated adults learn best with behaviorally based instruction (Bates, 1979). Trainers need to teach adult learners to view themselves as the source of their behaviors and not as manipulated pawns (DeCharms, 1976). Adult learners who view themselves as the source of their own learning behaviors are able to free themselves from feelings of helplessness, improve their academic achievement, and set more appropriate goals for themselves. In many cases trainers must first teach employees to "learn how to learn" before undertaking training in new job skills that can be applied to everyday work tasks.

The construct of motivation continues to add to our greater understanding of behavior. As trainers we need to be aware of motivational patterns among learners. If we know what motivates an individual, we can attempt to match instruction to individual needs. It is far easier to teach an accountant how to write clearly if he or she perceives that this will lead to professional success and advancement. A production worker may lack motivation for more job-related reading and math training until he or she can see the relevance of these skills for job advancement, personal use such as tax returns, or helping a child with homework.

These intrinsic and extrinsic motivational issues may appear cumbersome when considered by trainers for the first time. However, we have achieved a great deal of success in management and skill training programs when we made the effort to discover each employee's motivational training profile and built it into our training program objectives.

Information Processing

Learning and instruction can be made analogous to information processing by the modern computer. This cognitive model helps us explain and define our understanding of the development of memory and the operation of adult learning.

As we have seen, the use of advance organizers facilitates top-down processing. This allows the adult learner to organize and anchor new information from the general to the specific (Ausubel, 1978). We believe that the adult learner must be actively involved in the task in order to be able to learn and retrieve information. For this reason we encourage the use of creative role-playing and training simulations (Wittrock, 1978). Training activities such as summarizing, outlining, and graphing are useful internal organizers that may add to overall depth of understanding for most adult learners (Rothhopf, 1977).

Cognitive Style

Cognitive style also adds to our understanding of the teaching-learning process. It describes the ways adults differ in their personal perception and information storage. Global-style learners, for instance, tend to be more impulsive and to generalize information. Analytic-style learners, on the other hand, tend to be more reflective, detailed, and exclusionary (Kagan, 1966).

We can also consider adults to be field-dependent or field independent learners (Witkin et al., 1977). Field-independent learners tend to be more individualistic and less likely to want or need trainer assistance. They are internally motivated and more inner-directed with respect to acquiring values and goals. These learners tend to be more interested in abstractions and are often more self-assured and confident. They tend not to need other people for their definitions of self and often are found in leadership roles.

On the other hand, field-dependent adult learners tend to be other-directed, more dependent upon other people for cues. They are more likely to need trainer assistance, and look to other adults for a definition of self and personal values. As a trainer you will become aware of many different individual cognitive styles in a training class. You must consider how to make your training methods more adaptable in order to address the individual needs of the global versus analytic learner, or the field-dependent versus field-independent learner. A trainer's final outcome may often rest upon how effectively he or she adjusted training methods to match an adult's personal cognitive style.

CAN TRAINERS MODIFY INTELLIGENCE?

In recent years we have witnessed new trends in the conceptualization of intelligence and have reexamined our earlier notions of the nature of intelligence. New training programs have been developed to more accurately assess and improve individual intelligence. If assessment is merely an exercise in the placement or slotting of adults, few training/educational programs will offer personal growth. However, cognitive-based learning has broadened our notion of intelligence.

Trainers may now consider intelligence as something that is modifiable. Human assessment can be accomplished in many different ways. Adult learning is moving away from the "pigeonholing" concept of individual IQ and considers intellectual assessment as a beginning, not an end point for understanding the potential of further developing every employee's intelligence (Feuerstein et al., 1985; Gardner, 1983; Sternberg, 1985a).

This educational approach gives us a new instructional plan when working with problematic adult learners. Trainers must break down problem-solving tasks. We need to identify the information-processing components required in a training program. We need to use perceptual and cognitive-based teaching strategies. These ideas give trainers new tools to work with when dealing with adult learning problems. In subsequent chapters we will be examining these strategies in great detail.

THE COGNITIVE KEY TO LEARNING

The cognitive basis of individual differences for the problem adult learner and related instructional activities provides important links between cognitive learning theories and the design of training that better fosters individual leadership and personal empowerment. Detailed cognitive task analyses of instructional sequences are being done in both the corporate classroom and the schoolhouse. We will show how the training of metacognitive skills and problem-solving strategies helps adults master intellectual skills. This may be applied to the content of management development or an educational program.

The identification of individual differences in personal information-processing capacities is now being utilized to design effective instruction. We can compensate for specific learning deficiencies by providing learners what they cannot provide for themselves. By identifying individual information-processing deficiencies, we can supply the appropriate links that enable an adult to learn at the higher, more abstract thinking levels demanded by a twenty-first century work environment.

We believe that most of these cognitive variables are learnable by adults. Therefore, when designing new learning environments, trainers will be able to use instructional procedures that assess and modify these cognitive variables. A cognitive perspective on instruction has potential ramifications for daily instructional improvements in the corporate classroom. From ongoing, field-based research, the authors have considerable evidence supporting the use of cognitive instructional training practices in the workplace.

The following chapters will illustrate the possibilities of relating these cognitive variables to existing models of instruction. We will offer new instructional options that better describe how to minimize individual differences in learning. Our fundamental goal is to foster leadership through more pervasive human development at all levels of any organization.

REFERENCES

Ausubel, D. P. 1980. Schemata, cognitive structure, and advance organizers: A reply to Anderson, Spiro and Anderson. *American Educational Research Journal* 17 (3):400–04.

____. 1978. In defense of advance organizers: A reply to the critics. *Review of Educational Research* 48 (2):251–57.

Bar-Tal, D. 1978. Attributional analysis of achievement-related behavior. *Review of Educational Research*, 48 (2): 259–71.

Bates, J. A. 1979. Extrinsic reward and intrinsic motivation: A review with implications for the classroom. *Review of Educational Research* 49 (4):557–76.

Bloom, B. S. 1968. Learning for mastery. *Evaluation and Comment* 1 (2):1–12.

DeCharms, R. 1976. *Enhancing Motivation*. New York: Irving Press/Wiley.

Dillon, R. F., & Sternberg, R. J. 1986. *Cognition and Instruction*. New York: Academic Press.

Feuerstein, R.; Jensen, N.; Hoffman, N. B.; & Rand, W. 1985. Instructional enrichment, an intervention program for structural cognitive modifiability: Theory and practice. In J. W. Segal, S. F. Chipman, & R. Glaser, eds., *Thinking and Learning Skills* Vol. 1. Hillsdale, NJ: Erlbaum.

Gardner, H. 1983. *Frames of mind*. New York: Basic Books.

Garner, R., & Alexander, P. A. 1989. Metacognition: Answered and unanswered questions. *Educational Psychologist* 24 (2):143–58.

Glaser, R. 1990. The reemergence of learning theory within instructional research. *American Psychologist* 45 (1):29–39.

____. 1986. *Advances in Instructional Psychology* vol. 3. Hillsdale, NJ: Erlbaum.

____. 1984. Education and thinking: The role of knowledge. *American Psychologist* 39 (2):93–104.

____. 1982. *Advances in Instructional Psychology* vol. 2. Hillsdale, NJ: Erlbaum.

____. 1978. *Advances in Instructional Psychology* vol. 1. Hillsdale, NJ: Erlbaum.

Greeno, J. 1980. Psychology of learning 1960–1980: One participant's observations. *American Psychologist* 35 (8):713–28.

Kagan, J. 1966. Reflection-impulsivity: The generality and dynamics of conceptual tempo. *Journal of Abnormal and Social Psychology* 71 (7):17–24.

Maslow, A. H. 1954. *Motivation and Personality*. New York: Harper & Row.

Murray, H. A. 1938. *Explorations in Personality*. New York: Oxford University Press.

Rothhopf, E. Z. 1977. The concept of mathemagenic activities. In M. C. Wittrock, ed., *Learning and Instruction*, Berkeley, Calif.: McCutchan.

Sternberg, R. J. 1985a. *Beyond IQ: A Triarchic Theory of Human Intelligence*. Cambridge: Cambridge University Press.

____. 1985b. Instrumental and componential approaches to the nature and training of intelligence. In S. F. Chipman, J. W. Segal, & R. Glaser, eds. *Thinking and Learning Skills* vol. 2. Hillsdale, NJ: Erlbaum.

Weinberg, R. A. 1989. Intelligence and I.Q.: Landmark issues and great debates. *American Psychologist* 44 (2):98–104.

Weiner, B. 1986. *An Attributional Theory of Motivation and Emotion*. New York: Springer-Verlag.

Witkin, H. A., Moore, C. A., Goodenough, D. R., & Cox, P. W. 1977. Field-dependent and field-independent cognitive styles and their educational implications. *Review of Educational Research* 47 (1):1–64.

Wittrock, M. C. 1978. The cognitive movement in instruction. *Educational Psychologist* 13 (2):15–30.

Chapter 3

Back to Basics: Enhancing Learning In Training and Development

INCREASING WORKER COMPREHENSION

The drive to strengthen American competitiveness has resulted in new interest in finding training and development programs that support improvement in worker productivity at all business levels. Capital expenditures for the latest in high-tech equipment need to be accompanied by well-educated workers.

During most of the twentieth century the nation's schools were expected to produce mostly a grunt labor force of minimally educated adults working at mass-production, assembly-line jobs. Large numbers of public school students were never expected to achieve better than fourth-to-sixth-grade reading, writing, and math abilities. Since 1900 about 20 percent of the American population has remained at this educational level.

Technology and international trade have forced our educational expectations for workers up to at least the twelfth-grade level. By the year 2000, 80 percent of all jobs throughout the United States will match these educational requirements. With this target in mind, from 25 to over 80 million American managers, support staff, and production workers today (1993) compose an inadequately skilled and poorly educated job force. Too many Americans are rapidly becoming the "new peasants of the information age."

Quality management, team building, and leadership, among many training and development programs, are in many businesses at best producing only marginal results. Too often these programs merely increase employee frustration and are soon abandoned. They do not improve individual comprehension, understanding, insight, or motivation. Current research indicates that these inadequacies stem from the behavior-based training that predominates in American businesses. We believe that this behaviorist training approach provides an inadequate design for the increased demands of a twenty-first century workplace (Brown, 1978; Case, 1985; Glaser, 1990; Gordon et al., 1989, 1991; Levin & Pressley, 1983). (For additional discussion of this issue see chapters 5 and 6.)

American business desperately needs new practical approaches to training and development. The new workplace is characterized by many complex tactical and strategic tasks that require the assimilation of large amounts of new knowledge, personal thinking/application/problem-solving abilities, and high work loads with extremely variable content. This is a far cry from the assembly line of the past ninety years that emphasized unvarying, rote, fixed procedural sequences that relied heavily on psychomotor skills. In the service sector the response to high technology and deregulation has placed the same educational demands on management and support employees.

What training areas need this attention? They are far broader than at first realized by business, since they are needed by many managers, support staff, and production workers. The authors' ongoing, field-based research projects have uncovered a multitude of work force education needs. They include reading, math, grammar training, management writing skills, office practice, computer skills, software knowledge, English as a second language, foreign-language skills for business, problem-solving abilities, conducting meetings, meeting participation, report/form writing, blueprint reading and other functional educational areas. These are the work force education areas that TQM, ISO 9000, and other advanced managerial quality-control systems take for granted as the minimal abilities of all production or service employees. The question remains, How do we train the majority of our adult workers to meet the educational requirements of twenty-first century business?

PATHWAYS TO EMPOWERING THE MIND

Three instructional models have served as the basis of the authors' research in training and development programs for work force education: mastery learning, personalized systems of instruction, and tutoring. These three models emphasize continuous assessment, remediation, encouragement, and support. We will learn throughout this book that many of the limitations usually placed on individual intellectual potential can be overcome by diagnosing and developing personal learning skills and application abilities.

We need to give specific attention to the alterable aspects of human thinking and problem solving. Through the use of insights derived from cognitive science, we believe that many personal learning problems may be remediated through the use of carefully crafted education programs. These include permanently expanding the learner's ability to acquire knowledge, teaching enhanced language acquisition, improving personal auditory and visual learning abilities, modifying personal attitudes and expectations, controlling moods, and improving attention and problem-solving abilities.

In reviewing this material we hope to offer the trainer/educator a design for work force education that includes instructional procedures that modify the cognitive components associated with learning.

Mastery Learning

John B. Carroll (1963) proposed that the degree of learning is a function of the ratio of two quantities: (1) the amount of time a learner spends on the learning task, and (2) the amount of time a learner needs to learn the task (see Figure 3.1).

This model has served as a behaviorally based theoretical framework for much of Benjamin Bloom's (1968) work related to mastery learning instruction. Carroll's formulation implied that by allowing sufficient time to learn a task (i.e., permitting the numerator of the ratio to be larger), and by improving instructional conditions (i.e., decreasing the denominator), most students will be able to reach mastery. Mastery learning is an educational procedure in which a learning hierarchy is developed and learners are required to master each unit of the hierarchy prior to beginning a subsequent unit. Mastery usually is determined by end-of-unit tests that learners must pass.

However, most tutoring and mastery learning theorists acknowledge that during the initial learning sequences, extra time must be provided to less able learners. However, this extra time is viewed as a temporary crutch that becomes less and less necessary with practice (Bloom, 1976).

A number of critics of mastery learning instruction (Anderson & Burns, 1987; Buss, 1976; Greeno, 1978; Guskey, 1987; Guskey & Gates, 1986; Mueller, 1976; Resnick, 1977; Slavin, 1987a, 1987b) have argued that additional time must be provided for both learners and teachers in order to bring less able learners up to the desired mastery level. Mastery learning may help slower-learning adult students but at the expense of those who learn faster. Trainer time and attention may be used to benefit the slower learners at the expense of faster ones.

From the results of numerous investigations, we know that mastery learning programs, compared with traditional approaches to instruction, produce positive gains in academic achievement and student attitudes (Block & Burns, 1976; Carroll, 1989). Considerable evidence indicates that effectiveness of mastery

Figure 3.1
Carroll's Model of Mastery Learning

$$\text{Degree of learning} = \frac{\text{of time spent on a task}}{\text{amount of time needed to learn the task}}$$

learning depends on the length of the program and the type of outcome measured. For example, training programs lasting four weeks or longer yielded more positive findings than those lasting less than four weeks (Slavin, 1987a, 1987b).

Personalized Systems of Instruction

The personalized system of instruction (PSI) strategy was developed by F. S. Keller (1968). It evolved from Skinnerian behavioral theory and has had its major impact on technical training for blueprint reading, welding, and other areas.

The basic components of PSI include self-pacing, the use of proctors, the mastery requirement, immediate personalized feedback, and frequent testing on relatively small units. PSI argues that regular teaching procedures do not encourage enough responses or provide enough opportunities for reinforcement. Instead, subject matter should be divided into brief instructional units that enable students to study at their own rate, then progress to the next unit when mastery (an 80 to 90 percent correct score) is achieved. Those students who do not master an instructional unit the first time are given additional time and tutoring until mastery is achieved (Keller 1968).

Compared with traditional instruction, PSI produces superior student achievement, considerably less achievement variation, and higher student evaluations of college courses. In addition, PSI procedures have been found to be unrelated to increased study time or course withdrawals (Kulik et al., 1979).

PSI gets generally favorable marks when compared with traditional classroom instructional methods. Since students work independently, teacher time and attention are not used to benefit slower learners at the expense of their faster peers. It appears to be easily adaptable to a wide variety of instructional situations and has few, if any, negative side effects.

Tutoring

For many centuries tutors have demonstrated that a child's education is a highly personalized process, supported by the family and guided through the assistance of literate teachers. At their best, tutors are the best equipped to assess individual differences among their students and to engineer stimulating learning environments (Gordon & Gordon, 1990).

In the nineteenth and particularly in the twentieth centuries, tutoring became an actual part of schooling. Some of the most important philosophers of the West developed educational theories based upon their practical experience as tutors. Their tutorial philosophy led to the development of many of our modern educational principles, such as continuous assessment, remediation, encouragement, and support. Some of these principles are the same as those assumed to be of importance to advocates of mastery learning and PSI instruction.

A review of the literature indicates that tutoring usually produces positive results. Tutoring procedures appear to produce good effects on both tutees and tutors (Annis, 1983). Summaries of research on tutoring show that these positive effects have been consistently found on assessment of the learner's achievement, self-esteem, and personal interest in the subject matter being taught (Cohen et al., 1982; Gage & Berliner, 1988). In addition, the results from numerous cross-age, peer-tutoring studies conducted with learners of many ages have yielded positive findings. Tutoring appears to be a very powerful technique for enhancing adult learning across a wide variety of content areas (Lippitt, 1969; Lippitt & Lippitt, 1968, 1970).

INDIVIDUALIZED INSTRUCTIONAL PROGRAMS (IIP)

Based on the authors' ongoing, field-based research program conducted within many production and service businesses, we have embellished the behaviorally based mastery learning model originally proposed by Carroll (1963) to include a number of cognitive variables. Our embellished cognitive science model of mastery learning, PSI, and tutoring instruction is presented in Figure 3.2.

From a cognitive learning perspective, individual differences in student aptitude would consist of differences in personal attention, individual temperament, maturational stages of development, existing knowledge and language base, cognitive learning styles, personal attitudes, individual expectations, and mood. Quality of instruction is related to the ability of the trainer to organize instruction and to set up situations that enhance meaning and contribute to the development of critical thinking and problem-solving skills.

Trainers are unable to modify biological differences in temperament and maturational stages. But most of the other components that appear in our embellished cognitive science model are teachable. We can enhance individual knowledge and language bases. We believe that how efficiently we learn depends to a great extent on what we already know.

From a cognitive learning perspective, the major limitations for problematic adult learners are their very limited knowledge base and ability to use language to classify and store new information. Years of school attendance give most of us a "literate bias." We tend to believe that it will take any adult many years of "schooling" to achieve effective thinking and problem-solving behaviors. We also assume that this "literate bias" allows the expert adult learner to interpret

Figure 3.2
The IIP as an Enhanced Model of Mastery Learning

Degree of learning =

$$\frac{\text{time spent (willing or allowed)}}{\text{time needed (aptitude, i.e., individual differences)} + \text{(quality of instruction x ability to understand instruction)}}$$

Where: Learner <u>aptitude</u> consists of the biological differences of personal attention, individual temperament, and maturational stages of development and the psychological differences of existing knowledge and language base, cognitive learning styles, personal attitudes, individual expectations, and mood.

Quality of instruction is viewed as the ability of the trainer to organize instruction, to give it meaning, and to set up problem-solving situations that enhance critical thinking.

Ability to understand instructions consist of the same components as quality of instruction.

---

environmental events in a different way than the novice adult learner.

But consider the following scenario. Two employees are part of a company's customer service operation. The first worker is a senior manager with an MBA degree. The second is a first-line manager who finished two years of college. Because of the literate bias in schooling, most observers will assume, when comparing the two employees, that the senior manager has a greater overall depth of understanding, pays more attention to details, and will be able to offer a better overall analysis of the company's customer service program. Can the senior manager's more advanced interpretive, analytical skills be taught to the supervisor through cognitive-based training? Must it take as many years as the formal schooling process? In later chapters we will review how to shorten these pathways to enhanced personal intelligence for many employees.

IMPLICATIONS FOR TRAINING

The authors are not advocating a diagnostic-prescriptive framework for improving the achievement of learners. This approach focuses too narrowly on deficiencies, does not recognize and build on personal learning strengths, and does not consider the complexity of learning (Arter & Jenkins, 1977; Kavale & Forness, 1987).

Much of what we are presenting is derived from the field of cognitive information processing. There are those trainers who claim that this field is too complex and the instructional procedures derived from it too cumbersome to use in the corporate classroom. Many other trainers agree that they should utilize these cognitive information-processing principles in curricula and instructional designs they create for all adult learners, if they are shown how to apply them for different training programs. We will make every effort to provide specific cognitive training examples throughout this book and information on cognitive training design (see Chapter 9).

To what extent can trainers realistically expect to change the cognitive information-processing abilities of adult learners? Can the individual adult's memory, expectations, learning style, and personal attention be significantly improved? Our research evidence and that of many others indicates that these learning enhancements are attainable for most adults through workplace training (Glaser, 1984, 1990; Good & Brophy, 1987; Gordon et al., 1991; Walberg, 1984; Wang et al., 1990).

THE TRAINING CHALLENGE

We believe that individual differences in cognition and perception can both limit and facilitate learning. Our identification of individual cognitive information-processing capacities has been utilized to design instruction that compensates for a particular learning deficiency. In effect, we are providing for learners what they cannot provide for themselves. Such information has been used to capitalize on the learner's strengths. It is particularly valuable for diagnosing current individual learning difficulties and in suggesting mastery learning, PSI, and tutoring instructional procedures (prescriptions) for overcoming them.

What we are proposing is a general information-processing approach to training and instruction. Instruction should be directed at modifying student attention, expectations, and memory. Cognitive information processing is enhanced when learners are actively engaged in the learning task, discuss, rehearse, analyze, problem-solve, use graphs to represent experience, and share observations, understandings, and knowledge. In the following chapters these methods will be explored in greater depth.

In the next chapter we will discuss in detail the authors' Individualized Instructional Program (IIP) that incorporates these cognitive aspects of learning into workplace skills training. In a later chapter we will present the authors' Management Insight Development Program (MIDP), which fosters these cognitive concepts for management development.

REFERENCES

Annis, L. F. 1983. The processes and effects of peer tutoring. *Human Learning* 2:39–47.

Anderson, L. W., & Burns, R. B. 1987. Values, evidence, and mastery learning. *Review of Educational Research* 57 (2):215–224.

Arter, J. A., & Jenkins, J. R. 1977. Examining the benefits and prevalence of modality considerations in special education. *Journal of Special Education* 11 (3):281–98.

Block, J. H. & Burns, S. 1976. Mastery learning. In L. S. Shulman, ed., *Review of Research in Education*, vol. 4. Itasca, IL: Peacock.

Bloom, B. S. 1976. *Human Characteristics and School Learning*. New York: McGraw-Hill.

_____. 1971. Mastery learning. In J. H. Block, ed., *Mastery Learning: Theory and Practice*, pp. 47–63. New York: Holt, Rinehart and Winston.

_____. 1968. Learning for mastery. *Evaluation Comment* 1 (2):1–12.

Brown, A. L. 1978. Knowing when, where, and how to remember: A problem of metacognition. In R. Glaser, ed., *Advances in Instructional Psychology*, vol. 1. Hillsdale, NJ: Erlbaum.

Buss, A. R. 1976. The myth of vanishing individual differences in Bloom's mastery learning. *Journal of Instructional Psychology* 3:4–14.

Carroll, J. B. 1989. The Carroll model: A 25-year retrospective and prospective view. *Educational Researcher* 18 (1):26–31.

_____. 1963. A model of school learning. *Teachers College Record* 64:723–33.

Case, R. 1985. A developmentally based approach to the problem of instructional design. In S. F. Chipman, J. W. Segal, & R. Glaser, eds., *Thinking and Learning Skills*, vol. 2. Hillsdale, NJ: Erlbaum.

Cohen, P. A.; Kulik, J. A.; & Kulik, C. C. 1982. Educational outcomes of tutoring: A meta-analysis of findings. *American Educational Research Journal* 19 (2):237–48.

Gage, N. L., & Berliner, D. C. 1988. *Educational Psychology*. Boston: Houghton Mifflin.

Glaser, R. 1990. The reemergence of learning theory within instructional research. *American Psychologist* 45 (1):29–39.

_____. 1986. *Advances in Instructional Psychology*, vol. 3. Hillsdale, NJ: Erlbaum.

_____. 1984. Education and thinking: The role of knowledge. *American Psychologist* 39:93–104.

_____. 1982. *Advances in Instructional Psychology*, vol. 2. Hillsdale, NJ: Erlbaum.

_____. 1978. *Advances in Instructional Psychology*, vol. 1. Hillsdale, NJ: Erlbaum.

Good, T. L., & Brophy, J. E. 1987. *Looking in Classrooms*. New York: Harper & Row.

Gordon, E. E., & Gordon, E. H. (1990). *Centuries of Tutoring: A History of Alternative Education in America and Western Europe*. Lanham, MD: University Press of America.

Gordon, E. E.; Ponticell, J. A.; & Morgan, R. R. 1991. *Closing the Literacy Gap in American Business: A Guide for Trainers and Human Resource Specialists*. New York: Quorum Books.

____. 1989. Back to basics. *Training and Development Journal* 43 (8):73–76.

Greeno, J. G. 1978. Review of *Human Characteristics and School Learning* by B.S. Bloom. *Journal of Educational Measurement* 15 (1):67–76.

Guskey, T. R. 1987. Rethinking mastery learning reconsidered. *Review of Educational Research* 57 (2):225–30.

Guskey, T. R., & Gates, S. L. 1986. Synthesis of research on the effects of mastery learning in elementary and secondary classrooms. *Educational Leadership* 43 (8):73–80.

Kavale, K. A., & Forness, S. R. 1987. Substance over style: Assessing the efficacy of modality testing and teaching. *Exceptional Children* 54 (3):228–39.

Keller, F. S. 1968. Good-bye teacher! *Journal of Applied Behavioral Analysis* 1 (1):79–84.

Kulik, J. A.; Kulik, C. C.; & Cohen, P. A. 1979. A meta-analysis of outcome studies of Keller's personalized system of instruction. *American Psychologist* 34 (4):307—18.

Levin, J., & Pressley, N. 1983. *Cognitive Strategy Research: Educational Applications*. New York: Springer-Verlag.

Lippitt, P. 1969. Children can teach other children. *The Instructor* 78 (9):141, 99.

Lippitt, P., & Lippitt, R. 1970. The peer culture as a learning environment. *Childhood Education* 47:135–38.

Lippitt, R., & Lippitt, P. 1968. Cross-age helpers. *NEA Journal* 57 (3):24–26.

Mueller, D. J. 1976. Mastery learning: Partly boon, partly boondoggle. *Teachers College Record* 78 (1):41–52.

Pressley, N., & Levin, J. (1983). *Cognitive Strategy Research: Psychological Foundations*. New York: Springer-Verlag.

Resnick, L. T. 1977. Assuming that everyone can learn everything, will some learn less? *School Review* 85 (3):445–452.

Slavin, R. E. 1987a. Mastery learning reconsidered. *Review of Educational Research* 57 (2):175–214.

____. 1987b. Taking the mystery out of mastery: A response to Guskey, Anderson, and Burns. *Review of Educational Research* 57 (2):231–35.

Walberg, H. J. 1984. Improving the productivity of America's schools. *Educational Leadership* 41 (8):19–30.

Wang, M. C.; Haertel, G. D.; & Walberg, H. J. 1990. What influences learning? A content analysis of review literature. *Journal of Educational Research* 84 (1):30–43.

Chapter 4

The Individualized Instructional Program (IIP) Training Alternative

WORK FORCE EDUCATION SKILLS

Since the 1970s American business has sought solutions that will improve employee productivity. In the first phase of their drive for competitiveness, high-tech equipment and computers were introduced into almost every office and plant. This led to the dramatic downsizing of management and production forces that still continues. In many instances high technology did fulfill its prophecy of accomplishing more work with fewer workers. Thus significant productivity gains were realized by American business in 1992, reversing the erosion of American productivity from the 1980s.

Business is now experiencing a realization by senior management that high-tech, computer-driven equipment requires better-educated employees than are generally available in sufficient numbers within most companies. Of far greater concern is the sobering fact that many managers, professional office support staff, and production workers require workplace educational programs to realize real productivity gains.

The growing necessity for lifelong employee education now exists throughout American business. The needs of many employees have outpaced the public school system's ability to educate or train. Higher education must update its degree programs to guarantee higher levels of personal literacy, (reading, writing, public speaking, research abilities, foreign language fluency), and broaden its applied professional preparation. By the year 2000, the U.S. Department of Labor estimates that 80 percent of all jobs will require from at least a twelfth-grade educational level to one or two years of college education. Eighty-four million Americans now in the workforce do not meet these educational standards (Gordon, 1991b).

America today needs more employees with much higher educational abilities than in past generations. Limiting this discussion to "basic skills" or "literacy" is totally insufficient for the United States to remain globally competitive in the industrial services or professional economic sectors. Twenty percent of American managers and professionals lack the educational abilities to perform their jobs successfully.

These work force education skills include "learning how to learn" (metacognition). Many people need to improve their personal skill competencies in reading, writing, mathematics, foreign languages, or English as a second language (ESL), but in a work-applied manner that will solve day-to-day and future workplace problems. Workers cannot be efficient team members if they are inarticulate. "Better communication abilities" means developing personal verbal and listening skills. As we have already discussed, improving individual self-esteem and motivation are critical for better management that empowers workers to think for themselves with less supervision. How well can we educate every adult worker to become more adaptable? Can we enhance personal creative-thinking, and problem-solving skills? These abilities are the foundation of the interpersonal and team skills needed for group effectiveness. All of these work force education changes are being driven by competitive necessity (Boyett & Conn, 1991; Gordon et al., 1991).

Work force education is a new strategic business paradigm that encompasses twenty-first century educational and training standards. Conceptually there is much more to work force education than merely acquiring better reading, math, writing or thinking abilities. This is a macroeconomic issue, not a technological problem to be solved, or just another business cost. To succeed in the twenty-first century workplace, senior management must acknowledge work force education as the driving activity that supports quality management and the work-team empowerment process. Work force education is the strategic linchpin of modern productivity, business innovation, and renewed employee commitment (Gordon et al., 1991).

Work force education has long been the "poor man" of corporate training and the "bastard" of the American educational system. Born in adversity and mired in political controversy, until now it has remained isolated from the mainstream of business training and development.

Before 1980 this was not a popular training issue. Most businesses vehemently denied that managers or workers experienced this problem. They would never consider an in-house education solution. However, by 1984 some businesses began using computer-based training and classroom instruction to raise educational levels. Unfortunately, the majority of these programs typically experienced dropout rates of at least 50 percent. Employees saw little connection between the training activities and their day-to-day job needs. Instructional materials were often inappropriate for the workplace, and instruction was "lock-step" rather than individualized to meet the adult's personal learning problems (Gordon, 1991a).

Findings from current and emerging research suggest that the behaviorist tradition, which permeates much of current practice in adult training and instruction, provides an inadequate design for the demands made by more sophisticated workplace environments (Brown, 1978; Case, 1985; Glaser, 1990; Gordon et al., 1989, 1991; Levin & Pressley, 1983). New approaches to training and development are needed because complex tactical and strategic tasks now require the assimilation of large amounts of new knowledge and high workloads. Outmoded, fixed assembly-line sequences relied heavily on employee psychomotor skills. Now productivity demands innovative work force education training that fosters better universal worker thinking skills. Brains have become more valuable than brawn.

The nature of these new training approaches is emerging as a growing area of research and interest in business and industry. For many years we have been studying the results of the Individualized Instructional Program (IIP), a specially designed tutoring curriculum used by management/employee/union teams to provide sequentially arranged, systematic applied workplace training for individuals and small groups. A number of specially crafted curriculum scripts were designed to teach employee competencies at introductory, maintenance, and/or mastery levels. Over 300 learning descriptors were systematically developed and are being used to document academic achievement, social-emotional outcomes, and selected job-related skills. Those interested in reading a description of our research program should refer to Appendix I.

THE IIP TUTORIAL TRAINING MODEL

As part of the FutureWork: Work Force Education Triad (see Chapter 1) we have designed a tutorial delivery system for business skills that helps the employee learn more efficiently, master subject material and improve long-term retention (see Figure 4.1). Adults are motivated by the immediate application of these new skills. Our on-site tutorial program integrates the learning of job content material and instruction in reading, composition/grammar, applied math concepts, a foreign language, or English as a second language.

Tutoring is already widely used in the corporate training environment. One example is the Johns Hopkins University Directed Listening-Language Approach (DL-LEA) (Cohen Gold, 1982), a tutorial method of teaching adults reading. The DL-LEA method integrates the learning of any subject matter and a tutorial reading program. Since 1989 Boston University's Corporate Education Center has trained thousands of employees using Accelerated Learning Techniques (ALT). This program uses tutorial methods to decrease the amount of time required to cover a given subject area. Skills are taught in intense, short time frames. Accelerating learning is possible if training programs are designed by content/learning/training experts who determine how to break a job down into tasks, functions, skills, and related competencies.

Another important component inherent in an organized tutorial system is a

Figure 4.1
FutureWork: The Work Force Education Triad

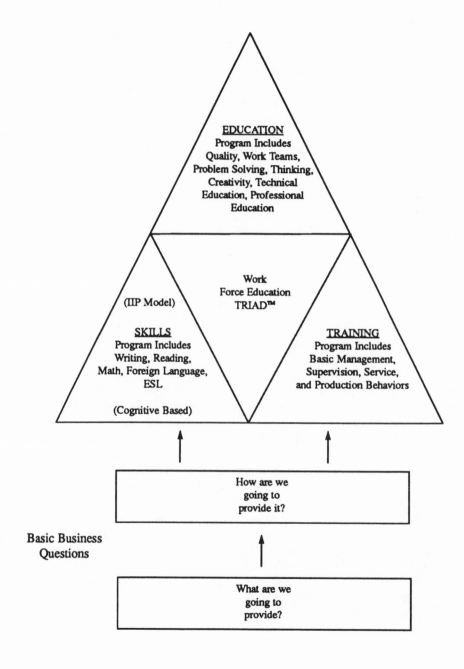

personal needs assessment that determines employee training capabilities. Tutoring will more efficiently answer the primary question of what must be learned by the individual employee. This is a difficult and painstaking task that is far more important than computer-based training's high-tech bells and whistles, or physically attractive corporate training environments. Tutoring facilitates the collection of information on the employee that can be used to modify the work force education program. It also establishes criteria for individual employee success. An ongoing tutorial-training evaluation process will provide for a continual modification of the work force education program based on an individual employee's learning needs and occupational skill/application requirements.

The work force education skills program developed by the authors has been used in many corporate settings with hourly workers, office support staff, and business managers. It is based on a cognitive, mastery learning model that offers fifty-two curriculum scripts designed to diagnose specific adult learning problems while tutoring for mastery of related job skills. It is designed around a carefully arranged sequence of individualized learning goals tracked by written instructional objectives related to those goals.

The Individualized Instructional Programs (IIP) are specifically designed to bring about rapid, verifiable skill training. Each IIP, with its associated written methods and reporting materials, helps the trainer follow a thoughtful, sequentially arranged, systematic presentation with a group of up to five adult students or on a one-to-one basis. The IIP program emphasizes administrative quality control, student learning awareness, and ongoing feedback to company management during the training.

The IIP curriculum was written in an attempt to avoid duplicating many of the pitfalls of traditional large-group classroom instruction. Many illiterate adults dropped out of school to become entry-level employees because of personal underachievement and frustration in the classroom. The IIP small-group (one instructor with up to five students) or individual training format takes into account individual differences among the participants. It is easily adapted to many different learning problems.

A typical IIP (small-group) training module consists of forty hours of instruction. Classes meet for two hours and are held twice a week for ten weeks. (One-to-one instruction is done during one hour classes held twice a week for ten weeks, totaling twenty hours.) This tutoring module structure recognizes the importance of extending learning over time rather than offering short-term massed practice. Time is needed to assess how an adult learner approaches the learning task; to discover what specific sequential subject-matter skills are missing; to reorganize the adult's achievement/study habits; and to assess and improve employee motivation that supports learning related to the workplace. The hallmark of the IIP program is precise individualized diagnosis and applied training that allow employees to learn at their own pace.

In order to facilitate better individualized tutoring across types of educational/job-related skills, specifically crafted curriculum scripts have been designed to teach job skill competencies at the introductory, maintenance, and mastery levels. We have systematically designed into these IIP curricula over 300 learning descriptors that are used to document academic skill achievement, selected job-related competencies, and personal motivational outcomes. These learning descriptors are assessed throughout the forty class hours by tutor observations, diagnostic/developmental testing, criterion-referenced tests, and normed achievement testing.

Structure

How does a trainer decide if an employee has learned a particular skill concept or work procedure and is ready to move on? The IIP curriculum script is a loosely ordered but well-defined set of skills and applied work concepts that the adult is expected to learn. What drives the instructional process is the skills the employee brings to the learning task. The IIP facilitates the gathering of this information individually from student performance cues (300 skills) and student learning strengths to attack learning difficulties or skill misconceptions.

The content areas used to teach these new skills are taken directly from the daily work assignments or future jobs in the office or factory. Thus the IIP curriculum script is the major determinant of the content for the tutoring class, not a trainer's rigid, developed lesson plan. Curriculum scripts used in our research program include basic reading and math, learning disability areas, grammar training, managerial/executive writing skills, English as a second language, fifteen foreign languages (including French, Spanish, German, Italian, Portuguese, Japanese, Russian, Chinese), and office practice (typing, shorthand, computer literacy, computer software).

The IIP's formal/informal test-teach-test format helps establish meaningful personal employee learning goals and objectives. Attainment of specific job-related skill goals is reported in great detail back to the adult student throughout the training classes. The use of realistic skills and job-training goals and objectives motivates adults to persist to any desired level of literacy or advanced educational fluency. The IIP gives a concrete picture of their progress and establishes a positive self-motivational training process.

The IIP curriculum script provides an overall inclusive structure that is used to track the daily performance of a particular tutoring class. A primary component of each class is the tutor's ability to use task analysis to track the sequence of successive steps the adult must take to attain a particular learning goal. For each of the written learning objectives that the tutor records, task analysis describes exactly what skills the adult must learn to achieve mastery. Task analysis has been used by human resource development for many years to break down job-training requirements. The IIP has taken it a step further by including both educational skill requirements and employee learning aptitudes. Thus the IIP not only serves as a diagnostic tool uncovering employee learning difficulties but also recognizes the importance of laying out for the trainer specific subject-matter content. Our attempt to better organize and structure skill content related to on-the-job performance has improved the rate of sustainable adult learning and retention over time (see figures 4.2 and 4.3).

These applied individualized tutorial programs (forty hours) have shown a distinctive pattern for employee learning. Initially the learner makes negligible gains because of unresolved interrelated learning-skills problems. Then there is gradual progress while basic skills are being diagnosed, reorganized, and taught. A significant breakthrough usually occurs at about the fifteenth hour of instruction as the student responds to the IIP restructuring of abilities and learning materials. Performance differences over time (fewer than ten hours of tutoring, ten to twenty hours, twenty to thirty or more hours) have been documented repeatedly by the authors. Maximum grade-level improvement occurs around the thirtieth hour of tutoring. The majority of individuals enrolled in IIP work force education module of twenty to forty hours attain six months to a year of skill improvement. (See Appendix II for IIP statistical research data.) At the end of an IIP training module, employees needing additional training are easily regrouped with others who have been diagnosed as needing similar assistance (see Figure 4.4).

Learning Disability Factors

Individualized diagnosis of learning disabilities (LD) is embedded in IIP small-group tutorial classes. The anecdotal account of actual class work is recorded on both a short class outcome report and the appropriate IIP checklist. A trained tutor closely observes and records student learning skills on a class-by-class basis. An accurate diagnosis of specific learning disabilities can be made by observing for particular learner behaviors in areas of vision, hearing, speech, and achievement.

Visual memory/tracking/discrimination, auditory discrimination/attention/memory, and achievement/work ethic attitudes are some of the learner characteristics that may be related to a learning problem. Each of these categories is defined, and specific observable aspects of learning are rated by the tutor. If visual tracking (the ability of the student's eyes to follow written material from left to right without moving his or her head) is a problem, the student possibly ignores punctuation; loses his or her place in a sentence, a paragraph, or a page; is easily distracted; or tires easily. The tutor observes and documents these characteristics and rates the student on visual tracking errors during the course of the tutoring classes.

Figure 4.2
IIP Comprehensive Reading Checklist

Directions: Please check appropriate box as an indicator of skills levels and developmental progression. This is FOR YOUR USE WITH <u>EVERY</u> CLASS. After the last class for this unit, you must indicate the Final Instructional Skill level.

Example: 3^1 (first 3 mos. of grade level) 3^{mid} (4 to 6 mos. of grade level) 3^2 (7 to 9 mos. of grade level)

ACTUAL GRADE PLACEMENT _____

	FINAL INSTRUCTIONAL SKILL	INTRODUCING SKILL	EMPHASIZING SKILL	MASTERING SKILL
A. Sight Vocabulary				
B. Acquired Vocabulary				
1. Context Clues:				
a. pictures				
b. listening				
c. verbal				
d. word meaning				
C. Visual Discrimination & Analysis				
1. Developing left to right sequence				
2. Recognizing letters, capitals and lower case				
3. Likeness and differences in word forms				
4. Reverses letters				
5. Inverts letters				
D. Total Phonetic Skills (See attached Phonetic Skills Checklist)				
1. Single Consonants				
a. initial				
b. final				
c. medial				

Figure 4.3
IIP ESL Beginning Level: Speaking

Directions: Please check appropriate box as an indicator of skills levels and developmental progression. This is FOR YOUR USE WITH <u>EVERY</u> CLASS. After the last class for this unit, you must indicate the Final Instructional Skill level.

Example: 3¹ (first 3 mos. of grade level) 3ᵐⁱᵈ (4 to 6 mos. of grade level) 3² (7 to 9 mos. of grade level)

ACTUAL GRADE PLACEMENT _____

Procedure: All structures should be taught in the affirmative, negative and question forms, if possible. Unless otherwise specified, verbs should be taught in the form of action verbs and <u>to</u> <u>be</u> verbs.

A. <u>Structures</u>	FINAL INSTRUC- TIONAL SKILL	INTRODUCING SKILL	EMPHASIZING SKILL	MASTERING SKILL
1. This/that				
2. Verb <u>to be</u> - is/am/are				
3. Singular/plural noun forms (regular and irregular)				
4. Possessive adjectives (my, your, etc.)				
5. Personal pronouns in subject and object forms. Example I/me, she/her, etc.				
6. Contrast of statement and question forms with verb <u>to be</u> Example: The book is white/Is the book white?				
7. Imperative forms Example: Go to the store/Don't sit there.				
8. Present continuous Example: I am walking/You are walking, etc.				
9. There is/are Example: There is an elevator in the building.				
10. The habitual present tense Example: I go to class every Monday.				
11. The future tense with <u>will</u> Example: I will go				

Figure 4.4
Comparison of Instruction Modes to Academic Gains

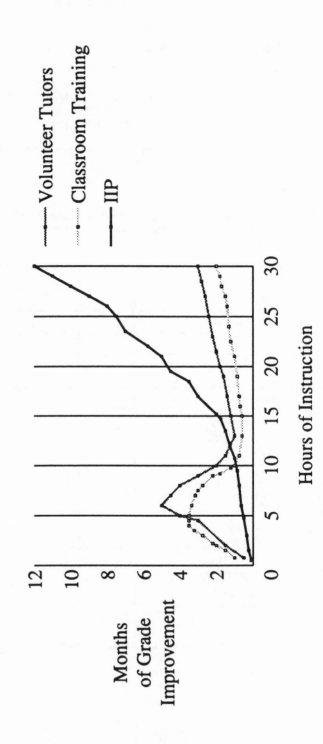

If the number of errors is high, diagnostic tests are used to pinpoint specific visual/perceptual skill problems. Remedial work is then done by the tutor to improve visual tracking skills, using employee work-related materials (see Figure 4.5).

We have found that the IIP LD curriculum scripts are very accurate at pinpointing specific learning disabilities by using this tutor-test-tutor approach rather than administering lengthy, comprehensive LD diagnostic tests. The curriculum script is in itself a diagnostic test that allows for maximum class time to be used for job-skill tutoring, and a minimum for necessary testing. The IIP helps minimize the risk that important LD skills areas will be inadvertently overlooked by the tutor. Finally, it should be noted that diagnosis is an ongoing IIP process throughout all the classes, rather than bunched in pretesting, as occurs in many traditional adult classroom programs of study.

Methods

The IIP curriculum scripts are updated as the tutor teaches each class. The tutor fills out the checklists after the first class to indicate skills observed at a "mastery level" (the specific grade level that has been established for this group as a final target by the end of the ten-week module of classes). Specific skill weaknesses observed in student class work are supplemented by diagnostic tests. As a student maintains or achieves mastery over designated job-related skills, these skills are tracked class by class on the appropriate IIP checklists by the tutor. Over forty different subject-area curriculum script checklists have been developed and tested within the context of our ongoing, field-based research project. Subject-area experts were formed into curriculum committees that systematically prepared and reviewed each subject-specific curriculum script. This field research process has extended over twenty-five years (1968–1993) with approximately 7,000 participating students. It is still an ongoing process. Every effort has been made to lay out and update the potential skills needed by a student in a wide variety of work-related academic areas. This has saved tutors a great deal of class time. They are now better able to concentrate on the diagnosis and analysis of individual employee's skill problems and to select the tutoring methods that maximize each adult student's learning.

Many adult students have motivational problems related to formal learning and a lack of a personal work ethic. They may possess a high aptitude but perform poorly on the job because of undiagnosed learning problems not uncovered in their school years. Employee educational skills may be uneven (i.e., math computation skills high, reading comprehension skills low).

In order to motivate the adult learner, we begin the IIP tutorial process by working at an independent skill level (with skill-related materials that give the positive reinforcement of immediate personal success). Adults' recognition of their own

Figure 4.5
IIP Vision and Motor Skills Checklist

Directions: Circle the number that best describes the student's performance of each individual skill. For each given category that you have observed and tested, mark the skill, using the 1-5 point rating scale. Comment sections are provided for further amplification. THIS IS FOR YOUR USE WITH EVERY CLASS.

Number Key: 1 - Excellent
2 - Very Good
3 - Good
4 - Fair
5 - Poor

Visual Memory:

The ability of the student to retain and recall information assimilated through visual means.

Time durations to be considered by teacher:

One minute to another:	1 2 3 4 5
Early to later part of same class:	1 2 3 4 5
From class to class:	1 2 3 4 5
From beg. to mid UNIT:	1 2 3 4 5
From beg. to end of UNIT:	1 2 3 4 5
Follows written directions:	1 2 3 4 5

Circle: Adequate   Fair   Inadequate

Comments:

ability to achieve begins the enhancement of personal motivation and builds a positive self-image as a student. An example of this method is to allow employees with reading problems to use actual workplace vocabulary materials that demonstrate their current understanding of job-related safety rules. The tutor moves rapidly to the adult's capacity level of learning. Here the student can perform the skill functions but must rely on the tutor as a resource for coaching. At this stage the tutor is continuing to rebuild the adult's self-confidence in the classroom and gain his or her personal trust as a mentor. The instructional level of tutoring can then be introduced by the tutor without running the risk of traumatizing the learner. This stage presents new material that can be introduced/reinforced/mastered by using the IIP's tutor-test-tutor learning system. The IIP process avoids tutoring at the "frustration level" that duplicates many adults' previous learning failures in large classes.

At every step of these instructional activities the adult learner has a need to know "How am I doing?" Immediate feedback to the adult student is critical for improved motivation. The greatest risk at the initial stages of a work force education program is that the employee will come to think that the learning task is impossible. The IIP tutorial process is ideal in breaking down long-term learning goals into small information chunks that adults can recognize, understand and master at their own pace.

However, this ideal is not always possible, since significant skill problems are often related to poor study skills. Far too many adults have few if any specific learned, study-skill strategies. They easily become overwhelmed and distracted when presented with complex independent homework/classroom exercises. In many instances, study skills were never formally taught in school; in other cases, the student ignored or misunderstood the material. Of course, a lifetime of study-skills deficiencies is not changed in one tutoring class. Assigning a large amount of homework at the beginning of a work force education program invites student failure and demotivates many adult learners. Formal study-skill habits must be taught gradually. They can be included as part of realistic work-related skill exercises rather than presented independently, out of context. The tutor teaches more complex study skill concepts as the adult progresses from the independent skills level to capacity and instructional skill levels. Homework assignments now take on an added work realism that encourages better study habits.

With these improved skills, student homework/independent work activities show adults their own small but recognizable steps in learning. This new learning self-awareness builds self-motivation. As a result, adult learners enrolled in IIP work force education come to see learning new ideas as a personal challenge that is attainable, not as a punishment to be feared or avoided.

Testing is another difficult hurdle for adults who experienced repeated test failures in their formal education. They sense that skill tests will only prove how much they do not know. Instead of administering a long pretest, the IIP utilizes shorter subtests over several class sessions. The IIP format of comprehensive, observable curriculum-scripted checklists eliminates the need for many diagnostic tests. Instead, the tutor makes consistently recorded skill observations of each student's daily class work. Testing becomes largely unobtrusive because it is part of a regular class learning exercise.

Tutor Training Concepts

H. S. Barrows (1988), in his research on the tutorial process, uncovered several additional tutorial concepts for consideration in training tutors using the IIP. A tutor's primary task is to ensure that no part of the skill-learning process is passed over or neglected until it has been fully understood by the adult student.

Each phase of the learning process must be taken in its proper sequence. For example, some adults are poor readers because of specific learning disabilities. Until these LD problems are diagnosed and remedied, the adults will not significantly improve their reading ability. That is, offering only reading instruction becomes a self-defeating process.

Educational diagnosis means early recognition not only of learning disabilities but also of reasoning difficulties, failure to understand concepts, or weak application skills. The tutor must be certain that the student has reached the level of understanding appropriate to on-the-job applications. A tutor must push the student to bring out what this learner already knows and to achieve better problem-solving and thinking skills. Constantly asking the appropriate who, what, when, where, or why questions will help the adult develop alternative solutions to an on-the-job problem. Learning will be geared not just to new skill acquisition but ultimately to success at work.

The IIP small-group learning format helps adult students recognize and freely admit what they do not know. This is essential to stimulate new learning. All of us have probably felt the embarrassment associated with admitting our personal ignorance in a classroom environment. Small-group tutorials help everyone relax. Adults want to learn and will aid each other in areas of personal strength. The social context of this group learning process is a powerful incentive that helps adults make open, unembarrassed statements of what they do not know or understand.

The IIP offers a special curriculum written for trainers to individualize instruction for almost any adult student. Most significantly, the IIP work force education program is flexible enough to accommodate a wide variety of learning problems based upon careful observation and continuous re-evaluation class by class. Skill training is built on an assessment of what the student already knows, then matching the tutoring/learning techniques considered to be most appropriate for that adult learner.

Tutoring Instruction Alternatives

The IIP was initially developed for one-to-one tutorials. Adults requested private instruction at home on work-related applied skill training. This assured total privacy, since employees did not always wish their employers to know they lacked basic educational skills. These programs proved highly successful in developing both diagnostic strategies and accelerated learning methods inherent in the IIP process. This field research formed the basis for the IIP tutorial program's professional recognition and accreditation in 1982, by the North Central Association of Colleges and Schools, as a "special function" educational service. It was the first instance in the history of American education that any tutorial program had achieved professional, public recognition.

These highly individualized one-to-one programs have also been used in-house by corporations to train managers and professionals in all levels of writing, fifteen foreign languages, English as a second language, public speaking, speech elocution, blueprint reading, speed reading, basic reading, basic math, and learning disabilities programs. Administrative assistants and secretaries have used the one-to-one IIP for grammar training, shorthand, typing, and computer skills.

The one-to-one format has the advantage of shortening training time. A typical module consists of twenty classes one hour in length. Two classes are held each week, over a ten-week period. Precise individualization, accelerated learning, and improved retention was attained at a ratio of 1:5 compared with conventional classroom instruction (i.e., the educational/training curriculum tutored in a 20-hour, one-to-one IIP module would require at least 100 hours of classroom teaching to achieve comparable results). Our short-term long-term analysis of results indicate an 80 percent information-retention ratio six months after the students finished their IIP tutorials. This exceeds standard classroom information-retention standards.

Our many corporate training applications indicate that one-to-one IIP management/staff training has a very high cost-benefit ratio. Increased productivity far exceeds program cost. Corporate competitiveness issues are dramatically increasing the demand for training programs such as the IIP that will rapidly accelerate adult learning and improve long-term retention.

In other instances where the number of employees to be trained was large, the IIP was conducted at a ratio of 1:5. These small-group tutorials consisted of twenty two-hour classes. Two classes were held each week over a ten-week period. Adult learning occurred at a ratio of 1:3 compared with classroom teaching (i.e., the educational/training curriculum tutored in a forty hour, 1:5 IIP module required at least 120 hours of conventional classroom attendance for an adult to achieve the same results). Small-group IIP long-term retention rates were found to be similar to the one-to-one tutorial program. Training content for the IIP small-group programs included all of the areas taught on a one-to-one basis.

Groups of two to five adults tutored in this manner have consistently shown the above rates of learning. Our research with the IIP tutorial model indicates that accurate diagnosis and individualized instruction significantly declines beyond a five-student class size.

Another format for IIP, work force education programs is the use of cross-training (i.e. peer tutoring). In this instructional program one employee tutors another employee. Peer tutoring has been used successfully for decades in American education. D. G. Ellson (1976), G. Von Harrison and R. E. Guymon (1980), and B. Bloom (1989), as well as other researchers, have long advocated the use of peer tutors as a powerful supplement to standard classroom teaching. E. E. Gordon and E. H. Gordon (1990) have chronicled peer tutors' success in tens of thousands of one-room American schoolhouses for over 100 years. And in the cities peer tutors helped to instruct small groups of students in nineteenth-century "monitorial" schools.

Cross-training is also being used for work force education programs. For example, Best University at Inland Steel has used managerial volunteers to teach workers basic skills. At IBM's Chicago office, manager volunteers on company time at their corporate worksite have tutored local unemployed community residents.

The IIP easily can be adapted for use by company peer tutors to reinforce the classes taught by subject-specialized tutors. For the cross-training to have maximum effect, peers must tutor peers. A literate shop worker will be more effective in tutoring a less literate peer than a supervisor or a management volunteer tutor. Why? They speak the same language. Research has shown that a student will be better able to explain what he or she does not understand to a peer than to a manager. Adult student's inhibitions are reduced with other adults drawn their own work group. Peer-tutor explanations become more relevant because the information can be given in the work context of both tutor and tutee. Fear of displaying ignorance subsides because the student knows the tutor is a peer.

There are several key considerations that will enhance a cross-training program. Peer tutors must receive formal training in tutoring techniques that motivate adult learners. A special subject-related curriculum must be laid out step by step so that the tutor can easily follow it. Tutors need to record daily results in a simple reporting log. Peer tutors should receive basic methods instruction in reading, math, learning disabilities, or the appropriate skill areas for a specific company. They will also need periodic retraining while participating in the cross-training program. Finally, peer tutors need the back up of subject-trained specialists who can intervene when the volunteer tutor hits a major learning roadblock that stops an individual adult's skill-building progress. Besides helping a fellow worker succeed, the company work force education program must offer other incentives to recruit peer tutor volunteers. Peer tutors will probably never possess the technical expertise of a degreed teacher. However, human resource professionals should not be intimidated by the acronyms of education. Intelligent adult volunteer tutors can teach basic skills and observe or remediate LD problems. Their rate of progress with the tutee will be slower than that of a teacher. However, furnished with an organized curriculum script, peer tutors can make a valuable addition to your company's work force education program.

An IIP train-the-trainer program will be particularly useful if large numbers of employees need an in-house program. Can current corporate trainers be prepared to tutor small groups in basic reading, math, learning disabilities, or writing skills? We believe this approach will be successful if they are trained to use a mastery-learning program with a curriculum-scripted format. Like peer tutors, trainers must learn the use of effective tutorial and skill-content methods in any train-the-trainer program. Content specialists need to back up these trainers' ongoing work, offer retraining sessions, and provide direct intervention with more difficult adult-learner problems. Company trainers will prove even more effective than volunteers as tutors because many have already had positive experiences motivating adult learners.

During the 1990s the use of properly written train-the-trainer programs, in combination with cross-training and tutoring by subject-area specialists, will emerge as "jump-start" solutions to America's work force education dilemma. They are cost-effective remedies that will reach large numbers of adult workers at all levels. These tutorial formats will enable corporate human resources departments to train the "untrainable" through specific diagnosis and enhanced remedial education. Such training will prepare for work countless adults who otherwise cannot be hired, may quit their jobs, or act as an ongoing drag on company productivity. For managers this specialized tutorial format offers human resources a flexible tool for key executive training and individual career development.

CASE-STUDY REPORTS

What we have reported on the IIP's results sounds impressive. But how practical have the actual business applications been?

The employee groups that have been trained using the IIP include professionals, managers, office support staff, production/service workers, and technical trainees. The IIP skills content areas used in these programs were reading, math, writing, English as a second language, foreign language, and office practice (see Figure 4.6).

Managers/Professionals

Written Communications

Accounting firms began competitively marketing their services in the 1980s. As a result, the writing skills of CPAs have come under increased client scrutiny. The jargon and acronyms of the accounting profession often create an unintelligible audit report, document, or annual accounting letter for the client's board of directors. Besides their technical inscrutability, these documents are often boring, with little variation in basic analysis from year to year. Few college schools of accounting offer students serious business writing programs. CPAs, until the current era, had little opportunity or inclination to improve their writing skills. More than one CPA has admitted to the authors that being able to avoid writing projects in college was one reason why they chose accounting as a profession.

Accounting firms have lost clients to competitors due to unintelligible or boilerplate reports. Accountants must now be able to produce financial reports that are individually written, clear, concise, and punctuated with careful recommendations for improving corporate financial management.

Price Waterhouse, a "big six" accounting firm, worked with the authors in offering their CPAs an advanced writing communications program. Individual CPAs were trained by a writing specialist with a background in financial reports. The one-to-one IIP tutorial was conducted on-site, with two sixty-minute classes held each week for ten weeks. The key element in business writing training is for the executive to practice, not listen to a lecture on "good writing habits." We have repeatedly tutored managers who had attended in-house writing-skills seminars. Even though some seminars are conducted over several sessions, there is little time to practice writing, critique the result, and try again.

An individual CPA's written reports were studied by the trainer prior to the program. The accounting firm selected specific examples of "model letters" as course goals. These documents reflected the firm's management perspective, tone, and accounting philosophy. The training modules were designed to diagnose specific writing weaknesses and promote individual skill improvements to attain the firm's writing standards. Allowances were made for the individual writing style of the CPA. This advanced written communication work force

Figure 4.6
IIP Workplace Programs Overview

POPULATION TUTORED

COMPANY	Professionals	Managers	Office Support	Production	Service	Technical
Angus Chemical Co.			X			
Christ Hospital			X			
Clorox				X		
Continental Can	X[1]					X[2]
Courtyards by Marriott					X	
First National Bank of Chicago	X					
FMC Corporation			X			
Fox Secretarial College			X			
Homequity			X			
Indramat	X					X
KDK Job Training Service			X[1]	X[2]	X[2]	
Marriott Residence Inn					X	
Metra Railroad	X[1]				X[2]	X
Morton International		X[1]	X[2]			
Motorola	X[1]	X[2]	X[2]			X[1]
Newly Weds Foods		X				
Northern Trust	X					
Nutrasweet		X				
Premark International			X			
Price Waterhouse	X					
Santa Fe Railroad		X	X			
Schless Construction		X				
Tellabs		X				
U.S. Gypsum		X				
W.W. Grainger		X				

Source: Imperial Corporate Training & Development, Oak Lawn, IL
Notation 1,2,3 pairs "Population Tutored" to "Tutoring Content" for end program.

COMPANY

TUTORING CONTENT

Company	Reading	Math	Writing	ESL	Foreign Language	Office Practice
Angus Chemical Co.			X			X
Christ Hospital						X
Clorox	X	X				
Continental Can	X	X	X²	X²		
Courtyards by Marriott				X		
First National Bank of Chicago				X		
FMC Corporation			X			
Fox Secretarial College	X	X	X			
Homequity			X			
Indramat					X	
KDK Job Training Service	X³	X³		X²		X²
Marriott Residence Inn	X	X		X		
Metra Railroad	X³	X³	X²	X²		
Morton International			X²	X²		
Motorola	X³		X²	X²	X²	
Newly Weds Foods			X²		X	
Northern Trust	X				X	
Nutrasweet						
Premark International			X			
Price Waterhouse			X	X		
Santa Fe Railroad			X			
Schless Construction			X			
Tellabs				X		
U.S. Gypsum			X			
W.W. Grainger				X		

Source: Imperial Corporate Training & Development, Oak Lawn, IL.
Notation 1,2,3 pairs "Population Tutored" to "Tutoring Content" for end program.

Figure 4.6 continued

education program is used as individual needs for continuing professional education are identified by Price Waterhouse (Chicago).

The authors have assisted many other organizations with basic, intermediate, and advanced managerial writing programs based on the IIP format. This has included executives at U.S. Gypsum, the Santa Fe Pacific Corporation (railroad), and Carson Pirie Scott & Company (retailer).

The engineers of the international division at Continental Can and Metra (Chicagoland commuter railroad) participated in a technical writing program. This professional education program helped these technical professionals improve communication with nonengineering staff. A technical writing professional taught this IIP tutorial on a 1:5 basis to sharpen the engineers' writing skills for clarity, nontechnical vocabulary usage, conciseness, and organization. The principles of effective technical writing were practiced with typical business memos, reports, and internal or client correspondence.

These successful business writing work force education program are not dissimilar to management development in team building, project management, change management, or other executive development areas. The goal is acquisition, review, and application of abstract, cognitive thinking skills for written communication. The test-tutor-test IIP format on a 1:1 or 1:5 basis allows executives extended, applied, confidential practice.

English as a second language (ESL)

During the past twenty years large numbers of foreign students have attended U.S. universities for their professional and technical education. Many have remained to work for American companies as mid- and upper-level management employees. On the whole, they have exceptional business/technical abilities and read English well. But their ability to speak, understand, and write in contemporary American English is often inadequate. The authors have worked with many organizations (W. W. Grainger, Morton International, Tellabs, Continental Can) to help foreign-born engineers or executives improve their interpersonal and group communication skills on the job. Specialized industry vocabulary and specific common written documents were included in the IIP tutorials.

Both American and Japanese companies are relocating Japanese and other foreign nationals for a tour of duty in the United States. In the case of Japan, the government operates Japanese schools in the United States for these executives' children while they live overseas.

Though the average overseas executive's prior foreign language training is considerably more advanced than that of his or her American counterpart, these businesspeople often arrive at an American company with an unacceptable English fluency level. The authors worked with several corporations (Motorola,

Panasonic, Honda) in providing IIP tutorials for these managers and, in some instances, their entire families. Our ESL training increased proficiency in spoken English, identified pronunciation problems, and dealt with idiomatic business expressions.

Foreign Languages for Business

The world market has arrived for North America, Europe, and Japan. Any company that hopes to remain an industry leader with a product or service for which there is international market has to compete in this global arena. Any company that needs to export its products or services had better get busy if it wants to remain healthy and profitable.

As the world marketplace continues to merge overseas corporations with their American operations, it is necessary for American executives to function effectively in languages other than English. Few corporate training programs are geared to teach foreign languages applied to a specific industry's vocabulary and terminology.

Indramat is an automotive engineering and manufacturing company headquartered in Frankfurt, Germany, with U.S. operations in Chicago's northwest suburbs. To aid their job performance, the American engineers received German-language training focused on three types of communication with their Frankfurt colleagues: written correspondence, telephone conversations, and face-to-face negotiations. The training was given through small tutorial groups of five engineers led by a German-language trainer using appropriate IIP materials. Grammar, vocabulary, and usage were specifically linked to content areas of automotive engineering and manufacturing. Twenty class modules were used, built one upon another, until the individual engineers reached the proficiency level required by their job assignment. This work force education program was conducted over a two-year period with over forty participating engineers. The authors will resume the program as Indramat hires new engineers who require German-language training.

Expanding U.S. international business operations requires the preparation of American managers for overseas assignments. Motorola used a small-group IIP French-language tutorial for international marketing staff. NutraSweet had the authors develop an advanced Portuguese-language program to help their sales representatives better penetrate South American markets. One NutraSweet manager was specifically trained in Chilean-dialect Spanish. The IIP gave these managers precise individualization for their company's products and a shortened time frame to achieve job-related fluency.

Production Employees

The Clorox Story

The suburban Chicago plant of Clorox employs approximately 100 hourly workers and managers. Clorox distributes its household products through such plants strategically located across the United States. Each location assembles a finished product from the raw materials delivered at each site. Local manufacturing and product testing have become much more sophisticated during the past decade. In response to Workforce 2000 and changing demographics, Clorox is attempting to upgrade its workers' skills for the future introduction of high-tech manufacturing/assembly equipment.

As is true for the majority of U.S. manufacturers, Clorox's present work force includes individuals who never attained the high school educational skill levels needed for operating the new equipment. These adults are good workers. Many have been with the company for ten, fifteen, or even twenty years. Management realizes that it is far better to retrain these loyal employees rather than to seek new hires in an even tighter, uncertain job market. Some of these adults already have failed GED classes. Others have never voluntarily admitted any educational problems to their employer.

A voluntary work force education program was begun by Clorox with several orientation sessions announcing the availability and content of the classes, and answering specific employee questions.

The company paid for the entire program. The employees attended classes after or before their work shift. A two-hour class was held on-site twice each week for a period of ten weeks, totaling forty hours of training. The IIP curriculum was used with each employee.

Prior to the first classes the program's trainers conducted a detailed analysis of employee job content, the work site, and potential program goals and objectives. Also, the readability levels of the technical manuals for the new production line equipment were determined.

Two classes with five workers each were formed. Initial testing showed that individual educational skills in reading and math ranged between the fourth-grade to prereading levels. Some of these adults had significant learning disabilities that had prevented success in school. We found, almost without exception, that once their learning disabilities were diagnosed, they were capable of rapid skill growth and information retention. Overall, worker achievement averaged twelve months of skill growth over the ten-week training period. However, performance varied, with one adult advancing only by six months and another by two years. These variations of individual learning rates were traced to the presence or absence of personal motivation, aptitude, or, in some cases, learning disability issues. One employee related how happy he was to be able to read the daily newspaper. For over fifteen years he had come to work everyday with a rolled-up newspaper in his back pocket. He wanted to be like everyone else so at breaks and lunch he would "read" his newspaper, even though he understood very few words. Now that he can actually read his newspaper, his personal motivation for learning and belief in himself are at an all-time high.

After the initial program, workers were regrouped and began follow-up training for another ten-week period. Our immediate goal remained: the elimination of significant learning problems. The program's long-term goal was ultimately to raise skills to the seventh-grade level, enabling the adults to attend local GED classroom instruction.

A second long-term goal was to reach all local Clorox employees with work force education needs. This will assure that the plant will be ready to use the high-tech equipment arriving within the next several years. It has been our experience that a program's first successful volunteers offer their peers much needed encouragement to participate. In many instances these first testimonials for the work force education program prove to other workers that it is practical and useful, and makes a daily job simpler, safer, and perhaps even enjoyable.

Supervisors were surveyed at the end of each ten-week class period. We needed to determine if the employees' job performances had improved during the training process. Of equal importance was raising their awareness that work force education was making a noticeable difference in employee work patterns. Supervisory support of the program is essential to encourage active worker participation. They reported that among employees who participated in the work force education program, production errors dropped, employees became more interested in advancing to more complex jobs, job problem-solving/troubleshooting skills increased, and personal job motivation improved.

There are now men and women at Clorox in Chicago who have just begun experiencing the pleasure of success in learning on the job and at home. Their worries over how they will cope in an increasingly complex high-tech manufacturing environment have begun to fade. Instead, these employees are more optimistic about themselves, their products, and their future at Clorox. The local human resources manager felt that "ten tons had been removed from my back" with the initiation of the work force education program. The demographics of the work force, and a lack of information on how to address this issue, had given him few alternatives. He can now partner with his workers to face successfully the high-tech factory of the twenty-first century that will arrive soon at his plant.

Technical Employees

The Metra Story

The Northeast Illinois Regional Commuter Railroad Cooperative (Metra), the commuter rail division of the Regional Transportation Authority, provides all commuter rail service for the six-county Chicago metropolitan area. Begun in 1982, Metra is the second largest commuter rail system in the United States. It generates over 270,000 trips on an average weekday using over 11 lines radiating north, south, and west of downtown.

Metra has one of the best railroad safety records in the country. It intends to maintain its excellent safety/customer service record, and it wants to utilize the latest technological innovations in passenger railway service. Microprocessors are now in every locomotive. Computers operate advanced signaling devices. High-speed/high-tech trains are now operating daily in Europe and Japan at speeds of 125 mph to 170 mph. Can the ever greater suburban sprawl make this an attractive future consideration for a railroad that wants to increase its ridership by shortening travel times over expressway alternatives?

Metra's work force education program was designed to train current workers who had educational skills below the tenth-grade level. This "people program" gave an older, well-established work force the opportunity to improve their reading, math, and communication skills (such as English as a second language). Employees participating in the program were specifically interested in improving current job skills or gaining promotion to a new job at Metra.

Classrooms were located in the Metra railroad marshaling yards scattered throughout the Chicago metropolitan area. This placed the training program near the individual employee's daily work activities. In the briefing sessions held for all employees before the program began, workers were told, "This program is like a floating crap game. It can go wherever you want it to go." From the beginning a key concept was building the entire training effort around what Metra's training manager described as "on-the-job trust."

In the two years prior to the program, Metra stressed its commitment from the top down. The executive director made a major commitment to the concepts behind this work force education effort. Fifteen unions were briefed and lent their support to beginning the program. Question-and-answer presentations on work force education were made during a general management and small committee meetings.

An information campaign was then begun for all 2,100 Metra employees. Flyers were distributed to all employees, and information was published in the Metra newsletter (see Figure 4.7). Of even more importance, face-to-face briefing sessions were held in Metra rail yards for all employees, who attended

Figure 4.7
Metra's Workforce Education Bulletin

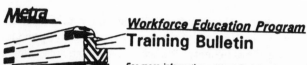

Workforce Education Program
Training Bulletin

For more information contact Training & Development at 8913, 8932 or 8922; We're at your service.

Workforce Education Program

A new educational opportunity will soon be coming our way--Metra's *Workforce Education Program*. This training program, open to all employees, will provide customized instruction in math, reading and language skills. This is an opportunity to brush up on some old skills or even learn a few new ones.

Metra has been awarded a grant from the Illinois Secretary of State to implement this "pilot program". The grant provides matched funding for 30 Metra employees who will receive forty hours of customized instruction in the educational skills they want to improve.

The classes will be small--5 to a class. What's also interesting is the approach. Metra's Training Division will be working with an outside expert in the field of adult education--Dr. Ed Gordon. "This is a people program..." said Dr. Gordon (he prefers "Ed") at a presentation to the members of our Labor/Management Technical Skills Task Group. Dr. Gordon stressed the fact that each class will incorporate "real world" examples from the job or other areas of personal interest to participants. "For example, we might use a racing form to work with fractions..."said Gordon, "...anything to make it more enjoyable."

This program has received the glowing endorsement of many of our Labor

officers. One highly supportive General Chairman (Mark Wimmer, General Chairman B.M.W.E.) wrote to the Director of Training, John Wagner, commenting on the *Workforce Education Program* "...Metra appears to be very committed to enhancing basic education, as well as work skills...most importantly in a confidential and non-threatening environment." Participation is voluntary and costs the employee nothing. The classes will be provided after hours utilizing Metra facilities easily accessible to the employee.

Field presentations to explain the Workforce Education Program will take place in mid-November. Following these presentations, interested employees can arrange for an orientation session with Dr. Gordon's staff to discuss their particular interests.

Programs using the same approach are being provided by Federal Signal, First National Bank of Chicago, Nabisco and by many other Illinois employers. It is worth noting that among the 57 grants awarded by the State, Metra's Workforce Education Program was the only transportation entity and the only public sector employer to be successful. For additional information on the program you can call the Training Division (X8932).

on a voluntary basis. Metra's work force education program was offered to all employees who wished to volunteer for the training classes. All program test scores were kept confidential by the authors. Progress reports on each worker were given to Metra's human resource department rather than the employee's immediate supervisor.

At its inception approximately 200 Metra employees volunteered for the program. Maintenance-of-way personnel, coach cleaners, engine machinists, and workers in many other job classifications were tutored in groups of five, using the IIP curriculum scripts and the tutorial methods previously described. Every effort was made to use realistic, on-the-job training materials and other tutoring materials applicable to personals interest or daily life. Each ten-week, forty-hour program consisted of a two-hour class meeting twice each week. At the end of a ten-week module, employees needing further training could be regrouped on the basis of similar educational needs, and the training continued.

Metra has made a budgetary commitment to do whatever it takes to meet all the educational needs required for work by all their employees. Its program was partially funded by a grant from the Illinois Secretary of State's Work Force Education Program. The Metra work force education program is a serious, long-term commitment to broaden the availability of training and development services for all workers (Gordon, 1993).

Service Employees

The Marriott Story

The Chicagoland Chamber of Commerce (CCC), a nonprofit business-economic enhancement organization, partnered with the authors to provide work force education company models for small and medium-sized companies. CCC piloted groups of workers with their companies for skills training through On-the-Job-Training programs. They fund this program through the Job Training Partnership Act, which helps organizations hire and train economically disadvantaged adult workers.

With the Marriott organization, we trained workers in CCC's Future Tech Program for basic reading and math applied to the housekeeping function. Another group of maids was enrolled in an ESL program. The small-group tutorial classes met on-site over a ten-week period.

One of the results of the training was that the daily newspaper became user friendly to the students. During the tutoring classes, they read help-wanted ads to learn about their job requirements and specifically about hotel positions that will become available to them as they acquire more knowledge and problem-solving skills. CCC placed them with a hotel because it provided good upward career ladders. However, without this work force education program, they would not have known about higher-level jobs or how to apply for them.

The basic skill trainer characterized some of their work with the following comments:

> They [the students] talked about recipes and reinforcing measuring skills. The use of the newspaper to increase knowledge of current events and job responsibilities helped reinforce good basic living-job skills. General information of all sorts that is sometimes taken for granted by many of us was eagerly learned by these adults. Sometimes thought of as trivial information, this was found to be beneficial to these adults. They had never been exposed to, or taught, such knowledge.

The fact that their employer offered training that will improve their quality of life had a major motivational impact on these employees. In too many instances the unemployed minority worker is viewed by companies as a high-risk employee. The authors believe that work force education programs have considerable potential for providing life-style-related work "anchors" that build a more stable, dedicated work force.

The ESL students had very different experiences. Their ability in their native language was at best near the third-grade levels. Their language training focused on housekeeping vocabulary and vocabulary commonly used with hotel guests. The ESL trainer typified their work with these comments:

> The ESL training provided them with a good inner feeling that each of them is capable of learning! They were surprised with their own learning ability and realized that with more exposure and practice, they could each begin to speak English....This exposure to the English language and to a learning environment gave them an incentive to learn to communicate better.

Imparting this employee incentive translates into transferring the work ethic to the present American generation. We believe this to be an achievable goal for work force education programs.

CCC has learned through these program experiences that the training must be scheduled at least partially during working hours. Students had been volunteering an hour at the end of the workday. Many ended up with poor class attendance that reduced individual skill gains. Also, the company has to designate a permanent training classroom so everyone knows where to report and can acclimate to the setting. It is not recommended that the training be moved to whatever space is available that day.

CCC and the participating companies recognized the value of a one-to-one or small tutorial group setting. The IIP offered them a prescriptive learning method that tailored the program content to the individual student's best learning abilities. Even though these tutorial classes are more expensive in comparison to traditional classroom teaching, the learning outcomes are far greater with the corollary of a positive training experience that enhances employee motivation. Given these positive results, CCC has continued these Work Force Education Skills Programs with the authors, and has great confidence in the future enhancement of worker performance.

Office Support Employees

Office support positions employ millions of workers who must have skills at a high-school level or above. However, too many employees have very poor academic preparation to work in a high-tech modern office. Thousands of companies have experienced a steep rise in personnel screening costs to find competent office support employees. However, even the best recruitment efforts still leave many companies with many individuals who are poorly trained in office skills.

In 1984 the authors were contacted by corporations looking for a successful solution to this workplace dilemma. Many companies had already tried in-house training classes, public seminars, or local educational programs, but office workers were still making many of the same errors. Corporations took an unprecedented step (for 1984) by asking us to tutor their secretaries on a 1:1 or 1:5 basis at their office during the workday.

IIP tutorial programs in basic, and sometimes intermediate, written communication skills were provided to these secretaries, with programs lasting from six to twelve months in order to cycle all the office workers through the classes. Some needed only review work; others needed extensive skill building and practice. Prior employee work was analyzed for errors by our business English tutors. Company "model letters," documents and reports were incorporated into the IIP tutorial content.

Work force education programs for office practice have covered an array of business skills, including grammar, spelling, punctuation, proper business letter forms, writing, speed typing, shorthand, PC use, and PC software. Executive secretary business communication training helps employees learn how to edit the writing errors of top-level managers. The secretaries became proficient in such areas as correct use of pronouns and modifiers, punctuation, parts of speech, and sentence structure.

These office practice areas are part of the literacy-fluency gap that permeates the U.S. work environment. Many companies must now hire marginally educated entry-level clerical workers. As they are incorporated into the support service, a company may find promotable individual through their daily performance record. However, many cannot be advanced because of their weak educational preparation. Even major law firms have contacted the authors for secretarial training programs that focus on specialized legal vocabulary, legal correspondence, and legal documents.

Many secretaries are now called upon to assume managerial responsibilities. A newly promoted headquarters secretary found her responsibilities included interoffice memos. Her training included learning advanced vocabulary and the proper use of colons and semicolons. At the end of the one-to-one writing program she was able to compose appropriately worded, clear, and concise memos.

In another instance, a corporate vice president dictated letters without following the basic rules of business writing. His secretary already possessed excellent grammar and punctuation skills. The IIP sessions emphasized establishing the proper tone of a letter, smooth topic transitions, getting to the point, filling in details, and a proper summary close.

Health care and insurance organizations have used our IIP programs to improve accuracy and speed in patient data entry. Data entry clerks have received PC training that taught them both PC usage and software capabilities. At a major insurance company, grammar and speech skills were improved by taping conversations and learning correction through listening.

A leading Chicago law firm requested the authors' assistance in sharpening the shorthand skills of two executive secretaries. While both individuals had a good knowledge of Gregg Shorthand, they found it necessary to increase their speed and accuracy to meet the demands of a more advanced assignment. An IIP tutorial increased their shorthand speed from 60 wpm to 100 wpm. Not only was their accuracy greatly improved, but they were able to read other secretaries' shorthand notes. This has proven to be a labor-saving skill since letters do not need redictation if the secretary to whom they were dictated is absent. Companies that have participated in these IIP office-support skills programs include FMC, Premark International, Homequity, Angus Chemical Company, Morton International, and EHS Health Care.

LESSONS FOR TRAINERS

Several important factors have emerged from our work with the IIP as an embellished training model based on concepts found in mastery learning, Personalized Systems of Instruction, tutoring and cognition. (Our quantitative data on the results of the IIP are presented in Appendix II.) These general training concepts are as follows:

Time

1. The amount of time that adult learners are actively engaged in a

learning task is important (Fisher et al., 1978; Stallings, 1980).

2. From a cognitive science perspective, the performance of a task becomes more automatic with repeated exposure to small, meaningful components of the task consistently presented over a period of time (Myers & Fisk, 1987).

3. Learning is enhanced by instruction that breaks down complex tasks into small meaningful components that are taught individually.

Applying New Learning to Existing Knowledge

1. Knowledge, from a cognitive perspective, is viewed as organized in schemata (hierarchical mind structures or networks of abstract concepts, components, and interrelationships). Increasing an individual's ability to develop more elaborate schematas, to access them more easily, and to systematize learning procedures will make learning easier for adult learners.

2. Instruction that facilitates students' relating new information to old is useful. New information is more readily learned when it is organized and presented in a conceptual structure, using associations, advance organizers, topic headings, and mnemonics.

3. It is important to teach the prototype first (i.e., concepts, rules, principles), then variations, including real-world examples and applications. It is also important that students see the alignment among goals, content, instruction, task, and evaluation.

Continuous Feedback and Assessment

1. Research indicates that adult learning is enhanced by detailed and specific feedback, not only on the correctness of responses but also on the appropriateness of learning strategies (Brophy, 1981; Guskey & Gates, 1986; Walberg, 1984; Wang et al., 1990).

2. In addition, feedback is important not only on total performance but also on specific task components, so that the learner can discover sources of error. Continuous assessment that is integrated with instruction enhances the learner's ability to identify useful program-solving strategies.

3. Individual or small-group tutorials feature both continuous feedback and assessment for the adult learner.

Metacognition: Learning How to Learn

1. Our research and that of others indicates that effective learners use mental models to conceptualize their tasks. This process also includes methods for accomplishing the task and establishing relationships to other similar ideas (Brainin, 1985). The best problem solvers develop a detailed mental representation of a problem before attempting its solution (Norman & Rumelhart, 1981).
2. Metacognition recognizes that learners can be explicitly taught to use learning models and thinking skills (Scardamalia & Bereiter, 1983). It is important to find out from adult learners what models they already use in everyday work or life situations. Learning is enhanced when these existing models are elaborated and refined through the instructional process.
3. For these reasons, effective task analysis enables the learner to identify the development of individual learning models. In addition, using learners' existing models provides examples and counterexamples for the adult to try on the job.

Motivational Links to Learning

1. Adult learners use two kinds of knowledge to learn: task knowledge and motivational knowledge (Ames & Ames, 1984, 1985, 1989; Winne, 1991).
2. Motivational knowledge influences learning involvement and stimulates how adults feel about the learning experience (Winne, 1985). Motivators for adult learners include the following (Morgan et al., in progress):
   a. A stress-free learning environment
   b. Peers' support of learning
   c. A business culture that emphasizes learning and work-related performance
   d. Easy program accessibility
   e. A sense of group "oneness" among training participants
   f. Employer commitment to the program's success
   g. Individual employees' personal values of persistence

APPLYING THE IIP TO SPECIFIC TRAINING PRACTICES

The authors' diverse company, multilevel employee work force education research has produced specific guidelines for future business program planning. We have summarized them in these ten "best training practice principles":

1. Instruction needs to modify student attention, expectations and memory. Cognitive information processing is enhanced when learners are actively engaged in the learning task (e.g., discuss, rehearse, analyze, problem solve, use graphs to represent experience) and share observations, understandings, and knowledge.
2. Find out the learning strengths and problems. Diagnose the adult's learning problems. This includes not only giving a normed pre/post-test in reading, math, problem solving, grammar, writing, or other pertinent skills but also making careful observations for potential learning difficulties and/or disabilities. Additional diagnostic tests can be used, if needed, to determine the direction for remedial training.
3. Use relevant adult training materials. Teaching materials must be realistic for each individual's present or future job requirements. The curriculum for a manager, secretary, or plant worker must be organized around actual job tasks. Training must be built on the employee's knowledge of job content. It is very important to include non-job materials based on the employee's personal interests, hobbies, and daily needs. Seeing broader, immediate payoffs in daily life will sustain the individual's interest and motivation.
4. Social learning. When possible, give employees an opportunity to work together and learn from each other. Social learning gives the adult an opportunity to imitate the successful learning behaviors of others (i.e., trainers, peers, even managers).
5. Feedback. Adult learners need constant feedback on their progress. When learning tasks are grouped into smaller segments, the trainer has the opportunity to give periodic progress reports to each adult learner. Verbal reports, progress charts, checklists, and certificates of completion are techniques that can be adjusted for the intended audience.
6. Evaluation. Effective work force education programs use an array of evaluation methods to improve content, training methods and overall employee success. Standardized tests alone will not do the job. They may even give a false impression of skill needs or overall program results.
7. Sustaining individual enrollment. To lower the dropout rates typically found in these programs, individual job goals and objectives must be clearly defined before employees enroll. While these issues may change once workers put their personal expectations in writing, the learners will become more goal-directed and will persevere when struggling to acquire or apply new knowledge.
8. Sustaining organizational support. Company goals must reinforce the goals

of participating employees. This will keep everyone's expectations realistic and help avoid the quick-fix mentality found in too many work force education programs.

9.   A multilayered approach. There is no one best training and development answer to the work force education puzzle. A company will usually need a multilayered program that offers a variety of approaches. This recognizes the different levels of personal experience and employee readiness to learn. Our research has rated these different alternative training methods in descending order of effectiveness:

   a. Small-group tutorials (or even one-to-one instruction based on a modified mastery learning model)
   b. Cross-training (peer tutoring)
   c. Computer-based Training
   d. Programmed learning materials
   e. Traditional classroom instruction (at or above the seventh-grade level).

10.   The IIP work force education approach, as an enhanced mastery learning model, yields significant results in the diagnosis and training of adult workers. Most important, these on-site company programs have demonstrated the adaptability of cognitive research to practical, job-training applications for managers, office staff, and production or service employees.

We have now completed the review of the skills segment of FutureWork's Work Force Education Triad, using cognitive concepts that are based on the authors' ongoing field research. Can these principles also be adapted to enhance management development programs?

The next two chapters will provide both the theoretical framework of behavioral/cognitive learning theory, and practical training applications. This will help establish a context for the cognitively based Management Insight Development Programs (MIDP) that the authors have developed through ongoing field research applications with many businesses.

REFERENCES

Ames, C., & Ames, R. E., eds., 1985. *Research on Motivation in Education.* Vol. 2, *The Classroom Milieu.* Orlando, FL: Academic Press.
____. 1989. *Research on Motivation in Education.* Vol. 3, *Goals and Cognitions.* Orlando, FL: Academic Press.
Ames, R. E., & Ames, C., eds., 1984. *Research on Motivation in Education.* Vol. 1, *Student Motivation.* Orlando, FL: Academic Press.
Barrows, H. S. 1988. *The Tutorial Process.* Springfield, IL: Southern Illinois University School of Medicine.

Becker, S. 1986. What you should know about tutoring centers. *Instructor* 95 (6):88–90.

Blazey, M. L., & Davison, K. S. 1990. Keeping up with the factory of the future. *Training* 27 (2):51–55.

Bloom, B. 1984. The search for methods of group instruction as effective as one-on-one tutoring. *Educational Leadership* 41 (8):4–17.

Boyett, J. H., & Conn, H. P. 1991. *Workplace 2000*. New York: Penguin Books.

Brainin, S. S. 1985. Mediating learning: Pedagogic issues in the improvement of cognitive functioning. In E. W. Gordon, ed., *Review of Research in Education*, vol. 12. Washington, DC: American Educational Research Association.

Brophy, J. 1981. Teacher praise: A functional analysis. *Psychological Review* 88 (2):93–134.

Brown, A. L. 1978. Knowing when, where, and how to remember: A problem of metacognition. In R. Glaser, ed., *Advances in Instructional Psychology*, vol. 1. Hillsdale, NJ: Erlbaum.

Case, R. 1985. A developmentally based approach to the problem of instructional design. In S. F. Chipman, J. W. Segal, & R. Glaser, eds., *Thinking and Learning Skills*, vol. 2. Hillsdale, NJ: Erlbaum.

Cohen Gold, P., & Johnson, J. A. 1982. Prediction of achievement in reading, self-esteem, and verbal language by adult illiterates in a psychoeducational tutorial program. *Journal of Clinical Psychology* 38 (2):513–22.

Ellson, D. G. 1976. Tutoring. In N. L. Gage ed., *The Psychology of Teaching Methods*. Chicago: NSSE.

Fisher, C.; Filby, N.; Marliave, R.; Cahen, L.; Dishaw, M.; Moore, J.; & Berliner, D. 1978. *Teaching Behaviors, Academic Learning Time, and Student Achievement*. Final Report of Phase III-B Beginning Teacher Evaluation Study. San Francisco: Far West Laboratory for Educational Research and Development.

Glaser, R. 1990. The reemergence of learning theory within instructional research. *American Psychologist* 45 (1):29–39.

Goldstein, I. L., & Gilliam, P. 1990. Training system issues in the year 2000. *American Psychologist* 45 (2):134–43.

Gordon, E. E. 1993. *Summary of Selected Client Programs in Educational/Skill Training*. Oak Lawn, IL: Imperial Corporate Training & Development. (Report available upon request; write to 10341 South Lawler Avenue, Oak Lawn, IL 60453-4714 or call 708-636-8852).

_____. 1991a. *Individualized Instruction Program (IIP) Curriculum, Administration and Methods Manual*. Oak Lawn, IL: Imperial Tutoring and Educational Services.

_____. 1991b. Managing the diverse skills of America's new workforce. *Managing Diversity* 1 (3):1, 4, 6.

_____. 1988. The implications of integrating business skills with appropriate content areas. *Training Today* (October), 8–9.

_____. 1983. Home tutoring programs gain respectability. *Phi Delta Kappan* 64 (6):398–99.

Gordon, E. E., & Gordon, E. H. 1990. *Centuries of Tutoring: A History of Alternative Education in America and Western Europe*. Lanham, MD: University Press of America.

Gordon, E. E.; Ponticell, J. A.; & Morgan, R. R. 1991. *Closing the Literacy Gap in American Business: A Guide for Trainers and Human Resource Specialists.* New York: Quorum Books.

_____. 1990. A report on results of the IIP literacy training program: Implications for the literacy issue in American business. Paper presented at the annual meeting of the Midwest Education Research Association, Chicago. October 19.

_____. Back to basics. *Training and Development Journal* 43 (8):73–76.

Guskey, T. R., & Gates, S. L. 1986. Synthesis of research on the effects of mastery learning in elementary and secondary classrooms. *Educational Leadership* 43 (8):73–80.

Harkins, P. J. 1991. The changing role of corporate training and development. *Corporate Development in the 90s,* supplement to *Training* magazine, 26–29.

Levin, J., & Pressley, N. 1983. *Cognitive Strategy Research: Educational Applications.* New York: Springer-Verlag.

Morgan, R. R.; Gordon, E. E.; & Ponticell, J. A. In progress. *Enhancing Learning in Training and Education: A Guide for Trainers and Human Resource Specialists.*

Myers, G. L., & Fisk, A. D. 1987. Training consistent task components: Applications of automatic and controlled processing theory to industrial task training. *Human Factors* 29 (3):355–368.

Norman, D. A., & Rumelhart, D. E. 1981. The LNR approach to human information processing. *Cognition* 10 (1-3):235–240.

Putnam, R. T. 1987. Structuring and adjusting content for students: A study of live and simulated tutoring of addition. *American Educational Research Journal* 24 (1):13–48.

Scardamalia, M., & Bereiter, C. 1983. Child as co-investigator: Helping children gain insight into their own mental processes. In S. Paris, G. Olson, & H. Stevenson, eds., *Learning and Motivation in the Classroom.* Hillsdale, NJ: Erlbaum.

Stallings, J. 1980. Allocated academic learning time revisited or beyond time on task. *Educational Researcher* 9 (1):11–16.

Von Harrison, G., & Guymon, R. E. 1980. *Structural Tutoring.* Englewood Cliffs, NJ: Educational Technology Publications.

Walberg, H. J. 1984. Improving the productivity of America's schools. *Educational Leadership* 41 (8):19–27.

Wang, M. C., Haertel, G. D., & Walberg, H. J. 1990. What influences learning? A content analysis of review literature. *Journal of Educational Research* 84 (1):30–43.

Winne, P. H. 1985 Steps toward promoting cognitive achievement. *Elementary School Journal* 85 (5):673–693.

Winne, P. H. 1991. Motivation and teaching. In H. C. Waxman & H. J. Walberg, eds., *Effective Teaching: Current Research.* Berkeley, CA: McCutchan.

Chapter 5

Behavior-Based Instruction: Missing Pieces of the Training Puzzle

IMPLICATIONS FOR TRAINING

How we learn is a matter of great debate! Different theorists have different views to explain why, how badly, or how well we perform in training and learning tasks in general. Reading, writing, language, listening, studying, remembering, analyzing, synthesizing, motivating, problem solving, comprehension, and creativity are but a few of the factors required to do well in learning tasks related to the modern workplace. We will briefly consider some of the major behavioral theorists and how they explain learning in general.

Behavior-based learning models have long dominated training in the corporate classroom. Let us explore the many useful ideas offered by this mode of training/instruction. We will also review behaviorism's broader implications in addressing contemporary adult training issues.

MODELS OF LEARNING

Two basic models of learning, behaviorism and cognitivism, are competing for use by trainers in a business setting. Each has had its own unique evolution.

In this chapter each specific learning model is briefly described and compared with other models. A practical training example is given to better explain each model's characteristics and how they might be applied to the workplace. Cognition will be presented in Chapter 6.

Additional sections of the chapter include a brief discussion on the special place of motivation within learning theory. We will conclude by weighing the limitations of behaviorism as it affects contemporary issues such as teaching for quality, team building, problem solving, and other education areas related to the workplace.

BEHAVIORISM MODELS

Classical Conditioning

In the classical conditioning learning model, stimulus-stimulus learning takes place when two stimuli are paired for a number of trials. One stimulus is referred to as the unconditioned stimulus (UCS) and the other as the conditioned stimulus (CS) (see Figure 5.1).

Pavlov

In the original 1927 experimental demonstration of classical conditioning, Ivan Pavlov (1960) paired food powder (a UCS) with the ringing of a bell (CS) for a number of trials. Before the experiment, Pavlov observed that presentation of food to a dog elicited salivation. Pavlov attempted to train the animal to salivate when a bell rang. To do so, he paired the two stimuli (UCS and CS) for a number of trials. With repeated pairings, the animal gradually learned to salivate when the bell rang.

Watson

Using the same model, Watson and Raynor (1920) designed an experiment in which they demonstrated that early emotions are acquired through the classical conditioning procedure. Using a child as a subject and pairing a loud sound (UCS) with a rabbit (CS), they found that the child learns to fear the rabbit. The Watson and Raynor study is considered by most learning theorists to be of crucial importance. Why? Because the study represents a demonstration that early learning takes place through a process of stimulus pairing and that emotions (fear in this instance) are not necessarily innate; they can be learned.

Training Applications

In U.S. Army basic training, recruits are taught how to crawl across an active battlefield to reach an enemy target. The key lesson to be learned is to crawl as close to the ground as possible, in order to offer the smallest possible target. The training's ultimate practice test is a simulated field exercise during which live ammunition is fired over the heads of the trainees.

The CS is the protective crawling tactic. The UCS is the sound of gunfire whizzing overhead. Hopefully, the soldiers will learn always to use their crawling tactic in the presence of the enemy, whether or not they experience gunfire. They will have thus better learned a basic battlefield behavior: personal survival. To explain adult training using classical conditioning, the unconditioned-stimulus (UCS) is the gunfire whizzing over the recruits' heads.

Figure 5.1
Learning Theory Overview

Characteristics	BEHAVIORISM			COGNITIVISM		
	Classical Conditioning	Operant Conditioning	Social Learning	Gestalt	Developmental	Information Processing
1. Theorists	Ivan Pavlov J.B. Watson E. Guthrie	E. Thorndike Clark Hull B.F. Skinner	Albert Bandura	E. Tolman Kurt Lewin W. Kohler	Jean Piaget Malcolm Knowles	Benjamin Bloom R.M. Gagne R. Feuerstein R.J. Sternberg R.R. Morgan
2. Definition of Learning	Conditioning	•Reinforcement •Habits	•Observation •Modeling	•Past Experience •Habits •Remolding Experience	Problem Solving Developed over Time	Strategies for •Thinking •Problem Solving •Recalling New Information
3. Definition of Human Nature	Stimulated by Environment	Responds to •Rewards •Correctives	Emulate Rewarded Behavior	Assimilation of Old Information with New Information	Children & Adults Approach Learning Differently	•Attention Develops •Memory Develops
4. Role of Trainer	Model	Shaper	Socially Correct Model	Organize Suitable Learning Environment	Adjust Learning to Specific Audience	Facilitate Mind-Activating Activities
5. Role of Learner	Passive	Manipulated	Imitating	Harmonize Learning	Interaction with Environment	•Motivated •Active •Eager
6. Typical Training Offered	•Simple Service or Assembly •Army Combat Training	•Assembly-Line Mass Production •Introductory Selling •Telephone Operator	•Consultative Selling •Supervisory Training •Waitress •Receptionist •Bank Teller Training	•1st-Line Manager Skill Training •Skilled Trades	•Management •Complex Manufacturing Process •Customer Service	•Management •Teams •Leadership •Professional Development •Quality Issues •Communications

This is paired with what you want them to learn, crawling close to the ground (the neutral stimulus). This allows for the transfer of learning to a more complex task. This is why trainees will remember to hug the ground on a battlefield (conditioned response).

Operant Conditioning

E. Thorndike, B. F. Skinner, and Clark Hull developed the operant conditioning model. They used reinforcement and corrective procedures to shape learning behavior (see Figure 5.1).

Thorndike

Edward Thorndike (1874–1949) dominated the field of educational psychology from about 1915 to 1935. He was a stimulus-response-stimulus theorist who emphasized reinforcement and practice. He believed that skill training was highly specific, and he expected little generalization to occur across different learning tasks. Often introductory sales training is designed around these concepts.

Thorndike's strict behavioral, noncognitive notions of learning have been severely criticized (Bower and Hilgard, 1981). We now know that information (Buchwald, 1967) and awareness (Estes, 1969) facilitate learning. For example, successful consultative selling training is often built around enhancing the adult learner's ability to gather information and increasing the learner's awareness of the buyer's personality needs. Thorndike refused to include these cognitive variables in his theory and viewed the learning process as being highly mechanical. History has not been kind to his views on learning. Nevertheless, he is given credit for establishing a laboratory approach to educational practice and for advocating that we carefully assess a learner's rate of progress.

Hull

Hull's (1943) theory was basically a reinforcement theory. However, he did allow some room for goal-directed cognitive mediation, which he called "habit chains," to occur between the stimulus and the response.

Hull assumed that knowledge was accumulated through experience. The greater the accumulation, the greater the adaptive ability, intelligence, and problem-solving skills of the learner. The role of a teacher/trainer is to increase the number of "habit chains." Creativity can be explained in terms of an accidental combination of two or more habit chains.

An example is telephone operator training based on teaching the individual to respond quickly to caller requests. The more variations learned in the basic operation of the switchboard, the greater the operator's ability to adapt and to route calls automatically. This training forms habits and "habit chains" for the telephone operator. Creativity is measured on how well and rapidly the switchboard can be operated with very few errors.

Hull related extinction to failure to receive reinforcement. He had many followers (Mowrer, Miller, Spence, Amsel, and Logan) and dominated the field of learning from 1935 to 1955.

Skinner

B. F. Skinner dominated the world of learning from about 1955 to 1970. His model of learning is an operant reinforcement model. He is viewed as a radical behaviorist since he advocates a response psychology, not an stimulus-response psychology. He focused his attention on the importance of arranging environmental factors to bring behavior under stimulus control.

Skinner provided evidence supporting the use of four basic ways to handle reinforcements and correctives (punishments) in order to bring about behavior change. For example, in quadrant #1 of Figure 5.2, an adult in a training situation answers a question that yields a positive consequence (a smile from the trainer). This is an example of positive reinforcement, and we expect this reinforced behavior to increase in frequency.

Figure 5.2
Skinner's Response Psychology Quandrants

QUADRANTS

	Produce	Withdraw
Positive + Consequence	+ reinforcement #1	+corrective by withdrawal #2
Negative - Consequence	- corrective by hurt #3	- reinforcement #4

In quadrant #2 we have a situation in which an adult learner engages in behavior that leads to something valued being taken away. For example, an adult learner is listening to a radio while engaging in a task. When the learner stops engaging in the desired task, the radio is turned off. If the learner resumes the task, the radio is turned on. You have set up a situation of punishment by withdrawal of reinforcement (i.e., rewarding on task behavior by allowing the radio to remain on). By definition, use of a punisher reduces the level of responding, and use of a reinforcer increases the level of responding. In this instance, if turning off the radio is truly punishing to the learner, off task behavior will decrease in frequency.

In quadrant #3, we have a situation in which an adult engages in behavior that produces a negative consequence. The adult starts an argument with another adult, and the trainer reprimands the first adult. If the argument is perceived by the adult as a negative consequence and not just an attention-getting device, the acting-out behavior will decrease in frequency.

Last, in quadrant #4, we have a depiction of a situation in which a negative reinforcement contingency is used to control behavior. For most people, the sound of an alarm clock is perceived as a negative stimulus. If one reaches over to turn off the alarm clock, he or she has engaged in behavior that has removed a negative stimulus. This behavior is reinforcing, not corrective.

Since these techniques seem to work so well in controlling basic adult behavior, trainers have often used Skinner's operant conditioning techniques of pairing reinforcing and corrective stimuli to control trainee learning. Even though trainers can control behavior by using punishment, there is considerable evidence in the research literature indicating that they not do so (Turkington, 1986a). Trainers tend not to punish adults in order to encourage better class attendance.

In addition to Skinner's pragmatic focus on reinforcement, he is credited with work related to using either continuous or intermittent stimulus reinforcement to control behavior. Some sales training programs attempt to teach correct employee behaviors by reinforcing specific selling steps. Trainees are videotaped constantly in role-playing exercises (continuous reinforcement) until they can repeat the desired reinforced selling steps. However, the effects of this sales training often quickly disappear after the videotape reinforcement is withdrawn. Employees will often revert to their old selling styles, having adopted few changes from the training program.

As an alternative training practice, the same group sales trainees are intermittently videotaped. This is done in follow-up practice sessions after the trainer's presentation and following self-practice exercises. Not every element of the sales training program is taped, only the specific areas where the trainee needs the most practice. If the trainer uses an alternative intermittent reinforcement schedule only to improve the trainee's weakest presentation skills, it may take longer to improve overall trainee selling skills; but once the desired behaviors are strengthened, they are seldom forgotten. Often the best arrangement is for trainers to use a combination of continuous reinforcement applied early in a learning sequence followed by intermittent reinforcement.

Skinner's operant conditioning model appears to be very useful with respect to explaining learning in terms of overt responses that can be selectively reinforced or corrected. Consider a situation where we want to increase class attendance. R. R. Morgan (1975) conducted a study in which he was able to increase class attendance by using a combination of material and social rewards. If learners do not attend class, the basic problem is that they do not perceive class as a social reinforcer. The job of the trainer is to set up reinforcing situations that will enhance trainees' class attendance.

Morgan designed a triad reinforcement procedure in which one problem absentee learner was paired with two nonabsentee friends. These friends were carefully chosen by the trainer and were believed to serve as social reinforcers for the absentee learner. The pairing used was that when the absentee learner came to class, all members of the triad received a reward. When the absent learner did not come to class, no reward was given to any of the three. Continuous reinforcement was used initially to get behavior going. Later, intermittent reinforcement was used to maintain the desired behavior. The results of the study supported the use of the triad reinforcement procedure for trainee class attendance.

Training Implications

The operant conditioning model is useful in explaining learning in overt response situations such as fire fighter, paramedic, and police disaster procedures; basic selling; and simple assembly-line production. Of great importance is that a chain of stimulus and response associations is presumed to exist to explain complex behaviors. A learner must make a series of overt responses that can be selectively reinforced or corrected.

One of the major criticisms directed at the model is that many of the most important behaviors of interest to trainers (thinking, problem solving, creativity, learning from attending a training class, reading, and imitation of a model) do not involve making a fine-grained series of overt responses that can be selectively reinforced or corrected by the trainer.

Training based on an operant conditioning model tends to reduce complex interpersonal business problems to rather simple behavior-based solutions. A group of bank customer-service representatives is shown a twenty-minute videotape on improving customer relations. The training's emphasis is that bank personnel must always remain cordial, and polite, and give the customer what he or she wants. This program demotivates the bank's trainees because they understand that many customer requests are complex and often cannot be fulfilled by the bank. They view customer service as requiring more of a problem-solving process, not just a set of behaviors. The operant model appears to have very limited application to many contemporary business training needs, such as team building, quality, or leadership programs that require individual development of higher-level thinking skills.

Another criticism of this model is that the use of extrinsic rewards (i.e., reinforcement) may undermine intrinsic interests (Bates, 1979; Deci, 1975; Lepper & Greene, 1978; Morgan, 1984). Material rewards do encourage most marketing personnel to sell more during a special campaign promotion. However, this procedure often backfires. It sometimes undermines the sales staff's motivation to sell on a day-to-day basis once this pairing is removed. The real goal is to get the employee to sell successfully by using a reward system, to make sure the marketer is learning effective selling strategies, and then to build a social support recognition system into the sales environment so that employees are motivated to continue to sell after the campaign ends.

A delicate balance exists between the proper use of extrinsic rewards and intrinsic interests. If a company has adopted a work-team bonus program, the extrinsic reward of the cash bonus may undermine the intrinsic interests of increasing personal job satisfaction, reducing job stress, or increasing personal flexibility. Company morale and individual performance may suffer unless other higher-level thinking skills are also developed so that the work team reaches a level of understanding that enables them to live with a bonus program's risks.

Social Learning

From a social learning perspective we learn by observing and modeling. We do not need to make an overt response that is selectively reinforced or corrected. In order to learn something, we are more likely to emulate a rewarded model's behavior than a corrected model's behavior. For example, in a training class adults will often model their behavior on another adult's actions that are rewarded by the trainer. For this reason it is very important to be careful with respect to exposing adult learners to antisocial role models.

Bandura

The social learning model is very important to trainers because a great deal of adult learning in the corporate classroom takes place in a social context where few overt responses are made. One of its chief advocates, Albert Bandura (Bandura, 1978, 1989) saw learning as having three interrelated components: the learner's behavior, individual differences between persons (i.e., intelligence and personality), and the learner's environment.

Training Implications

We learn by attending a seminar where we observe and listen to what is presented by the trainer. We imitate the behaviors of those around us (managers, trainers, peers, friends). Much adult learning takes place by reading. The trainers, managers, peers, and books serve as our role models. While learning to emulate these models, adults make no overt responses that are selectively reinforced or punished. The important lesson for trainers is that from a social learning point of view, what is taking place is the pairing of a stimulus with a response and the combining of the pair with thinking (i.e., cognition).

MOTIVATION AND LEARNING

To begin understanding how adults learn, we must offer some reasonable explanation of motivation. What is motivation? Most of us assume that motivation energizes behavior, gives behavior direction, and leads us to a goal. How can we best design motivation into a training and development program?

Each of the learning models we have discussed includes a motivational component (McCombs, 1984). Motivation in traditional classical conditioning models and some operant conditioning models consists of some sort of physiological drive mechanism. A more contemporary behavioral view of motivation is Skinner's use of schedules of reinforcement as motivators of behavior.

In order to give more meaning to the concept of motivation, we will examine it within the context of a latent learning example. "Latent learning" refers to learning without reinforcement. For example, a company has two sales representatives. One received a high personal incentive for learning by earning a large bonus. The second sales representative received a low personal incentive for learning by earning no bonus. What frequently happens is that the high-incentive, salesperson performs significantly better on the task than the low-incentive person. However, if the company suddenly gives higher-revenue-producing accounts, and thus the opportunity of a bonus, to the second sales representative, we usually find that he or she suddenly performs at a much higher level. In other words, the second salesperson was learning even in the low-incentive condition, but was not performing at a high level because a high-incentive system was not applied to his or her performance. Once incentives were made available, the low performer increased sales performance to match the higher performer.

Using this latent learning example, a motivator is defined as a stimulus that transforms learning into performance. In other words, we need a construct such as motivation (better-opportunity sales accounts) to transform an internal variable (learned sales abilities) into something external (sales).

The inclusion of a motivational construct within our learning theories allows us to connect the internal processes of learning with external performance. Use of a continuous or intermittent schedule of reinforcement, such as personal recognition, bonuses, or promotions, is using a stimulus to transform learning into performance. Use of cognitive conflict as a motivator in a problem-solving situation, such as the work of teams, also transforms simulated learning into performance on the job.

BEHAVIORISM'S TRAINING LIMITATIONS

Behaviorism has come under attack for its lack of a learning-performance distinction and its limitations in successfully addressing complex behaviors in the workplace such as thinking, problem-solving, or creativity-supporting programs for TQM, ISO 9000, team building, and other more demanding educational programs. It is estimated that only 10 to 15 percent of all contemporary training is retained by employees and used back on the job (Boyett & Conn, 1991). The uses of behavior-based management development programs or skill training for managers or nonmanagers is increasingly falling far short of the expectations and demands of a more competitive world. Quality, team-building, interpersonal communication, and leadership programs too often fall far short of their goals due to the limitations of behavior-based training.

Learning Versus Performance Distinctions

The distinction of learning versus performance has not been adequately accounted for by behaviorism. Behaviorism is basically a performance and reinforcement theory, not a learning theory. Studies of latent learning (e.g., Hull, 1943), or learning without reinforcement, indicate that reinforcement influences performance, not learning. Thus we can make a learning versus performance distinction.

The related issue of personal motivation also is difficult for behaviorism. It typically defines motivation as a variable that transforms learning into performance. This is a very awkward explanation for such an important element in the design of effective training outcomes.

The defense that behaviorists offer to these questions is that overt behavior must be kept as the unit of analysis. They state that it is unnecessary to go inside the person to ascertain what is "really" learned. Trainers/educators need not resort to mentalistic conceptualizations to adequately explain behavior (Skinner, 1989; Mahoney, 1989). The learning versus performance issue is further complicated by observational learning. There is considerable evidence to indicate that we can learn by observation (imitation of models, attending lectures, and reading) without making overt responses. How can the behaviorist adequately explain learning without an overt response?

Complex Adult Behavior for Learning

We believe the most damaging general criticism of behaviorism as a useful learning theory for training is that it is quite limited in terms of explaining complex human behavior. This severely limits the learning concepts that can be explained by the behaviorists. Such areas as thinking, problem solving, comprehension, and creativity, which do not entail an overt response, cannot be adequately explained by the behaviorist system. Also, the behaviorists have not provided a place in their learning system for the problems that can limit human learning. We can see from this analysis that the traditional behaviorist system is primarily appropriate for explaining performance rather than learning (Benjamin, 1988; Kipnis, 1987), and the behavior of animals such as dolphins (Turkington, 1986b). It is time for training and development to move on.

FUTURE TRAINING TRENDS

Since the 1970s, Skinner's contributions to learning have dominated the design of training and development (Mahoney, 1989; Zuriff, 1980). Present and future business trends driven by technology and competitive participatory management models are compelling many trainers to move toward models and methodologies that facilitate complex adult learning rather than a set of general behavioral laws.

In Chapter 6 we will examine how cognition deals with the complexities of thinking, problem solving, and workplace creativity. We will present our Management Insight Development Programs as a cognitive workplace learning model with specific business case studies of actual training program applications.

REFERENCES

Amsel, A. 1962. Frustrative nonreward in partial reinforcement and discrimination learning. *Psychological Review* 69:306–28.

Bandura, A. 1989. Human agency in social cognitive theory. *American Psychologist* 44 (9):1175–84.

___. 1978. The self system in reciprocal determinism. *American Psychologist* 33 (4):344–58.

Bates, J. A. 1979. Extrinsic reward and intrinsic motivation: A review with implications for the classroom. *Review of Educational Research* 49 (4):557–76.

Benjamin, L. T. 1988. A history of teaching machines. *American Psychologist* 43 (9):703–12.

Bindra, D. 1974. A motivational view of learning, performance, and behavior modification. *Psychological Review* 81:199–213.

Bolles, R. C. 1972. Reinforcement, expectancy, and learning. *Psychological Review* 79:394–409.

Bower, G. H., & Hilgard, E. R. 1981. *Theories of Learning*. Englewood Cliffs, NJ: Prentice-Hall.

Boyett, J. H., & Conn, H. P. 1991. *Workplace 2000*. New York: Penguin Books.

Breland, K., & Breland, M. 1960. The misbehavior of organisms. *American Psychologist* 6:81–84.

Brophy, J. E. 1983. If only it were true: A response to Greer. *Educational Researcher* 12 (10):10–12.

Buchwald, A. M. 1967. Effects of immediate vs. delayed outcomes in associative learning. *Journal of Verbal Learning and Verbal Behavior* 6 (3):317–20.

Burghardt, G. 1985. Animal awareness: Current perceptions and historical perspectives. *American Psychologist* 40 (8):905–19.

Capaldi, E. J. 1966. Partial reinforcement: An hypothesis of sequential effects. *Psychological Review* 73:459–77.

Deci, E. L. 1975. *Intrinsic Motivation*. New York: Plenum.

Deitz, S. M. 1978. Current status of applied behavior analysis: Science vs. technology. *American Psychologist* 33 (9):805–14.

Domjan, M. 1987. Animal learning comes of age. *American Psychologist*, 42 (6):556–64.

Estes, W. K. 1969. Reinforcement in human learning. In J. Tapp, ed., *Reinforcement and Behavior*. New York: Academic Press.

Gagne, R. M. 1985. *The Conditions of Learning*, 4th ed. New York: Holt, Rinehart, and Winston.

Geen, R. G. 1984. Human motivation: New perspectives on old problems. In *The G. Stanley Hall Lecture Series*, 5–58. Washington, DC: American Psychological Association.

Glaser, R. 1984. Education and thinking: The role of knowledge. *American Psychologist*, 39 (2):93–104.

Greeno, J. G. 1989. A perspective on thinking. *American Psychologist* 44 (2)134–41.

___. 1980. Psychology of learning, 1960-1980: One participant's observations. *American Psychologist*, 35 (8):713–28.

Greer, R. D. 1983. Contingencies of the science and technology of teaching and prebehavioristic research practices in education. *Educational Researcher*, 12 (1):3–9.

Guthrie, E. R. 1959. Association by contiguity. In S. Koch, ed., *Psychology: A Study of a Science*, vol. 2, 158–95. New York: McGraw-Hill.

Herrnstein, R. J. 1977a. Doing what comes naturally: A reply to Professor Skinner. *American Psychologist* 32 (12):1013–16.

___. 1977b. The evolution of behaviorism. *American Psychologist* 32 (8):593–603.

Hull, C. L. 1943. *Principles of Behavior*. New York: Appleton-Century-Crofts.

Kendler, T. S. 1964. Verbalization and optional reversal shifts among kindergarten children. *Journal of Verbal Learning and Verbal Behavior* 3 (5):428–436.

Kipnis, D. 1987. Psychology and behavioral technology. *American Psychologist* 42 (1):30–36.

Lepper, M. R., & Greene, D., eds., 1978. *The Hidden Costs of Reward*. Hillsdale, NJ: Erlbaum.

Logan, F. A. 1968. Incentive theory and changes in reward. In K. W. Spence & J. T. Spence, eds. *The Psychology of Learning and Motivation*, vol. 2. New York: Academic Press.

Luria, A. R. 1966. *Higher Cortical Functions in Man*. New York: Plenum.

Mahoney, M. J. 1989. Scientific psychology and radical behaviorism: Important distinctions based in scientism and objectivism. *American Psychologist*, 44 (11):1372–77.

McCombs, B. L. 1984. Processes and skills underlying continuing intrinsic motivation to learn: Toward a definition of motivational skills training interventions. *Educational Psychologist*, 19 (4):197–218.

McKeachie, W. J. 1976. Psychology in America's bicentennial year. *American Psychologist* 31 (12):819–33.

Miller, N. E. 1969. Learning of visceral and glandular responses. *Science*, 163:434–45.

Morgan, M. 1984. Reward-induced decrements and increments in intrinsic motivation. *Review of Educational Research*, 54 (1):5–30.

Morgan, R. R. 1975. An exploratory study of three procedures to encourage school attendance. *Psychology in the Schools*, 12 (2):209–15.

Mowrer, O. H. 1956. Two-factor learning theory reconsidered, with special reference to secondary reinforcement and the concept of habit. *Psychological Review*, 63:114–28.

Pavlov, I. P. 1960. *Conditioned Reflexes*. Translated and edited by G. V. Anrep. New York: Dover. (Original translation, Oxford: Oxford University Press, 1927).

Premack, D. 1965. Reinforcement theory. In D. Levine, ed., *Nebraska Symposium on Motivation* vol. 13, 123–80, 243–44. Lincoln: University of Nebraska Press.

Reese, E. P. 1986. Learning about teaching from teaching about learning: Presenting behavioral analysis in an introductory survey course. In V. P. Makosky, ed., *The G. Stanley Hall Lecture Series* vol. 6. Washington, DC: American Psychological Association.

Rescorla, R. A. 1987. A Pavlovian analysis of goal-directed behavior. *American Psychologist* 42 (2):119–29.

Rotter, J. B. 1966. Generalized expectancies for internal versus external control of reinforcement. *Psychological Monographs* 80 (1, whole no. 609).

___. 1954. *Social Learning and Clinical Psychology*. Englewood Cliffs, NJ: Prentice-Hall.

Samelson, F. 1980. J.B. Watson's Little Albert, Cyril Burt's twins, and the need for a critical science. *American Psychologist* 35 (7):619–25.

Schuell, T. J. 1986. Cognitive conceptions of learning. *Review of Educational Research*, 56 (4):411–36.

Sheffield, F. D. 1965. Relation between classical conditioning and instrumental learning. In W. F. Prokasy, ed., *Classical Conditioning: A Symposium*. New York: Appleton-Century-Crofts.

Sivan, E. 1986. Motivation in social constructivist theory. *Educational Psychologist* 1 (3):209–33.

Skinner, B. F. 1989. The origins of cognitive thought. *American Psychologist*, 44 (1):13–18.

___. 1977. Herrnstein and the evolution of behaviorism. *American Psychologist* 32 (12):1006–12.

___. 1938. *The Behavior of Organisms: An Experimental Analysis*. Englewood Cliffs, NJ: Prentice-Hall.

Spence, K. W. 1960. *Behavior Theory and Learning: Selected Papers*. Englewood Cliffs, NJ: Prentice-Hall.

Thorndike, E. L. 1949. *Selected Writings From a Connectionist's Psychology*. New York: Appleton-Century-Crofts.

Tolman, E. C. 1932. *Purposive Behavior in Animals and Men*. New York: Appleton-Century-Crofts. Reprinted, Berkeley: University of California Press, 1949.

Travers, R. M. 1982. *Essentials of Learning: The New Cognitive Learning for Students of Education*. New York: Macmillan.

Turkington, C. 1986a. Aversives: Report faulting institute refuels debate on its use. *APA Monitor* 17 (6):24.

____. 1986b. Dolphins: Responses to signs, sounds suggest they understand our orders. *APA Monitor* 16 (4):32–33.

Voeks, V. W. 1950. Formalization and classification of a theory of learning. *Journal of Psychology* 30:341–63.

Watson, J. B., & Raynor, R. 1920. Conditioned emotional reactions. *Journal of Experimental Psychology* 3:1–14.

Wittrock, M. C. 1979. The cognitive movement in instruction. *Educational Researcher* 8 (2):5–11.

Wolpe, J. 1981. Behavior therapy versus psychoanalysis: Therapeutic and social implications. *American Psychologist* 36 (2):159–64.

Woolfolk, R., & Richardson, F. 1984. Behavior therapy and the ideology of modernity. *American Psychologist*, 39 (7):777–86.

Zuriff, G. E. 1980. Radical behaviorist epistemology. *Psychological Bulletin*, 87 (2):337–50.

Chapter 6

Management Insight Development Programs (MIDP): A Cognitive Thinking Approach for Workplace Problem Solving and Creativity

REACHING THE GOALS OF EMPLOYEE INSIGHT

This chapter will explore the potentials for developing management insight. We will learn how the means of training are related to specific knowledge outcomes in an adult education program.

There has been much empty training rhetoric concerning "management creativity" or "critical thinking skills." Many promises are made, but few are able to design this elusive concept into most management training programs. The basic unanswered question remains "How can we teach more employees the critical thinking skills required to operate a twenty-first century business?" We do not have all the answers. However, we have conducted a variety of training programs based on a cognitive thinking approach, and will attempt to give the reader useful training best practices.

In this chapter the authors will present Management Insight Development Programs (MIDP), developed from an enhancement of Carroll's learning model. Our qualitative anecdotal business case studies will present the who, what, why, when, and how of our continuing, on-going, field-based research in management development. (Quantitative data on the MIDP is also presented in Appendix III.)

DEPARTING FROM BEHAVIORISM

Beginning in the 1970s, serious cracks appeared in the foundation of behaviorally based training programs, when they tried to enhance thinking and problem-solving skills. Behaviorism's response to training in these areas was grounded in the accumulation of habits and conditioning to explain thinking or creativity (Hull, 1943). This was far from an adequate model for designing effective management training programs.

McKeachie (1974) pointed out that many of the basic behavioral principles of learning are questionable:

1. Knowledge of results is not always necessary for learning.
2. Delayed knowledge of results is often more effective than immediate knowledge of results.
3. Rewards do not always improve learning, their effect depends upon the type of reward.
4. The careful planning of a learning program may be no better than a random sequence.
5. Depending on the learner, training by a sequence of small steps is often less effective than learning by larger jumps.
6. Defining objectives may not help improve student learning.

This does not mean that the behaviorists' attempts to influence training have been undesirable or without value. What they do mean for trainers is that since the 1950s, their systematic application to training and education programs has revealed that the general laws of behaviorism are mainly principles that hold true only under very limited conditions and not for all adult learners.

Behaviorally based systems of instruction such as programmed learning, computer-assisted instruction, and management behavior modification have been popular for improving organizational behavior control and acquiring rather simple supervisory skills. Unfortunately, most behaviors of interest to those of us working in an applied business setting involve situations in which adult learners do not make any overt response: role modeling, observational learning, attending seminars, and reading. For these reasons behaviorally based training efforts to enhance complex thinking, problem solving, comprehension, and creativity offer very limited results in most business settings. They fail to bring about the degree of complex change required in long-term thinking or educational skill acquisition by the adult learner.

We know that most extrinsically motivated adults learn best with behaviorally based training, while most intrinsically motivated adults learn best with cognitively based instruction (Bates, 1979). Extrinsic rewards are apparently most effective if the person is engaged in the job task or is in a situation where work performance is at a very low level. This includes many entry-level jobs, very simple service or assembly work. However, the use of extrinsic rewards is potentially detrimental if the individual is already highly motivated and is engaging in the work activity at a high level. Many managers and professionals seem to deal poorly with public recognition during training. This is because many adult learners receiving intrinsic rewards for a task feel personally responsible for their performance. However, when receiving extrinsic rewards, adult learners may feel manipulated, overtly controlled, and distrusted.

Even though traditional behaviorally based training has significant limitations, this does not mean that it is without value in the design of training and development programs. From what we have already stated, it is probably fair to make the following claims:

1. Knowledge of results is important for learning. This is particularly true when feedback contains information that may be used to improve overall performance. However, this feedback is of little value if the learner already has a good idea of his or her performance, or the information provides little insight on how to improve.
2. Relating a new idea to a familiar concept can facilitate learning, provided the adult does not soon forget the relationship. This method is of little assistance to learning if the adult can already remember the new material and spends more time thinking about it.
3. Rewards generally improve motivation for adult learning. The employee learns what activities lead to a reward. However, if these rewards are withdrawn, you may anticipate that many adults will lose interest in future training.
4. Planning and guidance of learning can be useful. However, the active participation of the adult in the learning activity will achieve far better results than passive learning. Similarly, adults exposed to meaningful, individualized learning programs of study will outperform those exposed to rote, behaviorally based, generic training programs (McKeachie, 1976).

THE GESTALT BRIDGE TO COGNITION

In the late 1920s and early 1930s, Western European Gestalt theorists made numerous contributions to the psychological literature of the period (Koffka, 1935; Kohler, 1925, 1929; Wertheimer, 1923). However, for the most part, Gestalt psychology was ignored by American psychologists and educators. Today, when we speak of cognition, the early contributions of Gestalt take on considerable importance in our effort to explain adult learning.

Gestalt theory is grounded in the psychology of perception (see Figure 6.1). From this perspective behavior-based training is a by-product of perceptual "mind chunk" development. Gestalt psychologists see these chunks of information growing in the adult's mind because of improved attention, perception, memory, and learning. Most perceptions are learned. These learned perceptions create perceptual templates through which a learner filters and pigeonholes new information. These learned perceptual templates can either facilitate or interfere with the learning process (see Figure 6.2).

For example, when an adult first learned how to read as a child in school, he or she established perceptual templates to acquire these skills and to add to them. Faulty templates can also be learned by the adult. These may have resulted from poor teaching, ineffective reading materials, or a personal learning disability (visual/auditory disabilities). If a faulty perceptual template is acquired as a child, the adult learner may continue to experience learning difficulties that interfere with reading (Gordon et al., 1991). Similarly, the

Figure 6.1
Learning Theory Overview

Characteristics	BEHAVIORISM			COGNITIVISM		
	Classical Conditioning	Operant Conditioning	Social Learning	Gestalt	Developmental	Information Processing
1. Theorists	Ivan Pavlov, J.B. Watson, E. Guthrie	E. Thorndike, Clark Hull, B.F. Skinner	Albert Bandura	E. Tolman, Kurt Lewin, W. Kohler	Jean Piaget, Malcolm Knowles	Benjamin Bloom, R.M. Gagne, R. Feuerstein, R.J. Sternberg, R.R. Morgan
2. Definition of Learning	Conditioning	•Reinforcement •Habits	•Observation •Modeling	•Past Experience •Habits •Remolding Experience	Problem Solving Developed over Time	Strategies for •Thinking •Problem Solving •Recalling New Information
3. Definition of Human Nature	Stimulated by Environment	Responds to •Rewards •Correctives	Emulate Rewarded Behavior	Assimilation of Old Information with New Information	Children & Adults Approach Learning Differently	•Attention Develops •Memory Develops
4. Role of Trainer	Model	Shaper	Socially Correct Model	Organize Suitable Learning Environment	Adjust Learning to Specific Audience	Facilitate Mind-Activating Activities
5. Role of Learner	Passive	Manipulated	Imitating	Harmonize Learning	Interaction with Environment	•Motivated •Active •Eager
6. Typical Training Offered	•Simple Service or Assembly •Army Combat Training	•Assembly-Line Mass Production •Introductory Selling •Telephone Operator	•Consultative Selling •Supervisory Training •Waitress •Receptionist •Bank Teller Training	•1st-Line Manager Skill Training •Skilled Trades	•Management •Complex Manufacturing Process •Customer Service	•Management •Teams •Leadership •Professional Development •Quality Issues •Communications

Figure 6.2
Gestalt Perception/Cognitive Information Processing

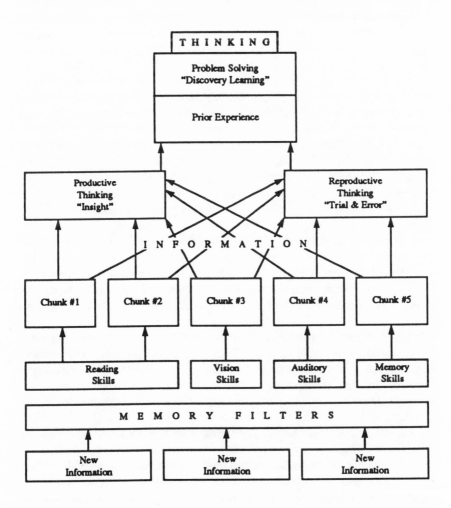

negative experiences of an adult learner who failed math courses in school can have serious consequences in an applied workplace math-training class. Likewise, failure to learn effective team-building concepts in a participatory management training class may be affected by the adult's previous experience of personal manipulation and harassment by a superior under the guise of a team-building program.

The Gestaltists view memory as nonpermanent and reconstructed. A common memory exercise that illustrates this is to have adults listen to a story individually and then pass the story along to others (Bartlett, 1932). Trainers find that the story changes radically as it is passed from person to person. The original story often is reconstructed because of the individualized pigeonholing and filtering process that takes place as each adult hears the story and adds his or her own cognitive-perceptual templates to the original story.

The Gestaltists link perception to the development of personal understanding and/or insight. They recognize two basic kinds of thinking. Productive thinking creates a new solution to a problem by creating a new idea. Reproductive thinking applies past solutions to a problem that merely reproduces old habits or behaviors. Productive and reproductive thinking can also be contrasted to the distinction between "insight" and "trial and error" behaviors.

An interesting contribution of Gestalt psychologists is that prior experience may have a negative effect on new problem-solving situations. Recall the examples of the negative experience of an adult learner who failed math courses in school or the management training class participant's experience with personal manipulation and harassment by a superior under the guise of a team-building program.

When designing instruction, Gestaltists saw the necessity of analyzing tasks into components and their subcomponents. Whenever possible, adult learners should be left to discover both the problem and its solution. This meaningful discovery learning is important to the development of creative, productive thinking. However, simply giving the learner the information results in rote learning that generally lacks personal meaning. As an alternative, the trainer can present interesting, thought-provoking problems to adults experiencing difficulty in problem-solving situations.

An example of this is the "tower building" exercise for a team-building class. In this team simulation, participants use discovery learning to build their personal awareness of how hard it is to apply principles they have been taught to make a work team function successfully (see Figure 6.3). These exercises are designed to focus the adult's attention on certain aspects of the problem structure in order to increase the likelihood of achieving personal insight. Gestalt psychologists enriched the study of thinking, problem solving, and creativity by introducing the idea that training in successful problem-solving techniques involves reorganizing or restructuring the problem situation.

Many contemporary cognitive approaches have worked on more practical applications of Gestalt learning theory for training (Ausubel, 1968; Glaser,

Figure 6.3
Simulation on Team Building: "Tower Building"

"TOWER BUILDING"

Directions:

1. Teams will be divided between participants and observers.

2. Participants:

    A.   You will be given the following building materials:

        1.   Three sizes of different color index cards:
            5 x 8, 4 x 6, 3 x 5
        2.   A roll of masking tape (2 inches/group)
        3.   A pair of scissors
        4.   A box of jumbo paper clips.

    B.   Rules:

        1.   Build the tallest "free standing" tower that you can.
            a.   You <u>cannot</u> tape the tower to the floor or table top.
            b.   You can tape the cards to each other or tape one level of cards to another.
        2.   In case of a tie, aesthetics will decide the winner.
        3.   You will be given 20 TOTAL MINUTES to build your tower:
            a.   <u>15</u> minutes must be used for "planning."
            b.   <u>5</u> minutes will be used for "building."
            c.   The entire team may handle during the "planning" phase only <u>1</u> size of each card type at anytime.

    C. **GOOD LUCK!**

3. Observers:

    A.   You will be expected to give feedback to the class on three aspects of team building as demonstrated by the team you observe.

        1.   How were conflicts resolved? What were the conflicts about?
        2.   In what ways did team members communicate with each other? Why did some team members fail to communicate?
        3.   How were decisions made? Who made them?
        4.   Any other general observations regarding how this group supported the team building process?

1978, 1982, 1986; Paivio, 1971; Rothkopf, 1977). Discovery learning and the use of imagery help adult learners store, retrieve, and organize information. New learning trained both verbally and visually will be better retained. This information imagery learning approach presents information in meaningful chunks. It is believed from research that the average adult learner cannot concentrate on more than seven information chunks, plus or minus two chunks, at any one time (Miller, 1956). This is a learning limitation that cannot be altered through training.

Remembering names at a business meeting can be an arduous exercise. Many businesspeople have learned memory exercises to relate a newly introduced individual's name to some other familiar idea to help its immediate recall. Unfortunately, in a large meeting only an exceptional individual can remember more than a few new names. If more informational chunks are presented by the trainer, personal low-priority information drops out before it can be permanently added to the individual's long-term memory.

There can be interesting exceptions to this rule. A trainer related to one of the authors a personal story regarding Mayor Richard J. Daley, the legendary mayor of Chicago from 1956 to 1978. In 1948, while serving as an election judge, she had met Daley, who was then Cook County clerk. She complained that suburban election judges were compensated at a lower daily rate than judges in the city of Chicago. Daley said he would consider the matter. In 1968, this same person was attending a political dinner for over 1,000 persons in the Grand Ballroom of the downtown Chicago Hilton. At the end of the dinner, Mayor Daley worked the crowd, shaking hands as he walked toward the exit. As he approached her, he said, "Suburban election judge, you wanted more pay. You got it, right?" She was struck speechless at Daley's amazing memory. One of the attributes of Mayor Daley's so-called political genius was his seemingly inexhaustible ability always to recall a person and his or her individual needs. This certainly contributed in a major way to his success as a political leader. Unfortunately, very few persons initially can learn low-priority information well enough to add it permanently to their long-term memory for later effective use.

For a successful discovery-learning training experience, we recommend that information be presented to the adult learner from the general to the specific. This procedure permits the anchoring of new information in what is already known. For example, in training customer-service representatives, in order to have them better understand what they are learning, you have each trainee work with key company people and departments. You assign each rep to meet and briefly interview key people appropriate to his or her job. During these interviews they will discuss what their relationship is, and what they need from each other in order to better serve their customers. Written notes are taken by the rep during these interviews (see Figure 6.4). With this activity the trainer strives to actively engage the employee throughout the learning activity. Whole concepts are presented first in class, then reduced to meaningful component parts during the interview exercise.

Figure 6.4
Discovery Learning for Customer Service

Interview Record

Date	Name	Title	What They Need From You And What They Expect To Give You

COGNITIVE LEARNING

Jean Piaget's (1896–1980) views are important for contemporary trainers and educators (see Figure 6.1). They provide a larger context regarding the acquisition of knowledge and competencies resulting from personal growth through interaction with the physical/social environment. Piaget forces us to study the developmental variables of growth and maturation. We must also focus attention, as a person ages, on the complex interplay between logic and psychology (Hilgard & Bower, 1975).

Piaget's Perspective

Piaget believed that knowledge is developed through personal maturation and appropriate experience (Resnick, 1976). A state of disequilibrium is created when learners are initially confronted with a problem (assimilation). The learner seeks a solution to the problem and in the process alters the existing schema (accommodation). This results in a return to an equilibrium. However, the learner is now considered to be at a higher level of logical thinking (see Figure 6.5).

Much of Piaget's research characterized cognitive development as a succes-

Figure 6.5
Piaget's Knowledge Development

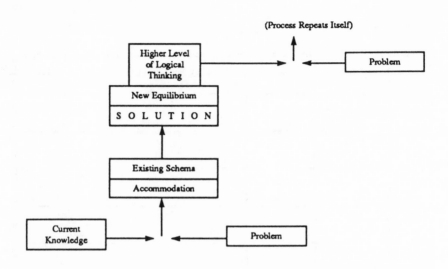

sion of logical cognitive structures acquired by individuals over time (stage theory). The case study used by Piaget was the long-term observation of his own children. This work yielded specific concepts that identified his children's learning responses to various cognitive problems. These cognitive concepts have been interpreted in terms of a learner "having" or "not having" cognitive structures of different kinds (Resnick, 1976).

Piagetian problem-solving tasks were chosen to typify universal cognitive structures. However, most such tasks are not typical academic tasks. One result has been a debate over whether Piagetian tasks can become the basis for teaching or training. In fact, are they teachable at all? Do they set limits on what other content can be assimilated and formally taught in the classroom? Some contend that the discovery of Piagetian learning tasks is interesting and well confirmed, but ask how important they are to instructional design (Hilgard & Bower, 1975).

We believe that Piaget's cognitive developmental approach to learning provides a unique theory of human cognition. This approach is heavily influenced by biological stage-theory concepts. Theories of human thought based on it remain quite limited because Piaget's biological analogy is not perfect. His most lasting contribution to instruction was his recognition that there are important cognitive developmental differences in the way children and adults approach certain instructional tasks.

This is well illustrated when an adult and a ten-year-old child decide to learn to play a game. The child will insist that all the rules must be followed in a literal manner throughout the game. According to Piaget, a ten-year-old child is at a "concrete operational stage" of learning. He or she feels most comfortable when allowed to assimilate new learning in this concrete manner. In contrast, the adult may wish to shorten playing time, or to combine or ignore certain rules, thinking that this approach will make playing the game more enjoyable. The adult has abandoned a literal interpretation of the game's rules, and abstractly creates improvements for playing, perhaps based on prior experience with other games. He or she is mentally operating at what Piaget calls the "formal operational stage" of adult creative thinking. The lessons for trainers are that children and adults learn in different ways, and that there is great variation in the ability of employees to reach the stage of formal operational thinking (abstract reasoning).

Cognition Beyond Piaget

Much research on Piaget has focused on locating specific cognitive concepts that improve performance on particular cognitive developmental tasks. There have been numerous studies designed to accelerate cognitive developmental stages (Gelman, 1983). There has been relatively little systematic study of task characteristics at the later stage of formal operational thinking (abstract reasoning).

Two basic task-analytic and acceleration strategies have been repeatedly tested. One has been to vary the cognitive problem-solving tasks and to examine (i.e., task-analyze) the cognitive processes being utilized by the subject in solving the problem. The second strategy is specifically to instruct learners on how to solve a Piagetian problem and then to test to see whether they can solve the problem after the instruction.

Current research supports the view that the acquisition of higher language skills and additional schooling is important in achieving abstract reasoning abilities by adult learners (Gelman, 1983). Acceleration training (providing needed experience) appears helpful only for learners from lower socioeconomic environments and learners who are in a transition from one stage to the next. Concrete operations problem-solving tasks are psychological indicators of general cognitive status rather than educationally important tasks (Gelman, 1983; Glaser & Resnick, 1972). However, formal operations (abstract reasoning) may need to be taught explicitly, since it is by no means clear that formal operational thinking is universally acquired by the majority of adults (Neimark, 1975).

Piaget's cognitive developmental approach has been criticized on several grounds. Many of his theories cannot be adequately tested because they are vague or ambiguous. Some of his theories that have been tested cannot be replicated. We believe that it is more productive for trainers and educators to focus their attention on the information-processing and modifiable components of cognitive development rather than on developmental stage theory.

WHAT DEVELOPS IN THE ADULT LEARNER?

Our response is that attention develops. As we noted earlier, the number of ideas an average person can remember at any one moment is limited. As a person ages, the number of informational chunks that can be remembered remains about the same. However, these informational chunks become embellished with additional symbols (particularly linguistic symbols). They become larger and more cognitively sophisticated. From a neo-Piagetian perspective, the differences between a child and an adult are considered to be similar to the differences between a novice and an expert. Children (like novices) and adults (like experts) perceive things differently because they are able to attend to different details of a problem, given their different perceptual-cognitive templates (see Figure 6.6).

In the 1990s most learning practitioners began comparing the problem-solving skills of an expert with those of a novice. In the first stage of acquiring a cognitive skill, the learner is receiving information and facts about the skill. With practice, this information becomes changed into proceduralized knowledge. Adult learners do not have to exert the same amount of energy at this stage.

Figure 6.6
Cognitive Novice/Expert,
Child/Adult Learner Model

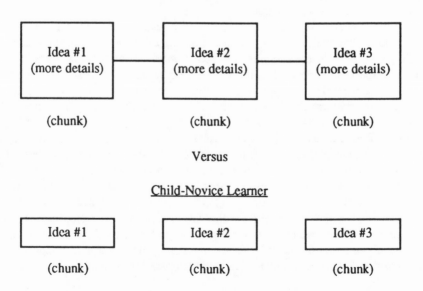

Adult-Expert Learner

| Idea #1 (more details) | Idea #2 (more details) | Idea #3 (more details) |

(chunk)   (chunk)   (chunk)

Versus

Child-Novice Learner

| Idea #1 | Idea #2 | Idea #3 |

(chunk)   (chunk)   (chunk)

They use those cognitive processes for other problem-solving tasks. It is a model that shows how a learner goes from "knowing what" to "knowing how" (Anderson, 1982).

These ideas seem to fit with other ideas of how information is organized, stored, and retrieved. As competence is attained, a person moves from being a novice to being an expert. The bits and pieces of information become more interconnected and grouped into meaningful chunks that are easier to access (Rumelhart & Ortony, 1977). The novice's information is considered to be spotty, consisting of terms and constructs in isolation. In contrast, the expert's knowledge is more integrated and connected.

Cognitive theorists claim that as we acquire knowledge, we acquire schematic representations. These representations evolve and are modified. In the process, more advanced forms of problem solving become possible because we have moved from merely "knowing what" to "knowing how" and "knowing that." The expert is thought actually to see a different problem representation than does the novice. When an expert and a novice view the same problem situation, the expert is operating on a different level, one not discernible to the novice. Novices are saying to themselves, "Okay, first ———, then —," whereas experts have sized up the overall problem situation, worked on a possible solution, and are thinking, "Next!"

Certain metacognitive abilities (executive and self-regulatory processes) appear to set experts and novices apart (Brown, 1978). An expert judges performance, engages in time-matching activities, evaluates outcomes, and so on. We believe that these metacognitive abilities can be taught (Garner & Alexander, 1989). The final overall goal of instruction using cognitive concepts is to foster independent learning (i.e., learn to learn) for the adult in the workplace.

An adult accompanied by a ten-year-old child arrives at an airport. What do they perceive? The child sees numbers of taller, older persons rushing about a building. There is a great deal of noise. Names are being called out from somewhere. There are many airplanes parked next to the building. It seems a hopeless task to determine which plane is the one they want. The adult also sees a busy terminal. Through the noise he hears an announcement of their flight number and gate assignment. He takes his son to the flight departure television monitors and rechecks his perception of the announcement. Then, following terminal signs, they walk down the long concourse until he sees the gate and the flight destination signs.

The principal differences between our novice and expert travelers were their overall perceptual levels. The adult was able to concentrate and understand numerous different information details of the departure time and gate. The child's perceptual-cognitive templates saw and heard the same information but could not filter out the essential details, and in the end was overwhelmed into a state of general confusion. However, if we placed this English-speaking adult in a restaurant in Frankfurt, Germany, many of his advantages would disappear.

Figure 6.7
MIDP: Cognitive-Based Instruction

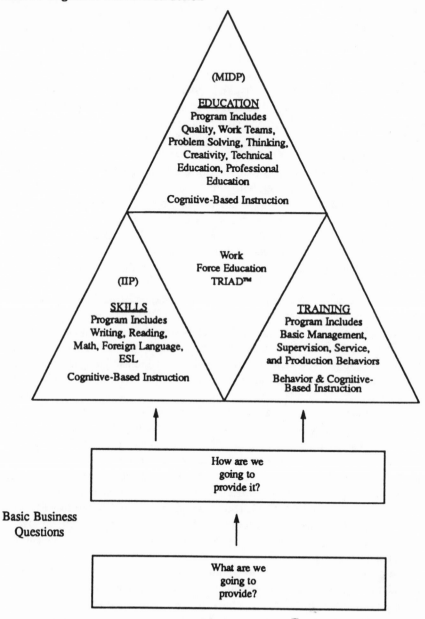

Without additional German-language perceptual-cognitive templates, the adult would perceive the menu and communicate with the waiter at the level of a novice learner (Gordon et al., 1991).

When do we learn new information? This happens when an individual is able to relate new information to existing cognitive structures. This is often done by means of language or numbers. We previously reviewed the authors' development of individualized instruction programs. This is an example of skills training designed on a cognitive learning model. Can the same be done for management development training, using cognitive concepts?

AN INFORMATION-PROCESSING APPROACH
TO TRAINING AND DEVELOPMENT

The authors have conducted a series of information-processing field-based programs designed to improve management training performance by using cognitive problem-solving training tasks (see Figure 6.1). Many of these information-processing training programs based on the authors' derived Management Insight Development Model were evaluated by the programs' ability to stimulate individual managers' thinking and problem-solving abilities. This is the "Education" part of the Work Force Education Triad (see Figure 6.7).

Active Engagement In Training

The Management Insight Development Programs (MIDP) of learning see the adult learner as active, not passive. The mind is a place where information is stored, assessed, and retrieved (see Figure 6.8). We teach adults strategies for effective learning and retrieving of new information. The adult learner literally "learns how to learn" by engaging in mind-activating activities. These include advanced study organizers, summary information statements, study guides, and the use of metacognition strategies such as a team-building simulation to increase awareness of the cognitive problem-solving process.

It is important to establish cognitive instructional objectives for adult participants (Wittrock, 1978). Behavioral instructional objectives generate learning or recall of information dealing with the specific objectives. However, cognitive instructional objectives generate more independent episodic learning that facilitates better long-term training results.

Such a program was established by U.S. Gypsum for sales training. It was totally self-driven by the trainees and featured traditional training seminars, one-to-one tutorials, audio, video, and self-study. The self-development guide was given to each sales representative at the beginning of his or her job (see Figure 6.9). The trainees initiated their own training activities to develop the skills

Figure 6.8
Memory as the "Storehouse of the Mind"

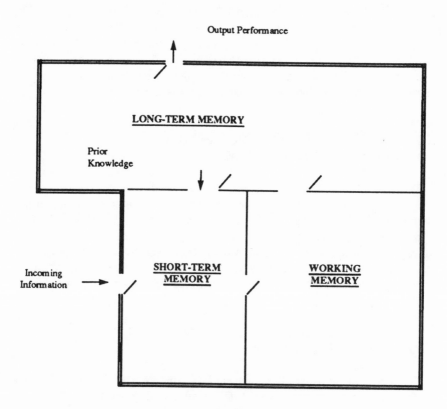

required in a fully skilled sales rep. They used the guide and were responsible for scheduling their own training, following an outline for each training area including meeting with the sales manager, writing reports, and attending a training class. As the sales reps completed these activities, they recorded each training component (see Figure 6.10). This training approach has the following objectives: making the sales reps accountable for their time, promoting independent thinking, building self-discipline, and making good decisions. These are the skills any company needs to have developed for a highly efficient sales force. This approach to training includes recognized important cognitive variables of field-dependent versus field-independent, of conceptually driven (from the general to the specific) or data driven (from the specific back to the general) (Wittrock, 1978). The training also took into consideration that by making learning independent and episodic, the sales force learned more and retained more information, skills, and useful self-knowledge.

Figure 6.9
Independent Episodic Learning I:
Self-Development Guide

A. YOUR CORPORATE
   RESPONSIBILITIES

   1. Know Your Position Responsibilities

   2. Know Your Benefits

   3. Know Your Company

   4. Work with Key Company People and
      Departments

   5. Know Plant Facilities

   6. Work with Your Manager

   7. Maintain Records and Files, and
      Submit Reports

   8. Maintain Corporate Assets

   9. Control Your Budget

   10. Represent the Company to Trade
       Factors, Business Groups and the
       General Public

   11. Inform and Advise Management

   12. Handle Special Assignments

   13. Know the Legal Aspects of Your
       Position

B. YOUR TERRITORY AND ACCOUNT
   MANAGEMENT RESPONSIBILITIES

   1. Cover Your Territory

   2. Know Your Competition

   3. Work with Trade Factors

   4. Work with Local Regulatory and
      Code Bodies

   5. Lead and/or Cooperate in Team
      Selling

   6. Participate In Special Marketing
      Efforts

   7. Identify Large Jobs

   8. Know, Sell and Service Your
      Assigned Accounts

   9. Identify, Approach and Qualify
      Prospective Accounts

   10. Plan and Initiate Account Calls

   11. Determine and Meet Account Needs

   12. Handle Pricing and Price
       Adjustments

   13. Handle Objections and Concerns

   14. Ask for Orders and Close Sales

   15. Follow Through on Sales

   16. Handle Complaints

   17. Expedite Credit, Collections and
       Claims

Figure 6.9 continued

C. YOUR PRODUCT KNOWLEDGE
   RESPONSIBILITIES

1. Know Sufficient General Technical
   Concepts to Deal Efficiently with
   Other Professionals

   a. Blueprint Reading

   b. Physics of Construction

   c. Chemistry of Gypsum Products

   d. Construction Process (Building
      Stages)

   e. Building Codes and Code Bodies

   f. Fire Safety

   g. Sound Control

   h. Use of Literature

2. Know Features, Applications and
   Benefits of Each Product Line and
   System You Sell

   a. Board Products

   b. Joint Treatment/Textures

   c. Construction Steel

   d. Plaster

   f. Systems

3. Become Familiar with Other U.S.G.
   Products

D. YOUR SELF-MANAGEMENT
   RESPONSIBILITIES

1. Know, Control and Motivate Yourself

2. Plan and Schedule Your Activities

3. Talk and Listen Effectively

4. Communicate Interpersonally

5. Read Quickly and Accurately

6. Write Letters, Memos and Reports

7. Gather and Organize Information

8. Identify and Solve Problems and Make
   Decisions

9. Develop and Make Persuasive
   Presentations

10. Conduct and Participate in Meetings

11. Establish and Maintain Productive
    Interpersonal Relationships

12. Practice Safety in Driving, Visiting
    Construction Sites

13. Project a Professional Image

14. Negotiate Agreements, Resolve
    Conflicts

15. Keep Current with Industry, Company
    and Professional Selling Developments

Figure 6.10
Independent Episodic Learning II: Training Progress Record

Sales Representative_____

Territory Number_____ Start Date _____

POSITION RESPONSIBILITY	DELIVERY SYSTEM	DATE COMPLETED TARGET	ACTUAL
Quarter 1			
A-1	Know Your Position Responsibilities	SDG	
A-2	Know Your Benefits	SDG	
A-3	Know Your Company	SDG	
A-4	Work with Key Company People and Departments	SDG	
A-5	Know Plant Facilities	SDG	
A-6	Work with Your Manager	SDG	
A-7	Maintain Records and Files, and Submit Reports	SDG	
A-8	Maintain Corporate Assets	SDG	
A-9	Control Your Budget	SDG	
A-11	Inform and Advise Management	SDG	
A-13	Know the Legal Aspects of Your Position	SDG	
C-1c	Products and Processes	SDG/LC	
C-2a	Gypsum Board Products	SDG/LC	
C-2b	Joint Treatment, Textures	SDG/LC	
C-2d	Plaster	SDG/LC	
C-2e	Acoustical Ceiling	SDG/LC	

NOTE: Quarter 1 Learning Center courses are contained in the product training binders

Quarter 2			
B-2	Know Your Competition	SDG/LC	
B-3	Work with Trade Factors	SDG/LC	
B-4	Work with Local Regulatory and Code Bodies	SDG/LC	
B-12	Handle Pricing and Price Adjustments	SDG/LC	
B-16	Handle Complaints	SDG/LC	
B-17	Expedite Credit, Collections and Claims	SDG/LC	
C-2c	Steel Framing Systems	SDG/LC	
C-2f	Gypsum Board Systems	SDG/LC	

NOTE: Quarter 2 Learning Center courses are the Phase 1 Selling Skills programs and the Advanced Systems Products courses.

Quarter 3			
B-1	Cover Your Territory	SDG/LC	
B-5	Lead and/or Cooperate in Team Selling	SDG/LC	
B-6	Participate in Special Marketing Efforts	SDG/LC	
B-8	Know, Sell and Service Your Assigned Accounts	SDG/LC	
B-9	Identify, Approach and Qualify Prospective Accounts	SDG/LC	
B-10	Plan and Initiate Account Calls	SDG/LC	
B-11	Determine and Meet Account Needs	SDG/LC	
B-13	Handle Objections and Concerns	SDG/LC	
B-14	Ask for Orders and Close Sales	SDG/LC	
B-15	Follow Through on Sales	SDG/LC	

NOTE: Quarter 3, where possible, should be timed to coincide with the division or area training conferences (Phase Two of Selling Skills).

SDG = Self-Development Guide
LC = Learning Center Courses
DC = Seminar: Division Conference
CC = Seminar: Corporate Conference

Figure 6.10 continued

POSITION RESPONSIBILITY	DELIVERY SYSTEM	DATE COMPLETED TARGET	ACTUAL
Quarter 4			
C-2 Know Features, Applications and Benefits of Each Product Line and Systems You Sell	SDG/LC		
D-3 Talk and Listen Effectively	SDG/LC		
D-4 Communicate Interpersonally	SDG/LC		
D-5 Read Quickly and Accurately	SDG/LC		
D-6 Write Letters, Memos and Reports	SDG/LC		
D-7 Gather and Organize Information	SDG/LC		
D-9 Develop and Make Persuasive Presentations	SDG/LC		
D-12 Practice Safety in Driving, Visiting Construction Sites	SDG/LC		

NOTE: Quarter 4 Learning Center courses are found in the Phase Three Selling Skills program (available 3rd Quarter, 1985).

POSITION RESPONSIBILITY	DELIVERY SYSTEM	TARGET	ACTUAL
Quarter 5			
A-10 Represent the Company to Trade Factors, Business Groups, and the General Public	SDG		
A-12 Handle Special Assignments	SDG		
B-7 Identify Large Jobs	SDG		
C-1 Know Sufficient General Technical Concepts to Deal Effectively with Other Professionals	SDG/LC		
a. Blue Print Reading			
b. Physics of Construction			
c. Construction Process (Building Stages)			
d. Building Codes and Code Bodies			
e. Fire Safety			
f. Sound Control			
g. Use of Literature			
C-3 Become Familiar with Other U.S.G. Products	SDG/LC		

NOTE: Quarter 5 Learning Center courses are the Applied Physics and Advanced Technical Knowledge courses in the Learning Center.

POSITION RESPONSIBILITY	DELIVERY SYSTEM	TARGET	ACTUAL
Quarter 6			
D-1 Know Control and Motivate Yourself	SDG/LC		
D-2 Plan and Schedule Your Activities	SDG/LC		
D-8 Identify and Solve Problems and Make Decisions	SDG/LC		
D-10 Conduct and Participate in Meetings	SDG/LC		
D-11 Establish and Maintain Productive Interpersonal Relationships	SDG/LC		
D-13 Project a Professional Image	SDG/LC		
D-14 Negotiate Agreements, Resolve Conflicts	SDG/LC		
D-15 Keep Current with Industry, Company and Professional Selling Developments	SDG/LC		

NOTE: Quarter 6, where possible, should coincide with a corporate conference (available in 1986).

Field Sales Manager _____

Division _____   Mail No _____

The authors conducted a "work-team communication" training program at Interstate National Insurance Company for new supervisors and middle managers. We used both bottom-up and top-down strategies to train how to apply specific feedback/facilitation skills on the job; how to obtain specific facts and feelings via active listening skills; and many other valuable communication areas. The two half-day sessions met these objectives by using group discussion (top-down); analyses of specific scenarios (bottom-up); role-playing of work-specific situations (bottom-up); and written activities and assessments (top-down). Personal written action plans were developed by each participant (bottom-up), and follow-up assessments were planned for one month and six months after the training.

How Are Memories Organized?

As previously mentioned, the famous Bartlett study (1932) of a memory exercise (where the content of a story changed as it was passed from one person to another) demonstrated that memories are essentially reconstructed by individuals. The organization or initial encoding of memory is influenced by a number of instructional variables: advance organizers, purpose (meaning), prequestions, and instructional objectives.

We believe, as do others, that knowledge is systematically organized in memory (Rummelhart & Ortony, 1977). For example, adults who are given a list of words in random order, will recall the words in self-determined categories. However, if they are presented with a list of words already arranged into semantically appropriate categories, retention is greatly improved. This finding supports the view that components of short-term memory assist in the organization of information before it is transferred to long-term memory for storage.

The instructional importance of organized rehearsal has been demonstrated in numerous investigations concerned with the order of presenting information (Bower & Hilgard, 1981). In the typical training program, items in a list are memorized; recall has been found to be best for the first and last items (see Figure 6.11). Recall was best for the last item on the list of "Customer Requirements," Expense, because it is in short-term memory, and it is easier to recall from short-term than from long-term memory. Recall was best for the first item, Produce or Service, because it was rehearsed more than the items in the middle of the list and presumably was better consolidated in memory.

Teaching cognitive organization strategies such as the use of acronyms on the Customer Requirements checklist (see Figure 6.11) may be useful in assisting trainees, particularly adult problem learners, to encode and retrieve information effectively. Problem adult learners, for example, often demonstrate difficulty in organizing input. They can be taught by using checklists like that in Figure 6.11, or other organizational aids or strategies to help them better remember new content and concepts. (See Chapter 9 for more details.)

Figure 6.11
Organized Rehearsal

CUSTOMER REQUIREMENTS

What do you need from me?

Product or
Service

Relationship

Integrity

Delivery

Expense

Information-processing analysis of instructional tasks is considered by most psychologists to represent a cognitive perspective. The information-processing approach to training can be clearly distinguished from behaviorally based training because it attempts to describe internal, unobservable cognitive processing components. Task analyses of instruction differ from the Gestalt and Piagetian analyses. Information-processing trainers engage in empirical attempts to describe thinking and problem-solving performance. Simulation techniques are designed to "restructure" management training information into specific role-playing situations or sequences of action. (See Chapter 9 for more details.)

A cognitively oriented team building training program was conducted by the authors at Interstate National Insurance. The natural work team experienced working together in a structured and controlled environment. The participants gave and received feedback while completing a series of exercises designed to provide them with information on personal management strengths and weaknesses as well as on the effectiveness of the team working together. Follow-up sessions were held for each team one, three, and six months after the initial two, half-day programs.

How Do Adults Organize Knowledge?

A schema (see Figure 2.1) consists of a learner's knowledge (Rumelhart & Ortony, 1977). We view this schema as denoting mental data structures for representing generic memory concepts. These generalized concepts are formed by networks of interrelations among represented objects, events, and situations. Four characteristics combine to make schemata powerful for representing knowledge in memory (Rumelhart & Ortony (1977):

1. Schemata have variables.
2. They can be embedded one within the other.
3. They represent generic concepts that vary their levels of abstraction.
4. They are encyclopedic, not definitional.

Schemata are considered to be prelinguistic. They can serve as a constraint on learning through the operation of the principle of proactive interference (i.e., the influence of existing knowledge structures with the acquisition of new knowledge). The more fully developed the schemata, the less likely that they will change.

All human knowledge is stored in a system of schemata or operational structures that are characterized as sets of executive strategies. Knowledge is retrieved by a process that allows for the convergence of information derived directly from input that leads to plausible new schematic representations of experience (Rumelhart & Ortony, 1977). This convergence is achieved by a combination of bottom-up (data-driven) and top-down (conceptually driven) processing. Existing knowledge is used in processing new information and in dealing with novel situations. Being viewed as the key units of the comprehension process, schemata serve as cognitive templates against which new inputs may be matched and in terms of which they can be comprehended.

Overall learning is faster with a combination of top-down and bottom-up processing. Adults who use mostly bottom-up processing tend to be easily distracted. We have attempted to teach distractable students the top-down strategies. Bottom-up processors are not less intelligent. They do very well when presented with a problem best solved by global processing (McKeachie et al., 1985).

One such training program that relied on what the trainer already knew was a train-the-trainer course conducted by the authors for the Illinois Department of Employment Security (IDES). It did not rely heavily on written materials but mobilized audio/video technology to enhance verbal instructional methods. In a previous reorganization, IDES had eliminated most of its training staff. It became evident after a period of time that the agency still needed to train employees in a cost-effective manner. The train-the-trainer course presented a four-day, hands-on workshop for participants. Many of these managers had previously been IDES trainers. Participants made three videotapes, and critiqued presentations, building on the skills they had learned with each successive presentation. The workshop presented practical concepts through a highly interactive learning process. The basic course foundation was broadened by the participants' observations, practice, and a wealth of personal experience.

This train-the-trainer program was very effective because it utilized the knowledge that the participants already possessed (schemata). This acted as the principal determinant of what they could learn from a new educational experience (Vosniadow & Brewer, 1987). The adult learner brings a knowledge base or schemata to the corporate classroom. In general, the learning process must deal with the formation and use of schemata — knowledge that will be learned and modified by training. The use of written language in learning appears to have great utility and survival value in our technological culture. However, the exclusive reliance upon text leads to an undervaluation of practical knowledge and verbal instruction.

R. M. Gagne and L. J. Briggs (1979) (see Figure 6.1) view knowledge acquisition in terms of learning the intellectual skills of how to comprehend and use language. Adults cannot acquire academic knowledge until they can manipulate language. Gagne proposes a skills-training approach to enhance the learning of language skills. The skills-training model, coupled with criterion-referenced testing, is promising because it recognizes that learning problems and prescriptions for remediation are the legitimate territory of the teaching process.

This is the central reason why the higher-level thinking skills required for quality programs, team building, and so on cannot be learned by adults unless they already possess advanced personal language skills (i.e., reading, writing, ESL). Therefore, this skills piece of the Work Force Education Triad must be in place before adults can move on to more quality or team-building education (see Figure 6.7).

The information-processing training approach provides a more detailed model of how intellectual operations are acquired and utilized, and how environmental and maturational factors can affect this process. We are beginning to identify "new aptitudes," interpreted in terms of cognitive information-processing variables and constructs. This offers the prospect that we will design training to adults' needs instead of forcing adults to fit the curriculum. We can help different levels of adult learners attain similar educational outcomes by using information-processing-based training (Glaser, 1978, 1982, 1986; Pressley & Levin, 1983).

A FUTUREWORK MODEL OF TRAINING AND DEVELOPMENT

It is the authors' view that it is time to embellish the behaviorally based learning models of instruction to include a number of cognitive variables. The authors' MIDP training models are field-based research attempts to construct useful management training programs that incorporate many cognitive variables. We believe that this has led to enhanced long-term general learning, as well as stronger thinking and problem-solving abilities (see Figure 6.7).

The MIDP represents an embellishment of Carroll's original mastery learning model (see Figure 6.12). From our perspective, individual differences in student aptitudes consist of differences in attention, temperament, maturational stages of development, existing knowledge and language templates, cognitive styles, attitudes, expectations, and mood. The MIDP is related to the ability of the trainer to organize instruction, to set up simulations, role-playing, exercises, and so on that enhance meaning and contribute to the development of critical thinking and problem-solving skills.

We recognize the inability to modify biological differences in temperament and maturational stages. But most of the other components can be learned in the cognitive science model of instruction. We know that we can enhance knowledge and language templates.

It is generally accepted that how efficiently we learn depends to a great extent on what we already know. From a cognitive perspective, a major constraint on normal or problematic adult learners is their knowledge base and limited ability to use language to code and store information. There is a literate bias in schooling that is viewed as enhancing our thinking and problem-solving behaviors. We believe that these educational skills can be taught by using the MIDP in developmental programs that improve individual thinking skills, enhance problem-solving abilities, and promote creativity in the workplace.

Our ongoing research findings support the need to establish a Work Force Education Triad in every company, to train and educate all employees for twenty-first century business (see Figure 6.7). The first piece of the triad,

Figure 6.12
The Management Insight Development Programs (MIDP)
as an Enhanced Cognitive Science Model of Mastery Learning,
PSI, and Tutoring Instruction

Degree of learning $=$ $\dfrac{\text{time spent (willing or allowed)}}{\text{time needed (aptitude, i.e., individual differences)} + (\text{quality of instruction x ability to understand instruction})}$

Where: Learner <u>aptitude</u> consists of the biological differences of personal attention, individual temperament, and maturational stages of development, and the psychological differences of existing knowledge and language base, cognitive learning styles, personal attitudes, individual expectations, and mood.

<u>Quality of instruction</u> is viewed as the ability of the trainer to organize instruction, to give it meaning, and to set up problem-solving situations that enhance critical thinking.

<u>Ability to understand instruction</u> consist of the same components as quality of instruction.

---

training, has been commonly restricted in the workplace to managers or foremen. Training will now be offered to far more employees at all levels. Its focus will shift from a command-and-control mode to a facilitator-monitoring role. Training will continue to use behavior-based instruction for simpler ideas, but it also will begin to rely much more heavily on cognitive problem-solving, outcome-based instruction.

The second piece of the triad, *skills*, will be offered to all people throughout the organization who need to improve language and math abilities. Cognitive-based curricula, such as the IIP, will help to individualize instruction, diagnose learning problems, and greatly increase long-term retention for workplace applications.

At the top of our triad, *education* will be supported by the skills and training components offered to all employees. MIDP or other cognitive-based instruction will prepare people for the complex thinking required by Total Quality Management, ISO 9000, business process re-engineering, high-tech workplace applications, and other new strategic business models as they are introduced by American business.

This is the authors' vision of FutureWork. Its components have already worked well for many different businesses, both small and large, presented in our case studies. How can you begin to apply this Work Force Education Triad to your company's competitive needs?

FUTURE TRENDS

The overall trend in learning theory has been a shift away from behavioral psychology and toward a cognitive psychology. Behaviorism has represented a learning theory that focused on observable behaviors and the stimuli that control them. A strict behaviorist does not accept the part played by internal cognitive forces such as purpose and will.

Today, the central information-processing (cognitive) view is receiving considerable support. This central cognitive-processing view (thinking, judging, and making decisions) has been confirmed with the use of technologies showing brain activity, such as the electroencephalogram, biochemical changes in glucose levels, PET scans, and magnetic resonance imagery.

The brain learns and remembers throughout life by constantly changing its network of trillions of connections between cells as a result of stimuli from the environment. New memory templates are created or diminished by means of this process throughout the adult's entire lifetime. This cognitive information processing acts like "little carpenters" constantly and quickly changing the "architecture of the brain" (Kotulak, 1993).

The cognitivists view learning as a reorganization of perceptions. It is a theory of learning that postulates cognitive intervening variables (e.g., expectations and verbal rules) in order to explain the learning process. In contrast, the stimulus-response theorists emphasize external reinforced responses and avoid the use of internal cognitive constructs as explanatory concepts. The cognitivists believe that all thinking is highly personalized and creative. Imagery is viewed as serving as a transition between perception and thought.

The results of our ongoing research on cognition and those of many other learning researchers has been presented in the hope of encouraging program designers and trainers of adults in the workplace to explore new cognitive instructional models. We are encouraged that many trainers now actively discuss these cognitive learning concepts. We are discouraged because many workplace programs that are reportedly designed to foster better thinking skills in reality reduce the training effort down to a simple stimulus-response behaviorist process that has little potential for enhancing the thinking, problem-solving process. Too many quality programs have failed to achieve their results because the higher-level thinking skills of employees cannot be fully developed by behavior-based training models. We believe that our quantitative and qualitative research findings support the use of these enhanced training methods. The cognitive training approaches of FutureWork will become the model of America's best training practices in the years to come. FutureWork supports the lifelong education of all employees as the best guarantee of American competitiveness in the world arena.

In the next chapter we address the difficult issue of how well training can increase the intellectual capacity of people. Is college the only educational means to prepare an adult for abstract reasoning? We think not! Let us explore how cognition provides a key to maximizing human potential in the workplace.

REFERENCES

Anderson, J. R. 1982. Acquisition of cognitive skills. *Psychological Review* 89:369–406.

Ausubel, D. 1968. *Educational psychology: A Cognitive View.* New York: Holt, Rinehart and Winston.

Bartlett, F. C. 1932. *Remembering: A Study in Experimental and Social Psychology.* London: Cambridge University Press.

Bates, J. A. 1979. Extrinsic reward and intrinsic motivation: A review with implications for the classroom. *Review of Educational Research* 49 (4):557–576.

Bower, G. H. & Hilgard, E. R. 1981. *Theories of Learning.* Englewood Cliffs, NJ: Prentice-Hall.

Brown, A. L. 1978. Knowing when, where and how to remember: A problem of metacognition. In R. Glaser, ed., *Advances in Instructional Psychology*, vol. 1. Hillsdale, NJ: Erlbaum.

Brown, A. L., & Campione, J. C. 1986. Psychological theory and the study of learning disabilities. *American Psychologist* 41 (10):1059–1068.

Gagne, R. M., & Briggs, L. J. 1979. *Principles of Instructional Design,* 2nd ed. New York: Holt, Rinehart and Winston.

Garner, R., & Alexander, P. A. 1989. Metacognition: Answered and unanswered questions. *Educational Pyschologist* 24 (2): 143-158.

Gelman, R. 1983. Recent trends in cognitive development. In J. C. Scheirer & A. M. Rogers, eds., *The G. Stanley Hall Lecture Series*, vol 3. Washington, DC: American Psychological Association.

___. 1990. The reemergence of learning theory within instructional research. *American Psychologist* 45 (1):29-39.

___. 1986. *Advances in Instructional Psychology,* vol. 3. Hillsdale, NJ: Erlbaum.

___. 1982. *Advances in Instructional Psychology,* vol. 2. Hillsdale, NJ: Erlbaum.

___. 1978. *Advances in Instructional Psychology,* vol. 1. Hillsdale, NJ: Erlbaum.

Glaser, R., & Resnick, L. B. 1972. Instructional psychology. *Annual Review of Psychology* 23:207–76.

Gordon, E. E. 1993. Case study files of client training programs. Oak Lawn, IL: Imperial Corporate Training & Development. (Report available upon request; write to 10341 South Lawler Avenue, Oak Lawn, IL 60453-4714 or call 708-636-8852.)

Gordon, E. E.; Morgan, R. R.; and Ponticell, J. A. 1991. *Closing the Literacy Gap in*

American Business. New York: Quorum Books.

Greeno, J. 1980. Psychology of learning 1960-1980: One participant's observations. *American Psychologist* 35 (8): 713-728.

Hilgard, E. R., & Bower, G. H. 1975. *Theories of Learning*. Englewood Cliffs, NJ: Prentice-Hall.

Hull, C. L. 1943. *Principles of Behavior*. New York: Appleton-Century-Crofts.

Koffka, K. 1935. *Principles of Gestalt Psychology*. New York: Harcourt, Brace and World.

Kohler, W. 1929. *Gestalt Psychology*. New York: Liveright.

___. 1925. *The Mentality of Apes*. Translated by E. Winter. New York: Harcourt, Brace and World.

Kotulak, R. 1993. Unraveling hidden mysteries of the brain. *Chicago Tribune*, 11 April, sec. 1, 1, 10.

McKeachie, W. J. 1976. Psychology in America's bicentennial year. *American Psychologist* 31 (12):819-833.

___. 1974. The decline and fall of the laws of learning. *Educational Researcher* 3:7-11.

McKeachie, W. J.; Pintrich, P. R.; & Lin, Y. G. 1985. Teaching learning strategies. *Educational Psychologist* 20 (3):153-160.

Miller, G. A. 1956. The magical number seven plus or minus two: Some limits on our capacity for processing information. *Psychological Review* 63:81-97.

Neimark, E. D. 1975. Current status of formal operational thought. *Genetic Psychology Monographs* 91 (2):171-225.

Olson, D. 1977. The languages of instruction: On the literate bias of schooling. In R. C. Anderson, & R. J. Spiro, eds., *Schooling and the Acquisition of Knowledge*. Hillsdale, NJ: Erlbaum.

Paivio, A. 1971. *Imagery and Verbal Processes*. New York: Holt, Rinehart and Winston.

Pressley, N., & Levin, J. 1983. *Cognitive Strategy Research: Psychological Foundations*. New York: Springer-Verlag.

Resnick, L. T. 1976. Task analysis in instructional design: Some cases from mathematics. In D. Klahr, ed., *Cognition and Instruction*. Hillsdale, NJ: Erlbaum.

Rothkopf, E. Z. 1977. The concept of mathemagenic activities. In M. C. Wittrock, ed., *Learning and Instruction*. Berkeley, CA: McCutchan.

Rumelhart, D. E., & Ortony, A. 1977. The representation of knowledge in memory. In R. C. Anderson, & R. J. Spiro, eds., *Schooling and the Acquisition of Knowledge*. Hillsdale, NJ: Erlbaum.

Vosniadow, S., & Brewer, W. F. 1987. Theories of knowledge restructuring in development. *Review of Educational Research* 57 (1):51-68.

Wertheimer, M. 1923. Untersuchung zur Lehre von der Gestalt, II. *Psychologisch Forschung* 4:301-50. Translated and condensed as Laws of organization in perceptual forms. In W. D. Ellis, *A Source Book of Gestalt Psychology,* 71-88. New York: Harcourt, Brace and World, 1938.

Wittrock, M. C. 1978. The cognitive movement in instruction. *Educational Psychologist* 13 (2):15-30.

Chapter 7

Defining Intelligence for the Training Arena

THE FUTUREWORK DILEMMA

For many in business the intelligence of "average" workers is unchangeable, defined by their formal education and role in the organization. However, the rise of quality, teams, and empowerment as FutureWork management issues has left many business leaders in a quandary. Suddenly, people are being asked to reason abstractly, to solve problems, and to reach workable solutions throughout the organization.

What if "average" workers do not possess the intelligence for FutureWork? Replace them? This is largely impossible and prohibitively costly. Teach them to become more intelligent? How? The practicality of this issue is well worth exploring if a business wants people who are abstract reasoners and problem solvers throughout its operations.

WHAT DOES "INTELLIGENCE" MEAN?

Intelligence has been defined by many as what an intelligence test measures (Weinberg, 1989). However, the use of intelligence tests has generated a great deal of controversy in recent years because many people have begun to question their nature and accuracy.

The traditional definition of intelligence becomes problematic when people who are not considered to be academically strong display enormous talent. John F. Kennedy was labeled learning disabled, yet he is now considered as having been a very thoughtful, charismatic president. George Washington's wife read to him, yet he distinguished himself on the battlefield. Abraham Lincoln received little formal schooling, yet many believe him to be America's greatest president.

Because of the apparent discrepancies in human ability and educational background, trainers continue to question the role of intelligence. What is intelligence? Can intelligence be improved through training?

The traditional definition of intelligence appears to be very limited with respect to addressing these two questions. The question has now shifted from "Who has it?" to "What is it?" The more important question for trainers is "Can it be improved?" Because of the many breakthroughs made available by cognitive-based learning methods, trainers can now profitably reexamine their assumptions about what adult learners can and cannot do in present and future job assignments.

We believe that intelligence is not limited to one aspect of human performance. IQ tests do not adequately measure all aspects of intelligence. For the purpose of training adults in the workplace, it is useful to make a distinction among three components of intelligence (see Figure 7.1). These are internal intelligence (content laden); external intelligence (situational); and interactive intelligence (the interaction of internal and external components) (Sternberg, 1985a).

Traditional IQ tests were designed to measure only one aspect of intelligence. This limits the utility of IQ tests to academic matters. The traditional IQ tests do a fairly good job of predicting who will do well in an academic training situation, and who will do well in school. However, they do not necessarily do a good job of predicting who will be successful in daily life. Other aspects of adult intelligence that deal with real-life social and problem-solving situations are not measured by the commonly used IQ tests.

Given this situation, is it surprising that the results of a number of studies (Feuerstein et al., 1985; Gardner, 1983) have shown that some adults with high scores on IQ tests as children, never attain successful personal careers? There are some differences between intelligence as measured by IQ tests and creativity (Sternberg, 1985a). An adult with a high IQ score is not necessarily creative. In fact, creativity has been found among some students with relatively low IQ scores (Ysseldyke & Algozzine, 1990). With a more contemporary information-processing view of intelligence, it has become important for trainers to design instructional situations that encourage academic intelligence, social intelligence, and creativity.

THREE COMPONENTS OF INTELLIGENCE

Major objections have been raised to the traditional methods used in assessing intelligence. R. J. Sternberg (1985a, 1985b) claims that present methods have little to do with understanding individual adult differences and are of little utility with respect to improving learning. His three components of intelligence are based on an information-processing approach to intellectual development. If properly applied to training methods, his framework has many pragmatic uses for educating adults in the workplace.

Figure 7.1
Three Components of Intelligence

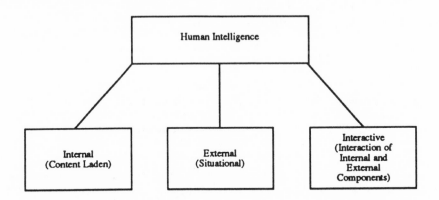

Internal intelligence (content laden) represents the "how" of intelligence (see Figure 7.2). An adult's executive processes (evaluating, planning, monitoring) regulate everything done both physically and mentally that directs learning. Direct teaching of the metacognitive strategies ("learning how to learn") has been found useful for slower adult learners. However, high-ability adult learners develop their own metacognitive strategies. Teaching them to use these strategies may conflict with their own well-developed problem-solving strategies (Garner, 1989; Brown, 1978).

Adult learners who have strong internal intelligence will do well in a training class because they will know how to analyze and solve problems, and will know exactly what the trainer expects during class instruction. This internal aspect of intelligence is what most traditional IQ tests are designed to measure.

In contrast, external intelligence (situational) is the practical component of adult intelligence (see Figure 7.3). This aspect of intelligence deals with real-life issues, the "what" and "where" of intelligence. Few IQ tests measure this type of human intelligence.

External intelligence is the ability to adapt environmental information to one's personal world. Most training programs fail to address this component of intelligence. We believe that in any training program it is essential to teach the adult learner to identify and solve real-world problems.

Interactive intelligence combines the adult's internal and external worlds (see Figure 7.4). People strong in this aspect of intelligence use their prior knowledge or experience when dealing with new life situations.

Few business problems have neat solutions. If we wish to measure intelligence, it is far more profitable to assess the adult's ability to deal with novel situations. Instead, we usually test academic problem-solving skills that come in neat little packages with specific solutions that have little to do with

Figure 7.2
Internal Components of Intelligence

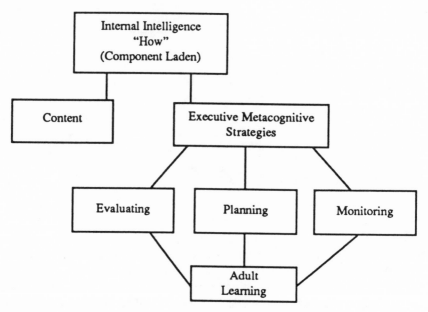

Figure 7.3
External Components of Intelligence (Social Dynamics)

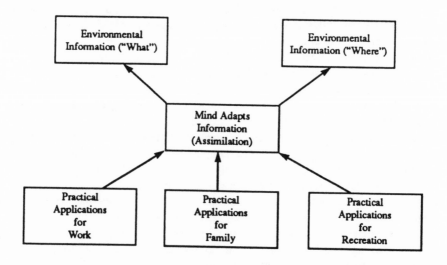

Figure 7.4
Interactive Components of Intelligence

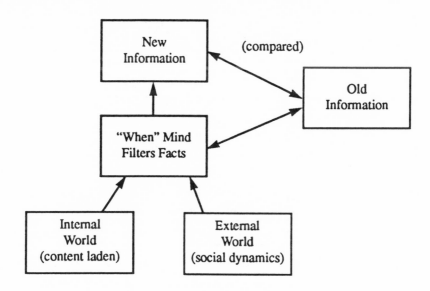

practical applications of intelligence. We agree with Sternberg that we need to nurture adult intelligence through the direct teaching of training situations transferrable to real-life work conditions. In this way trainers can "teach" workplace intelligence.

A SOCIAL LEARNING FRAMEWORK

Another approach to improving adult intelligence requires the trainer to carefully orchestrate the social learning environment to maximize new learning (Vygotsky, 1978). Here is how it works.

Initially in a new training program adult learners are other-directed, the trainer guiding their learning (see Figure 7.5). However, as the learners develop new knowledge as a result of the training process, they reach a point where they become self-directed. They now understand new information by internalizing the new with the old.

If any training program is going to optimize the intelligence of adult learners, it is very important for the trainer to know what the trainees know from the first day of class. You must bridge the knowledge gap between adults' independent learning level and their more advanced potential levels of learning. When we use a test-teach-test criterion-referenced form of assessment, it is far easier to design better training program content that builds adult intelligence. The IIP

Figure 7.5
Social Learning Framework Criterion: IIP Format

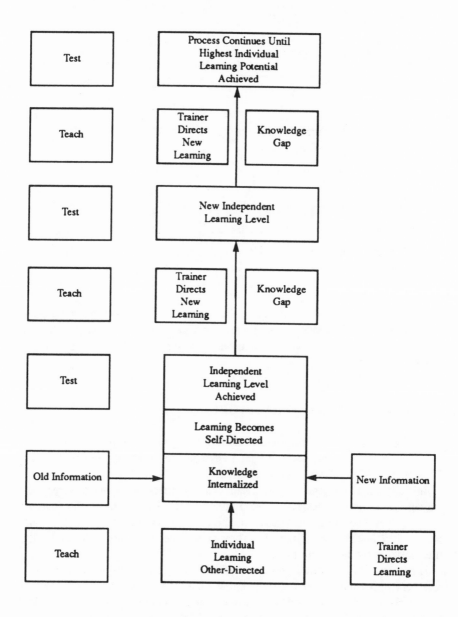

format that was described in Chapter 4 was designed around these principles. Its test-teach-test format gives a very accurate individual record of where the adult learner functions with little help from the trainer. The IIP assessment details exactly what additional help the adult needs to reach the maximum level of personal achievement from the training program (Gordon et al., 1991).

A related task-analytic test-teach-test approach to improving intelligence has some applicability to the workplace (Feuerstein et al., 1985). The initial test provides a task-analysis procedure to diagnose where the breakdown in learning has occurred for the trainee. The follow-up teaching is precisely modified to address the adult learner's diagnosed needs. Applying this test-teach-test approach to management development means that the trainer's testing of the trainee will uncover the specific problem-solving skills or concepts that are unknown or misunderstood. Subsequent training will be designed to modify identified misunderstanding or lack of content problem-solving skills.

This type of learning assessment/safeguard system enables trainers to conduct shorter knowledge checks during a training program and to modify instructional design content appropriately. By comparison, the alternative approach of only giving a program pre/post achievement instrument seems very limiting if we hope to achieve a maximum learning experience for the majority of adults in any training program.

In view of all these new developments in training, we believe that intelligence can no longer be viewed as static and biologically fixed for life. We will now discuss what can be done to help problematic adult learners minimize their individual differences and maximize their intelligence.

CAN INTELLIGENCE BE TAUGHT?

Fifty years ago, even twenty years ago, it was fairly preposterous to talk about "teaching intelligence." Intelligence was understood as the fixed score on an IQ test. A person's intelligence never changed. It was believed to be stable and static for life. One of the strongest arguments supporting this concept of the IQ was that it did not seem to change (much) over a lifetime. This point of view discouraged trainers from making serious attempts to improve an adult's intelligence in the corporate classroom (Sternberg, 1985b).

However, psychologists have long maintained that a significant amount of personal growth measured by intelligence test scores is fostered by individual heredity and an environment that stimulates learning. Based on discoveries in the past ten years, we may not be able to make a 70 IQ adult into a 120 IQ adult, but we can change the IQ as much as 20 points up or down, based on the environment and the exposure to better educational programs (Kotulak, 1993).

The authors' current field-based research and the work of many other researchers (Sternberg, 1985a, 1985b; Vygotsky, 1978; Weinberg, 1989) support the concept that intelligence can be taught through training and education. Sternberg's information processing model, and L. S. Vygotsky's novice-expert social interaction model have stimulated the development of the authors' training models that are designed to teach intelligence. We are trying to emphasize the metacognitive activities that foster individual learning and problem solving in the workplace.

Our approach forms important links to teaching adults how to regulate their planning, monitoring, and encoding of learning information through these training activities. Training based on building metacognition proposes that the adult learner's internal thinking mechanism processes information through planning, evaluating, and monitoring (see Figure 7.2). The adult learner is also taught to systematically compare possible solutions, to distinguish essential from nonessential details.

The authors' dynamic view of adult intelligence is that it can potentially be improved through training that uses a test-teach-test curriculum script (see Figure 7.5). The findings of the authors' Individualized Instructional Program (IIP) and Management Insight Development Program (MIDP) indicate that adult learners not only improve a specific skill but also become more intelligent problem solvers in the workplace.

The authors believe that we are at a point in our understanding of intelligence to be able to pinpoint how to improve an individual adult's specific learning skills. Our workplace programs have enabled adults to teach themselves how to strengthen their intellectual capacities for daily work activities.

RECIPROCAL TRAINING

Motorola has used this approach to initiate production employees into computer-integrated manufacturing. The trainees are paired up at a computer workstation. The trainer leads them step by step through the different types of equipment and computer controls. Trainees learn operation of the robot arm and simulated programming, and gradually become conversant in modern automated factory terminology.

By the end of this training program, assembly-line workers have achieved a higher level of personal understanding (intelligence) of how a computer will program a robot for creative job tasks. Production employees then begin to ask questions about applying robotics to their own specific jobs on the line.

This relatively low-cost reciprocal training program builds on a production employee's knowledge of practical, everyday technology by using dynamic test-teach-test social learning in small groups. It extends the adult's basic foundation of knowledge to include the training lab's robotic technology. The training equipment has the realistic features of industrial equipment but is smaller, far less expensive, and easier to operate (Cheng, 1990). These workers are walking away from their computer training program with cognitive learning strategies that increase both skills and personal intelligence. This will in turn enhance individual employee productivity and quality abilities for future manufacturing applications of many high-tech products (Gordon et al., 1991).

This is a practical example of the reciprocal training model (Brown & Campione, 1986; Palinscar & Brown, 1984) that is designed to explicitly teach metacognitive strategies, such as self-monitoring and rehearsal, within a cooperative learning workplace environment. This reciprocal training strategy encourages a gradual transition from the initial training situation, the teaching of problem-solving skills to the adult, to the employees themselves doing the actual training.

The trainer first teaches self-regulating strategies that increase adult learners' ability to predict results, analyze problems, summarize work strategies, and apply them broadly to their work. The second training phase allows practice of these skills in small teams, with different adults taking turns directing the learning/application process.

The reciprocal training process enables adult learners to realize a higher learning potential (intelligence). The metacognitive skills they learn give them insight into ways they can "learn how to learn." The employees move from external learning to internalizing the information and successfully applying it in diverse future work projects (see Figure 7.5).

In designing a new training program based on this metacognitive framework, we must pay attention to several adult learning factors:

1. What is the independent learning level of the adult for this specific training topic?
2. What is the adult's prior knowledge of the subject material?
3. What is this adult's learning potential?

THE BOTTOM LINE OF INTELLIGENCE

By using the test-teach-test format, the trainer will discover that as the adult learns more, individual learning potential will constantly fluctuate. Individual intelligence represents the ability of an adult to change as a result of instruction (see Figure 7.5). By teaching adults better procedures and strategies to "learn how to learn," we are increasing their personal intellectual flexibility in coping with future change by developing new self-learning techniques. The bottom line in developing a learner's intelligence is how far a trainer can increase these dimensions (procedures versus flexibility) as the individual faces new challenges in the workplace.

TRAINING ASSESSMENT AND INSTRUCTIONAL DESIGN

Traditional assessment procedures for training and development often have proven to be of little value in designing meaningful adult workplace learning programs.   The use of standardized achievement or IQ tests often yields misleading interpretations of how successfully an adult will perform on the job.

The development of behaviorally based company assessment centers was a popular alternative to trainers' total reliance on standardized tests.   These behavior assessment centers included direct behavioral observations under controlled conditions, self-assessment, and behavioral assessment reports or interviews completed with significant people in the employee's work environment, such as peers and supervisors.   In many assessment center programs, standardized testing supplemented these activities.   Business assessment center programs enabled the adult to be assessed within the context of a more natural workplace environment.

These behavior assessment center programs represent an improvement over a complete reliance on standardized testing.   However, neither of these assessment methods was designed to predict the individual adult's potential accurately nor to apply new problem-solving strategies successfully in the workplace (Feuerstein et al, 1985; Gardner, 1983; Sternberg, 1985a, 1985b).

As an alternative to these procedures, the authors' field-based research programs developed both the Individualized Instructional Program (IIP) for specific skill training and assessment, and the Management Insight Development Program (MIDP) for management development training and assessment (Gordon et al., 1991).   We attempt to identify the adult cognitive deficits and to assess learning potential.   The adult then participates in a series of individual tutorials or small-group tutorials (IIP), or classroom controlled-learning experiences (see Chapters 4 and 5).   This assessment is similar to R. Feuerstein et al.'s (1985) learning potential abilities device, where the learner is taught missing content and problem-solving strategies.

The test-teach-test approach found in the IIP and MIDP uses assessment to cover a wide range of practical work-content issues.   We are trying to relate formalized instruction to real-world problem-solving issues.   Sternberg (1985a, 1985b) does the same through the use of his multidimensional approach to assessing and enhancing intelligence.

The IIP, because of its tutorial nature, allows the trainer to interact directly with the adult throughout the testing/tutoring process to determine personal learning potential.   Its social interaction process is built on the concept that this more personalized social assessment more accurately reveals what the learner is able to do independently, what content or problem-solving skills are lacking, and what the learner's potential to move forward is (Vygotsky, 1978).

In order to better link testing to instruction, both the IIP and MIDP use a curriculum-based assessment (CBA).   This procedure uses the training curriculum as the basis for tracking learner performance.   There is a direct link between assessment and instruction.   Failures that occur in traditional testing may reflect a lack of exposure to the content material.   In contrast, individual failures in a CBA program are true learning failures.   Here the material is familiar to the trainees.   They just do not understand it.   (For more information on CBA see Chapter 8).

A primary reason that trainers and educators are turning to CBA is that they can develop a teaching plan directly from the assessment. CBA may also be very useful in training difficult adult audiences (Ysseldyke et al., 1982). It appears that CBA is less culturally and racially biased than other traditional assessment instruments used in training (Galagen, 1985).

Workplace assessment is now undergoing many fundamental changes. Traditional standardized assessment tests are not adequate for the training demands of the twenty-first century workplace. Standardized tests will always retain some value for trainers because of their comparison of an individual to a large representative sample. However, the overall trend in training is to develop the use of less formal and more varied curriculum-based assessment tools.

CAN TRAINERS MODIFY INDIVIDUAL ADULT LEARNING?

Traditional behavior theorists deemphasized individual learning abilities and focused on establishing general principles of behavior. However, increased attention to adult learning from a cognitive perspective highlights the importance of studying the individual differences among adults that might place limits on their learning activities. A detailed examination of these individual differences will facilitate trainers' understanding of the interaction among these limitations. This will also guide your design of effective training programs.

BIOLOGICAL LIMITATIONS TO ADULT LEARNING

Maturation and Temperament

Adult maturation and temperament are considered to be biological limitations that are not very amenable to change by trainers. Piaget viewed personal cognitive growth as the result of the gradual maturation in thinking that corresponds to the biological maturational stages of development. This view has been widely supported by research. The information-processing theorists view cognitive growth as a combination of qualitative and quantitative changes in knowledge. These changes are presumed to be a function of both physical maturation and experience. Information-processing theorists have observed differences between the way younger and older learners use cognitive strategies to solve problems.

In organizing a team to complete a work task or play a game, adults more likely will delegate the team's tasks to individual members who have demonstrated or volunteered expert skills that will help bring about a more successful team effort. Children are more likely to operate their team on the popularity of individuals and to have far less personal insight into the strengths or weaknesses of other team members. This makes team problem solving a far more difficult activity for children. Older learners not only learn and solve problems more rapidly, but also approach learning tasks in different ways than do children.

Individual Attention

The attention span of an individual is another biological limitation that may be only partially amenable to change. Attention or memory span refers to the amount of information that can be obtained from a single brief exposure to the learning task and immediately recalled from short-term memory (see Figure 2.2). The amount of information that can be remembered is believed to be limited to seven, plus or minus two, distinct ideas (Miller, 1956) (see Figure 7.6). With experience an adult is able to hold larger amounts of information in short-term memory by chunking or organizing lower-order units into seven or so higher-order units (see Figure 7.7). Learning becomes a matter of segregating, classifying, and grouping elementary elements into a smaller number of richer, more densely packed chunks.

PSYCHOLOGICAL CONSTRAINTS

Knowledge

From the information-processing perspective, knowledge is seen as arranged into hierarchies that gradually develop throughout our lives. A person first acquires lower-order thinking skills onto which higher-order thinking skills are anchored throughout the adult learner's lifetime (see Work Force Education Triad).

Learning occurs when the adult relates new knowledge to existing knowledge through the use of rules, particularly verbal rules, and through the development of higher levels of personal literacy (reading, writing, and math). A failure to develop lower-order skills or knowledge bases impedes the learning of higher-order skills which, in turn will impair adult thinking and problem-solving abilities.

Individual Memory Organization

Personal memory organization appears to be crucial with respect to the transfer of information from short-term memory to long-term memory. In fact, one of the major differences between problematic and normal adult learners appears to lie in the former's inability to organize information and use strategies (e.g., rehearsal) that enable the transfer of knowledge to the long-term memory system.

Figure 7.6
Individual Attention: Short-Term Memory Before Training

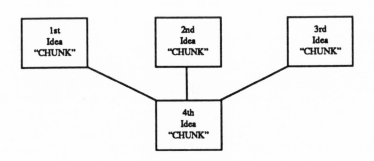

STM = 7 ± 2 Ideas

"REMEMBERED CHUNKS"

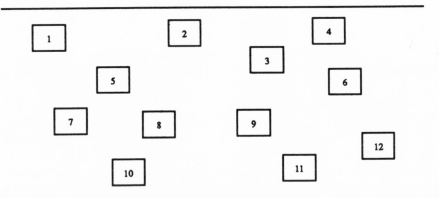

"FORGOTTEN IDEAS"

Figure 7.7
Individual Attention: Short-Term Memory After Training

STM = 7 ± 2 Ideas

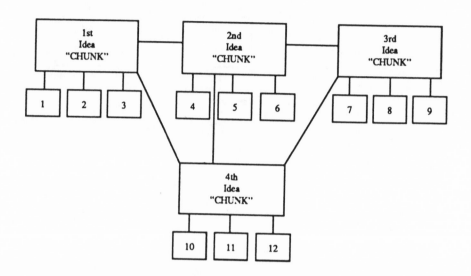

Emotions and Memory

Emotions may have a substantial impact on how information is processed during problem solving (Hooper & Hannafin, 1991). Pilots receive extensive behavior-based emergency-landing training. They do not have time to attempt elaborate cognitive problem-solving techniques. Instead, they rely mainly on "automatic" procedural trained behaviors that require very little creative thinking. Research has indicated that emotional reactions frequently reduce flexibility in some problem-solving situations and that frustration reduces fluency. Thus, some people experiencing strong emotional reactions may be less likely to access some of their knowledge and bring that knowledge into working memory.

Personal Mood

Personal mood may manifest its effects on adult learning in two ways: (1) the adult's mood may affect the nature of the materials selected for learning; and (2) personal mood provides access routes to past memories. There is ample evidence that the adult's positive or negative mood while in training has a direct correlation to the degree of learning that will result for that individual (Bower, 1981).

Language Fluency

Language appears to be an important force that drives the individual learning process. The achievement of higher thinking levels is closely tied to the development of individual verbal skills (speaking, reading, writing). Verbal memory is a very important component of the entire memory system. New knowledge is integrated into the existing verbal memory system. Other forms of personal memory usually remain at a relatively primitive level until the knowledge they contain can be represented in the adult's memory in a detailed verbal symbolic form. It is easy to understand why language is believed to be the key to success for academic intelligence and higher personal achievement in the workplace.

Individual Personality

Adult personality variables may either weaken or strengthen the learning process. A commonly seen personality dimension is the introverted or extroverted personality. These personalities may share problem-solving limitations, but for different reasons. Introverts may have difficulty detecting problems in their living environment, while extroverts may have difficulty properly understanding the basic causes of a problem. Personality differences among individuals are most evident when successful learning is dependent on the skills of problem detection, formation, and solution (Heppner & Krauskopf, 1987).

Individual Cognitive Style

How adults mentally process information (i.e., their cognitive style) is another major source of variation in personal performance and is related to success in thinking and problem solving. Several dimensions are useful for describing individual differences in cognitive style: reflective versus impulsive and field-independent versus field-dependent styles.

Reflective thinkers are usually more efficient problem solvers. Impulsive thinkers will plunge in, make mistakes, and then have to backup to arrive at a correct solution (Kagan, 1966).

Field-independent learners seem to learn more under internal motivational conditions. They have definite internalized values and standards in their personal behavior that help them persevere and are more systematic in their learning activities. In contrast, field-dependent learners have more success at perceiving social relationships when working with others. They are better at the casual learning of social nuances, and adapt better to new work/life requirements (Hooper & Hannafin, 1991).

An oil company research chemist is probably a field-independent learner and a reflective thinker. He or she will respond best to training designed around these cognitive styles. A colleague from the marketing department will tend to be far more impulsive and field-dependent. His or her success as a marketer often depends on these cognitive styles. Training for this marketer will be more effective if the design accounts for these variations in processing information.

Personal Motivation

How are an individual's actions selected and begun?   Motives regulate personal enthusiasm for learning and what is learned.   An adult possesses a cognitive system that remediates most internal or external motivators.   Both strong stimulation from the work environment and biological drives are controlled by this cognitive system. We may wish to travel extensively and have more leisure time. However, our need for a successful career identity and for ample food, shelter, and security are balanced out by our cognitive motivation system.   Rather than being moved by external forces, we are most often motivated by cognitive representations of future outcomes.

An additional source of cognitive motivation arises from our goal setting and self-reinforcement (Bandura, 1977). Self-motivation results from setting and making commitments to goals and defining standards that evaluate goal-attaining behavior.   Personal self-regulation largely explains achievement motivation, power motivation, competence motivation, curiosity, and thirst for knowledge of results.

THE FRONTIERS OF INTELLIGENCE

As we have seen many educators and trainers have assumed that the basic difference between the successful and the unsuccessful adult learner stems from disparities in mental processing ability.

What do we know about the differences in personal attention, memory, organization, and expectations among us? We know (Miller, 1956) that normal learners can concentrate on seven, plus or minus two things, at one time. Normal and problematic learners are thought to differ with respect to the bits of information they can remember without assistance.   We know that with increasing age and experience, the bits become more differentiated and sophisticated.

Successful efforts within educational contexts have been made to enhance personal attention. This includes work with training metacognitive skills (Brown, 1978). There is ample evidence supporting the notion that trainers can increase, direct, and control attention.

Personal expectations are of particular importance with respect to the stable ways in which a learner perceives, encodes, and stores information. Differences in these expectations among people divide adult learners into two categories, field-dependent and field-independent learners. Field-dependent learners are aware of cues, seek out reinforcement, and are sensitive to the feelings of others. Field-independent learners are more individualistic, intrinsically motivated, and less likely to seek out reinforcement (Witkin et al., 1977).

We believe there is a great need to deal simultaneously with individual learning differences and instructional programming (Brown & Campione, 1986; Cronbach, 1957). We need to establish an overall plan that will match individual differences in aptitudes to different instructional programs. We have seen from our ongoing field research that some people learn more easily with one method than another. If we look at individual differences and varying instructional strategies at the same time, we can develop an aptitude-treatment interaction methodology that provides a procedure to match aptitudes and different teaching methods. L. J. Cronbach's point was that you cannot separate the two.

We seem to need to free ourselves from the notion that intelligence is limited by individual differences and developmental constraints. Problematic adult learners may have deficient information-processing skills with respect to attention, memory organization, and expectations. However, our ongoing field research shows that we can modify these skills to minimize individual differences among adult learners that might have previously limited their learning activities and problem-solving performance. Based on the results of our cognitive-based training program, the authors believe that we can educate many adults for successful problem-solving, abstract reasoning activities tied to quality/team business efforts.

In the next chapter we will address the difficult issue of measuring training program results. Can we prove that training will work to improve employee skills and intelligence while also having a positive economic benefit on the bottom line?

REFERENCES

Bandura, A. 1977. *Social Learning Theory*. Englewood Cliffs, NJ: Prentice Hall.

Bower, G. H. 1981. Mood and memory. *American Psychologist* 36 (2):129–148.

Brown, A. L. 1978. Knowing when, where, and how to remember: A problem of metacognition. In R. Glaser, ed., *Advances in Instructional Psychology*. Hillsdale, NJ: Erlbaum.

Brown, A. L. & Campione, J. C. 1986. Psychological theory and the study of learning disabilities. *American Psychologist* 14 (10):1059–1068.

Cheng, A. F. 1990. Hands-on learning at Motorola. *Training and Development Journal* 44 (10):34–35.

Cronbach, L. J. 1957. Beyond two disciplines of scientific psychology. *American Psychologist* 30 (2):116–127.

Feuerstein, R.; Jensen, N.; Hoffman, N. B.; & Rand, W. 1985. Instructional enrichment an intervention program for structural cognitive modifiability: Theory and practice. In J. W. Segal, S. F. Chipman, & R. Glaser, eds., *Thinking and Learning Skills*, vol. 1. Hillsdale, NJ: Erlbaum.

Galagen, I. E. 1985. Psychoeducational Testing: Turn out the lights, the party's over. *Exceptional Children* 52:288–298.

Gardner, H. 1983. *Frames of Mind.* New York: Basic Books.

Garner, R. & Alexander, P. A. 1989. Metacognition: Answered and unanswered questions. *Educational Psychologist* 24 (2):143–158.

Gordon, E. E.; Ponticell, J. A.; & Morgan, R. R. 1991. *Closing the Literacy Gap in American Business, A Guide for Trainers and Human Resource Specialists.* New York: Quorum Books.

Heppner, P. & Krauskoph, C. 1987. An information approach to personal problem solving. *Counseling Psychologist* 15 (3):371–447.

Hooper, S., & Hannafin, M. J. 1991. Psychological perspectives on emerging instructional technologies: A critical analysis. *Educational Psychologist* 26 (1):69–95.

Kagan, J. 1966. Reflection-impulsivity: The generality and dynamics of conceptual tempo. *Journal of Abnormal and Social Psychology* 71:17–24.

Kotulak, R. 1993. Unraveling hidden mysteries of the brain. *Chicago Tribune*, 11 April sec. 1, 1, 10.

Miller, G. A. 1956. The magical number seven plus or minus two: Some limits on our capacity for processing information. *Psychological Review* 63:81–97.

Palinscar, A. S. & Brown, A. L. 1984. Reciprocal teaching of comprehension fostering and comprehension-monitoring activities. *Cognition and Instruction* 1 (2): 117–175.

Sternberg, R. J. 1985a. Beyond IQ: A Triarchic Theory of Human Intelligence. Cambridge: Cambridge University Press.

_____. 1985b. Instrumental and componential approaches to the nature and training of intelligence. In S. F. Chipman, J. W. Segal, & R. Glaser, eds., *Thinking and Learning Skills*, vol. 2. Hillsdale, NJ: Erlbaum.

Vygotsky, L. S. 1978. *Mind in Society: The Development of Higher Psychological Processes.* Cambridge MA: Harvard University Press.

Weinberg, R. A. 1989. Intelligence and I.Q.: Landmark issues and great debates. *American Psychologist* 44 (2):98–104.

Witkin, H. A.; Moore, C. A.; Goodenough, D. R.; & Cox, P. W. 1977 Field-dependent and field-independent cognition styles and their educational implications. *Review of Educational Research* 47:1–64.

Ysseldyke, J. G. & Algozzine, B. 1990. *Introduction to Special Education,* 2nd ed. Boston: Houghton Mifflin.

Ysseldyke, J. G.; Thurlow, M.; Graden, J.; Wessen, C.; Deno, S.; & Algozzine, B. 1982. Generalizations from five years of research on assessment and decision making. *Exceptional Education Quarterly* 4:75–93.

Chapter 8

Proving It Works!

TRAINING — THE "FIFTH WHEEL" OF BUSINESS?

Training and development's lack of accountability has for too long made it the optional "fifth wheel" of American business. Money may be set aside in a business' budget for training to improve an area of management failure. But how effective are the results? "The interpersonal skills of the managers are so bad they are chewing off the legs of their people. People are calling in sick. Productivity is down; turnover is high. So the company 'does motivational training' to help people feel good, keep them upbeat. Then it is back to work and business as usual" (Harte, 1990).

During a time of economic prosperity and business expansion, training most likely is still treated only as an option, not an essential, by most managers. Unlike our foreign competitors, training is readily cut in an economic downturn. Contrary to this basic intuition, hard times may be the best time to maintain or even expand company training efforts. This is supported by the fact that more slack time may exist for the workforce even if it is declining in size.

Another argument often heard is that training only encourages "poaching" by the competition. As Crawford and Webley state, does any company seriously consider its optimum human resource strategy is to keep its workforce so ignorant that nobody else will ever wish to employ them? (Crawford & Webley, 1992)

Employee loyalty to the organization rests on many other motivational factors besides money: self-fulfillment, improved self-esteem, and a need for personal affiliation. If a company's business culture places an emphasis on life-long employee learning, more individuals will see themselves as highly-appreciated members of the organization. This feeling of "being vested" is a powerful inducement to stay (Crawford & Webley, 1992). However, for the majority of managers there seldom exists any clear connection between training and the bottom line. Business wants financial results, not just "good feelings."

Other than a program's "smile sheets," trainers rarely gather information on any tangible results. Why? Here are the ten most common excuses offered by trainers regarding evaluation (Phillips, 1991):

1. It takes too much time.
2. My training program can't be measured for results; it's unique.
3. Evaluation is too expensive.
4. I can't get the cooperation of other departments to do it.
5. Nobody really cares. The CEO and my boss don't believe in it.
6. It's too hard. I don't have a Ph.D., or the funds to hire an expert to do it for me.
7. I'm afraid what we might find out.
8. You can't measure ROI for training.
9. Measurement is effective only in the production and financial areas.
10. I don't know how to get or where to go for useful information.

CEOs are demanding results from every part of their business. Unless training costs can be justified as an essential business operation, they will often be cut. Managers prefer to see their people working rather than in a classroom learning how to be more efficient. American business does not invest in educating its people because too many trainers do not know how to answer a basic economic question: "Will the time and money you invest today in training be repaid with interest in the next week, month, year or decade?" (Hassett, 1992).

HOW — THE TRAINING EVALUATION PYRAMID

The evaluation of training can be divided into four areas: reactions, learning, behavior and results.   The Training Evaluation Pyramid (see Figure 8.1) summarizes these different evaluation approaches. We will review the criteria and methods associated with each evaluation area. Before you begin training, time needs to be allocated for determining what you are about to train. Do you know how to conduct a training needs assessment for your business?

An accurate assessment of business needs will focus on linking real business problems to realistic training programs. The authors have too often encountered a training failure because the needs of the business were ill-defined, the training was not targeting the right audience(s), and/or a "training solution" was misapplied to a nontraining business problem.

We have assembled some of the key questions that may help you conduct a more meaningful training needs assessment (see Appendix IV). These questions will help you organize whatever approach is practical within your organization for the assignment at hand.   This may range from a comprehensive companywide survey, to a taskforce model, focus groups, or individual interview. The extent to which you address real business needs may often determine the breadth and depth of cooperation you receive from trainees and their supervisors when you begin to determine how well the training works.

Measuring Audience Reaction

At the base of the Training Evaluation Pyramid is the measurement of audience reactions (see Figure 8.1). This is by far the most widely used form of assessment across American business.

Audience reaction assessments attempt to gauge the trainees' impressions or feelings about a program. Sometimes called "smile sheets" or "happiness ratings," these assessments often yield highly subjective information. However, some research indicates that participants who enjoy the training program most are often the persons who achieve most back on the job (Elkins, 1977).

A properly designed audience reaction assessment may often have to suffice. This feedback questionnaire is certainly a critical part of any comprehensive, high-quality training evaluation. The most common types of audience feedback include the following (Phillips, 1991; see Figure 8.2):

- Instructor/speaker presentation skills
- Program content
- Program relevance to job
- Methods of instruction
- Training materials
- Program length
- Out-of-class work
- Facilities
- Overall evaluation
- Suggested improvements

The primary advantage of measuring a training audience's reactions is that it provides a quick, recent opinion while the information is still fresh in the participants' minds. Such questionnaires are easy to use, since they take only a few minutes to administer, and they can readily assess trainee satisfaction if tabulated, analyzed, and summarized. Moreover, this type of assessment can be useful in making adjustments for future presentations. It also provides one type of audience evaluation of the program's overall effectiveness (Jeleniewski, 1993).

There are clear disadvantages to this method of assessing training results. The questionnaire may offer superficial, subjective audience opinions and feelings. Personal bias, influenced by the trainer's presentation and interpersonal skills, may exaggerate the overall quality rating of the entire program. Also, the participants may not be the best judges of the trainer's performance. In some instances, trainees give a positive rating because of relief that the training is finished! Finally, even an excellent audience reaction gives little assurance that the participants will begin to use this information on the job (Jeleniewski, 1993; Phillips, 1991).

Reaction questionnaires offer an easy method to measure an audience's

Figure 8.1
Training Evaluation Pyramid

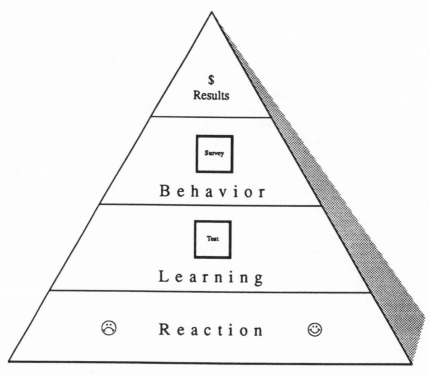

Source: Adapted from Jeliniewski, 1993.

impressions of an instructional program. However, trainers should consider them of only limited use in determining a program's overall effectiveness.

Measuring Learning

The measurement of learning is the next segment in the Training Evaluation Pyramid (see Figure 8.1). Considerable attention is now being paid to alternative forms of assessing learning. Why do we perceive a paradigm shift that is moving away from traditional, multiple-choice, standardized achievement tests to alternative forms of assessment? Why do we need a variety of strategies for tracking adult learner performance over time? Why is there renewed interest in finding more systematic ways of looking for connections between what we *do* in training and development and what *changes* occur in employee performance on the job?

Figure 8.2
Audience Reaction Questionnaire

Audience Reaction Questionnaire
by Edward E. Gordon, Ph.D.

Name of Program: _____ Date: _____

1. How would you rate the overall program?
   ___Excellent
   ___Very Good
   ___Good
   ___Fair
   ___Poor

   Comments:

2. The course goals and objectives were met.
   ___Very Much So
   ___Somewhat
   ___Not at All

3. The course content was logically organized and sequenced.

   ___Very Much So
   ___Somewhat
   ___Not at All

4. The exercises allowed me to practice what was taught.

   ___Very Much So
   ___Somewhat
   ___Not at All

5. There was enough time given for questions and discussion.

   ___Very Much So
   ___Somewhat
   ___Not at All

6. The training materials contributed to my learning.

   ___Very Much So
   ___Somewhat
   ___Not at All

7. The use of audio/visual aids helped me understand key points.

   ___Very Much So
   ___Somewhat
   ___Not at All

8. To what extent will it help you do a better job?
   ___To a large extent
   ___To some extent
   ___Very little

   Comments:

9. What were the major benefits you received? (Check as many as you wish)
   ___Helped confirm some of my ideas
   ___Presented new ideas and approaches I can use
   ___Gave me a chance to practice some newly acquired skills
   ___Gave me an opportunity to look objectively at how I perform

   Comments:

Figure 8.2 continued

10. Was the training program:
    ___Too long
    ___Too short
    ___Just right

11. What would have improved this program?

12. Rate the training program leader:

	Very Much	Some	Not At All
How well prepared			
Held interest of group			
Was enthusiastic			
Presented material clearly			
Helped group apply the material			
Involved the group			
Provided time for questions			
Used variety of methods			
Summarized			
Had knowledge of subject matter			

13. Additional Comments:

The Outcomes-Based Paradigm Shift

Granted, "paradigm" is an increasingly trendy word, but it does capture the dramatic shift that is occurring in how we think about about training and development.   Paradigms are rules and regulations, stated and unstated assumptions, models and standard procedures that shape our worldview or our understanding of the ways things are and work (Kuhn, 1970).

Paradigms shift when they no longer help us solve problems or explain powerful, fundamental, and emerging changes in our understandings, assumptions, and values.   Such a shift is occurring in how trainers view teaching, learning, and assessment.   We are beginning to question the accuracy of standardized tests in assessing outcomes important to a training or instructional program.   We have gotten too comfortable with designing training and instruction to match the format of multiple-choice testing items; thus, there tends to be overemphasis on drill and practice in discrete skills. This is problematic. The concept of learning as the accumulation of bits of knowledge is outmoded. Current models of learning based on cognitive psychology demonstrate that understanding is increased when learners construct their own knowledge and develop cognitive maps of interconnections among concepts and facts (Shepard, 1989).

To engage learners in the kinds of critical thinking that adults will need in the twenty-first century, we will have to shift to a paradigm that focuses on practice in solving real problems and comprehending complex tasks. The establishment of TQM, ISO 9000, business process re-engineering, teams, and other modern management systems requires new forms of assessment for outcomes-based training.

What knowledge, skills, and job orientations will adult learners need in order to be prepared to live in the more competitive twenty-first century? The next century will be characterized by an information society, global economic interdependence, cultural pluralism, rapidly expanding technologies, and decentralized social structures. Such a society is based on knowledge and the ability to put it to work to create, to invent, and to solve problems.

Emphasis for most workers on "basic skills" which characterized educational preparation during the twentieth century is no longer viable. Instead, capacities once demanded of only the top twenty percent of America's society will soon be required of the masses: to think critically and creatively, to solve problems, to exercise judgment, and to learn new skills and knowledge throughout a lifetime (Brown, 1991).

What Are We Learning About Assessment? This outcomes-based paradigm shift is also shaping how we view assessment. For decades, we assumed that assessment was an end in itself. Now we assume that assessment is a vehicle for learning improvement. An outcomes-based view of assessment begins with a vision of the kinds of learning we most value. These values or outcomes drive not only what we choose to assess but also how we do so.

What adult learners bring to the table is not that important. What has become crucial to business is what adult learners can be taught to do with new learning. Therefore, outcomes-based assessment requires a more diverse array of methods that measure actual learner performance over time to reveal change, growth, and increasing degrees of knowledge integration. In other words, our earlier assumptions about assessment as "one-shot" are giving way to an understanding that learning improvement is best facilitated when assessment entails a linked series of activities undertaken over time.

Outcomes-based assessment implies that we design and organize everything we do in training and education around the intended learning demonstration we want to see at the end. We base things on the outcomes so that the outcome will eventually occur for everyone (Spady & Marshall, 1991). What might an outcomes-based assessment mean for a management development training program?

We start with the program by identifying what is valued. The management development program might desire four general outcomes for participants: problem solving, analytic capabilities, value judgments, and decision-making skills. Participants do not take a multiple-choice content knowledge test under an outcomes-based paradigm. This test would only measure *what* discrete facts a person recalled from the training course. Instead, participants might be asked to work at an authentic task that will reveal their depth of understanding and applying the management course's new information.

For example, participants might be asked to select an action by an influential person in the company that had important consequences for that company. They are asked to determine the characteristics of the decision that had to be identified by this person before such an action was taken. What dilemmas did the person face? What alternative choices were available to this person when the decision was made? What criteria were the person likely to have applied in making the decision? What were the possible trade-offs in selecting one alternative over another? What were the risks, the rewards, and the consequences? How might these have been measured? Without benefit of hindsight, would you have made the same decision? Why or why not?

Such an outcomes-based task enables assessment of several indicators of good problem solving:

1. Clear definition of a decision question
2. Clear articulation of alternatives
3. Appropriateness of alternatives
4. Clear identification of criteria on which the alternatives were assessed
5. Value judgment of the importance of the identified criteria to the overall decision
6. Assessment of the extent to which each alternative included or matched up with each of the identified criteria
7. Commitment to a final selection among the alternatives
8. Adequacy of the final selection to the initial dilemma.

Criterion-based assessments and authentic tasks focus on what adult learners can eventually learn to do well, rather than on how well they do the first time they encounter something. Authentic tasks address the outcomes we value and simulate challenges facing an individual on the job. We will explore these specific notions of assessment in the sections that follow.

What Norm-Referenced Standardized Testing Can and Cannot Tell Us. What norm-referenced or standardized testing tells us is what learners know in general. If we look at a standardized reading test, for example, and focus on all learners with high scores and all learners with low scores, it is likely that more reading difficulties will exist among learners with low scores. Of what use is this kind of information? Standardized tests enable us to get a global picture. In general, are sixth graders learning reading at the sixth grade level? In general, are college algebra students learning college algebra?

However, what standardized testing does not tell us, nor is it meant to tell us, are "nuances of performance that characterize the full range of a learner's skill, ability, and learning style" (Worthen & Spandel, 1991). Just because a reader scores well on a standardized test, it does not mean that we can say with confidence that the person is a wonderful reader and always will be, in all circumstances.

Furthermore, traditional tests are arbitrarily timed, superficial in the content they test, and given only once or twice. They leave us with no way of gauging a learner's ability to make progress over time (Wiggins, 1989). So we must ask whether standardized tests provide sufficient information to allow intelligent instructional and program decision making.

For example, what does it mean if a learner ranks in the eightieth percentile on a reading test? We may say that person has performed better than 80 percent of the others who took the same test. This sounds impressive. However, a difference in performance on one test item can significantly raise or lower an individual's percentile ranking.

In addition, reading passages are generally shorter and less complex than the texts that learners encounter in daily work. Standardized reading tests use a small number of item types to avoid confusing test takers with frequent changes in format. This is problematic for there is considerable evidence that individuals "may appear to know a concept or skill when it is measured in one format but not know it if measured in another way" (Shepard, 1988). Given this, how much confidence do we want to place in standardized test scores for program and personnel decision making?

There are a multitude of complaints against standardized tests. As W. Haney and G. Madaus (1989) note, these complaints generally fall into four categories of recurring criticisms:

1. They give false information about the status of learning in the nation's schools.
2. They are unfair to (or biased against) some kinds of learners.
3. They tend to corrupt the processes of teaching and learning, often reducing teaching to mere preparation for testing.
4. They focus time, energy, and attention on the simpler skills that are easily tested, and away from higher-order thinking skills and creative endeavors.

Furthermore, the utility of norm-referenced tests is limited for two reasons (Webster, 1986). First, they tend not to be useful for monitoring progress and making instructional decisions. Second, since they generally do not relate to the content of specific program curricula, they may not be sensitive to progress made by adult learners in those programs.

There is no excuse for allowing standardized tests to be the *only* measure of learning in a training or educational program. It is important to supplement standardized measures with assessments constructed specifically to measure what the training or instructional program is attempting to accomplish.

When norm-referenced standardized testing is used, the issue of pre- and post-test reliability is an important one. Pre- and post-test reliability is primarily affected by two factors:

1. Carryover effects, by which the first test administration may influence the second (e.g., practicing on the test as a work assignment, remembering specific test items, changing attitudes about the test-taking experience).
2. Time effects, by which the length of time between test administrations affects the second test (e.g., short interval, making carryover effects due to practice, memory, or mood more likely; and long interval, making effects due to changes in information or attitude more likely).

Attention to testing conditions can help to reduce these effects. For example, it is wise to use alternate or parallel test forms. It is also wise to record the dates on which tests are taken. The interval between testings can be an important variable when interpreting certain performance traits. Furthermore, trainer/instructor and learner familiarity with the test's purpose, format, and directions makes for more consistent attitudes across test administration.

When we move to interpreting the data, the use of raw score (i.e., number of items correct) correlation, as opposed to percentage or normed scores, makes it possible to allow learners to indicate items on the test about which they have no knowledge. A simple method is to have learners circle the test items about which they have no knowledge, or no idea of how to start working on them. This proves useful in diagnosis of a learner's initial knowledge base.

Do standardized tests have value? Yes, they do. The most immediate value for pre- and post-standardized tests is as an indicator of a learner's initial, general knowledge base (see Appendix II for an example of how we have used test data in the IIP). However, as noted in our discussion of the nature of standardized norm-referenced tests, standardized tests are not generally aligned with training and development curricula. Thus, it is important to examine the match between competencies measured on a standardized test and the curriculum of the training or instructional program. It is also important never to assume that test scores are infallible or to use a single test to make an important decision about an individual or a program.

If the primary purpose of assessment is to guide instructional decision making and to provide feedback to learners, then standardized norm-referenced testing falls short of this purpose. More can be accomplished with a combination of methods that include, but are not limited to standardized measures. Pre- and post-standardized tests, when supplemented by criterion-referenced tests or alternative assessments, such as authentic tasks or curriculum-based measurements, can provide indicators of changes in a learner's knowledge base associated with a training or instructional program. In the following paragraphs, we will discuss such alternatives to standardized testing.

Criterion-Referenced Testing. Criterion-referenced tests are tests of specific skills that are scored with reference to examples of poor, fair, good, and excellent performance of those skills. Unlike norm-referenced or standardized tests, which compare any given student's performance in general with that of other test takers, criterion-referenced testing is interpreted in terms of performance criteria that can be more closely aligned with the content and conduct of specific training or instruction. Criterion-referenced tests tell us about a learner's level of proficiency in or mastery of some skill or set of skills. Learners are not compared with others, as in norm-referenced testing, but with a standard of mastery called a criterion.

Criterion-referenced testing helps us decide whether a learner needs more or less work on a specific skill or set of skills. It says nothing of the learner's place or rank compared with other learners. Hence, this kind of test provides constantly updated information about a learner's attained capabilities within a particular program of instruction or training. This information is far more useful in making ongoing training or instructional decisions. Criterion-referenced testing enables deficiencies to be precisely diagnosed and training or instruction to be targeted at addressing those deficiencies (Cancelli & Kratochwill, 1981).

Criterion-referenced tests must be very specific if they are to yield information about individual skills. Such specificity is useful for enabling teachers and trainers to be relatively certain that learners have mastered or failed to master the skill in question. The disadvantage is that a number of criterion-referenced tests are needed to make decisions about multiple skills.

Criterion-referenced tests require clear and measurable instructional or training objectives. A complete instructional or training objective includes (1) an observable behavior, (2) any special condition under which the behavior must be displayed, and (3) a performance level considered sufficient to demonstrate mastery. An example of a complete instructional objective for an adult basic-skills mathematics program would be "Given a calculator, the learner will multiply two-digit numbers, correct to the nearest whole number, with a 90% level of accuracy." An example of a complete instructional objective for a secretarial writing program might be "Given a dictionary, the learner will correct spelling errors in a sample letter of inquiry with a 95% accuracy level."

Both instructional and training programs can benefit from using a "test blueprint" or table that lists important objectives to be taught and the levels of student performance that can be expected from these objectives (Kubiszyn & Borich, 1987). The IIP curriculum script, for example (see Chapter 4), provides such a blueprint by which to measure learner performance. It is possible to note in the cells of the script the number of items on a given criterion-referenced test that match each topic or skill at a particular level of behavior. This enables both evaluation of an existing test with regard to how well the test compares in types and numbers of items with what has been taught, and planning a test with regard to the number of items that should be written for each major lesson or unit objective. The blueprint makes it possible to review individual test items from premade tests to determine if any of them match the content of any of the cells in the blueprint. This often precludes the need to write every test item from scratch.

As in norm-referenced tests, issues of validity and reliability are still important — that is, the capacity of a test to measure what it is supposed to measure and to consistently give the same or a similar score over repeated testings. The simplest form of validity is *content validity*, which is established by inspecting test items to see whether they correspond to instructional or training objectives. A test blueprint is especially useful for establishing content validity.

The reliability of a test refers to the consistency with which it yields the same, or nearly the same, score for an individual taking the test several times. The simplest method of estimating the reliability of a test is *test-retest*; the test is given twice, and the correlation between the scores is determined. Pre- and post-measurements of the skills being taught provide a concrete way of knowing if training and instructional programs are in fact achieving desired outcomes. Again, the test blueprint is useful in providing a way to track skill testing and attainment. The closer the correlation is to +1, the greater the reliability of the test. Generally, the longer the interval between test administrations, the lower the correlation.

Feedback on mastery of skills is important to performance improvement. To feel personal efficacy, learners need to know what areas are critical to their optimal performance and how much, if at all, they need to improve. The IIP curriculum script provides a means by which learners can focus on critical areas that require improvement, and by which instructional and training programs can be designed to reinforce those critical areas.

More than once we have noted that where criterion-referenced assessment is used, pre- and post-measurement of the skills that are critical to optimal performance is the only concrete way of assessing whether instructional or training programs are making a difference. We have also noted that it is important for learners to be able to track their own progress. In both program evaluation and learner feedback, the difficulty is always in finding a systematic way to examine key indicators that are valued in optimal performance.

The IIP curriculum script provides two important advantages: (1) it can serve as an important blueprint for aligning learning objectives and testing items; and (2) it can serve as a personal trainer, providing specific, systematic feedback to learners because they are able to track their progress and gauge their progress toward mastery through the skills and levels of performance appearing on the curriculum script.

Curriculum-Based Measurements (CBM). Because norm-referenced tests, and sometimes criterion-referenced measures, are intended for broad use, there is still considerable concern over the mismatch between content of such tests and the content of training or instructional programs. It is important to note, however, that standardized tests make no pretense of fitting training or instructional curricula precisely. What kinds of assessment might have a better fit in this respect?

Curriculum-based measurements (CBMs) are repeated measurements of an adult learner's performance on a single global task across time. They offer multiple assessments of adult learner progress toward a long-term course goal specific to mastering a task (Bean & Lane, 1990). CBMs use the specific curriculum provided in a training or instructional setting as the basis for tracking the adult learner's performance on specific desired outcomes. For example, at the beginning of a train-the-trainer program the adult learner is given a set of questions pertaining to the personal attributes of a "good" trainer. Using the provided CBMs rating scale, they determine their personal understanding of principles critical to the train-the-trainer learning process. At the end of the train-the-trainer course the adult learner again is assessed using this same CBM. Of critical importance is how well the rating scale tracks post-program changes in the degree of individual understanding of train-the-trainer "best training practices."

It is important in CBMs that learners review their performance before each assessment. The goal line, for example, helps learners to monitor their own progress. In addition, progress toward the estimated goal helps instructors make decisions about modifying instruction, changing the level of reading passages, or modifying the goal line.

A CBM that could be applied to a management development program would be to monitor and assess effective communication within a work team by using a two-minute reading/response passage for each participant. This reading passage might be used on a weekly basis and the accuracy of responses calculated. (See examples and data collected in the MIDP program in Appendix III).

Participants' progress (accuracy of responses) is graphed. An optimal performance, or goal line, might be determined by using the average of participants' performances on two baseline scenarios and adding a percentage of accurate responses to the score as a target for improvement. It is again important in CBMs that learners review their performance before each assessment to monitor their own progress.

Designing a CBM

Several factors must be taken into consideration when designing CBMs:

1. Select tasks that will represent those the adult learner is expected to perform in class/training sessions. Such tasks can be taken directly from sample curriculum materials being used.
2. Remember that CBMs are timed. Keep the measurement short (e.g., one to five minutes). The purpose of the CBM is to track learner performance in multiple tasks over time.
3. CBMs are most useful when they are given frequently (e.g., every other day, or twice a week, depending upon the length of the class/training session). Useful measurement occurs when the measurement task looks and functions like any other class/training

session task. In other words, learners should not feel they are taking a test.

4. CBMs can be normed. Give the same measurement to a sample of five to ten learners identified by the supervisor/employer as average peers of the learner. Or, if the trainer/employer wants to compare the learner's performance against optimally desired performance, the five to ten learners might be selected from among top-rated on-the-job performers. The performance of this sample of five to ten average or optimal learners sets the baseline for comparison of the individual learner's performance against the norm.

5. The most effective way to represent learner growth is graphically. Norm performance, or goal-related performance, and the learner's actual performance can be charted on a line graph (see Appendix III).

In general, the term "curriculum-based measurement" sounds much more complicated than it is. A CBM is nothing more than a task taken from the curriculum, except that the task is performed frequently, learner performance is tracked systematically, and learner performance can be compared against a norm of attendee average or optimal performance based upon the same task.

CBMs are also curriculum-, peer-, and individual-referenced. They are curriculum-referenced because the assessment tasks are drawn from the local curriculum, assuring content validity. They are peer-referenced because local norms can be collected to facilitate performance tracking (e.g., five to ten random subjects from an individual's peer group can be given the same CBM, and data gathered from the measurement can provide a general estimate of the level of performance of the "typical" learner in that peer group). CBMs are individual-referenced in that the measurements are designed to compare a learner's level of performance over time.

The primary advantage of CBMs is that learners are tested on the exact curricular task behaviors that they are expected to perform. A secondary advantage is that the learner's performance can be graphically tracked over time, thus providing a stable and immediate form of feedback to the learner.

They also ultimately provide senior management a graphic representation on how well groups of adults are learning in the company's training programs.

Authentic Assessment. Descriptions and views of authentic assessment tasks have some common characteristics:

1. Production-oriented. The task requires learners to use information that cannot simply be retrieved or recalled from memory. Rather, new knowledge must be created by the reorganization or manipulation of existing knowledge (Anderson, 1982; Wiggins, 1989).

2. Multidimensional. Diverse cognitive operations are used in the task. Authentic tasks draw upon multiple patterns of responses and behavior strategies for solving problems (Wiggins, 1989).

3. Nonroutine. The task is not performed in step-by-step, routine fashion that requires little thought. Rather, it may be executed in many ways and requires decision making with each execution.

4. Data-based. The task requires that the learner collect and assemble information,

generally from a number of primary sources (e.g., direct observations of, and artifacts from, the issue being studied).

5. Partially specified. Learners are free to specify the content and outcome of the task to some extent, in that they have wide latitude in the resources and information used, methodologies applied, and processes engaged. However, scoring criteria and standards are made explicit, so that learners know how their work will be assessed prior to doing it (Wiggins, 1989).

6. Long-term. The longer a task takes, the more learning probably occurs. Generally, in a typical classroom or training experience, "long-term" might refer to from two classes or training sessions to the entire term of the class or training program.

7. Domain-relevant. Tasks that are domain-relevant fall within content areas that are considered important to a particular instructional or training program.

8. Interdisciplinary. Ideally, authentic tasks cut across knowledge from two or more content domains, just as real-life tasks do.

9. Personally relevant. Those engaged in the task perceive it as falling within their set of personal goals. If tasks fit their goals, individuals utilize multiple talents and abilities when engaged in them (McCombs, 1984).

10. Learner self-assessment. Authentic tasks utilize learner self-assessment, providing situations and standards by which learners review and analyze their performance and provide themselves with feedback about their learning.

The previously discussed "Tower Building" simulation on team building (see Chapter 6 and Figure 6.3) is a good example of an authentic assessment. Adult learners use this hands-on exercise to discover how hard it is for any group of individuals to actually apply team-building concepts. This authentic assessment exercise focuses attention on specific aspects of how teams function and increase the speed at which individual adults reach higher levels of mastering and successfully using team structure back on the job.

Unlike standardized tests, authentic assessment has no pat item pool or step-by-step design process. You just keep tinkering with an authentic task design, piloting versions of it, and refining it as learners work with it in instruction or training contexts. Despite the frustrations and time invested in developing good authentic tasks, the payoff is in the ability of those tasks to assess process skills and intellectual habits that are mostly unassessed in traditional testing, but that will be increasingly required of all adults in twenty-first century society and work force contexts.

Some Implementation Issues. Alternative assessments take more time and require more individualization. In addition, alignment among training and development curricula and alternative assessments will most likely imply covering less material in order to achieve greater depth of understanding and transfer to job performance. Third, long-term education of instructional designers and human resource trainers will be needed if they are to create valid and reliable alternative assessments as learner measurers. Finally, there is a considerable battle to be faced regarding management's and the general public's acceptance of alternative assessments. We have come to rely so heavily and unquestioningly on standardized tests that perhaps the greatest challenge facing work force education is reeducating management and the general public regarding the differences between standardized and alternative measures, and the kinds of learner information to be gleaned from each.

However, alternative assessments have several characteristics of successful workplace programs, as noted by the U.S. Departments of Education and Labor (1988). First, alternative assessments utilize explicit standards for measuring success, and these standards are shared with learners before they complete an assessment task. Second, pre-tests, formative assessments, and post-tests that follow characteristics of alternative assessment simulate job tasks and contexts within which to measure learning. Thus, learners are assisted in diagnosing needs and strengths, and trainers/instructors can use such information in developing learning plans for participants. Finally, alternative assessments provide means by which frequent feedback can be given to learners and supervisors, and progress in job-related and contextualized tasks can be carefully documented.

Why Bother with Better Assessments? Unfortunately, there is a shocking lack of systematic assessment and applied research to enrich our state-of-the-art and best-practice knowledge about work force education (Gordon et al., 1991). Research and evaluation data tend to be collected in uneven ways. When programs are evaluated, assessment data are often limited to sketchy descriptions of program components, anecdotal recountings as indicators of effectiveness, questionnaires and surveys of program participants, and incomplete references to learner performance results (Mikulecky & D'Adamo-Weinstein, 1991). Occasionally, standardized test results may be provided, but standardized tests are useful indicators of general ability only. They are not specific to program curricula.

Better assessments are built upon three key assumptions. First, assessment is seen as integral to learning. The one-shot notion of assessment celebrated in standardized tests does not fit an emerging developmental and constructivist view of knowledge and understanding. The major purpose of assessment should be to aid learning. Assessment cannot be conceived as a series of discrete milestones but as part of a continuous and coherent learning process.

Second, assessment is linked to outcomes. Learning and understanding go beyond *what* one knows to what one *does* with that knowledge. Thus, it is important that assessments directly relate to instructional and training objectives. Assessments that reflect specific and explicit criteria for performance, continuous feedback, and self-assessment are more effective in capturing performance of valued outcomes over time.

Third, abilities must be developed and assessed in multiple modes and contexts. Most abilities and real-life situations in which they are tested are multidimensional and complex. Assessment should provide learners with repeated opportunities to experience, practice, and assess their performance in varied contexts and at varied levels of mastery (see Figure 8.3).

The more we understand about these alterable constructs associated with learning, as demonstrated in earlier chapters, the more likely we are to develop

Figure 8.3
Models of Learning Constructs and Assessment

Construct	Characteristics	Assessment Mode
Metacognition	Self-monitoring; self-regulatory and self-control strategies; Pattern and concept generalization	Curriculum-based measures; Authentic tasks
Alignment	Clearly stated outcomes; program content, instruction, learning task, and assessment coherence	Criterion-referenced tests; Curriculum-based measures; Authentic tasks
Time on Task	Increased amount of time in active engagement in learning task	Outcomes-based; Curriculum-based measures; Authentic tasks
Feedback	Frequent, outcome-specific; integrated with training and instruction	Criterion-referenced tests; Curriculum-based measures; Authentic tasks
Efficacy	Enabling beliefs in one's own ability to be successful	Criterion-referenced tests; Curriculum-based measures; Authentic tasks

training and education programs and assessments that contribute to greater learner success.

Measuring Behavior Changes

If we are to "prove that it works," skill and knowledge acquisition through training must translate into appropriate job behaviors (see Figure 8.1). Our aim is to measure how well these newly acquired skills are performed without the trainer's assistance in the individual's natural job setting (Patrick, 1991).

The most frequently used behavior feedback measure is a survey of the participant's supervisor. This evaluation uses a questionnaire designed to solicit specific information on the tangible results of the training program (see Figure 8.4). The specific survey questions are related to the problems originally identified by the training needs assessment. These are best written as clearly identifiable work behaviors familiar to the employee's supervisor. The supervisor's survey most often occurs immediately after the training program. However, it is often valuable to consider supplementing this information by conducting a second supervisor's survey six months later. This will assist trainers in better measuring long-term information retention and considering revisions of training course content areas (Phillips, 1991; Gordon, 1993).

These behavior change surveys are fairly easy to administer through direct interview or intercompany mail and are easy to tabulate. They provide a valuable additional perspective on program impact for the trainee. The long-term and short-term evaluations help measure the permanent effects of the training.

Figure 8.4
Work Force Education Skills Training Program
Supervisor's Post-Program Evaluation

Date: _____   <u>CONFIDENTIAL</u>

Participating
Employee: _____   Supervisor: _____

Directions: Recently your worker(s) completed a Work Force Education Training program in basic skills to make them more job ready. We are interested in the results that relate to changes in their work habits. Please answer the following questions by circling the appropriate answers. Feel free to give us your additional thoughts on this training program. Thank you for your help. (NA = Not Applicable)

1. Work-related errors:

    1   2   3   4   5   NA
  Decreased   No Effect   Increased

    Comments:_____

2. Number of accidents:

    1   2   3   4   5   NA
  Decreased   No Effect   Increased

    Comments:_____

3. Requests for additional work directions:

    1   2   3   4   5   NA
  Decreased   No Effect   Increased

    Comments:_____

4. Reduced absenteeism:

    1   2   3   4   5   NA
  Decreased   No Effect   Increased

    Comments:_____

Figure 8.4 continued

5. Job related problem solving/trouble-shooting skills:

1	2	3	4	5	NA
Decreased		No Effect		Increased	

Comments:_____

6. Improved job productivity:

1	2	3	4	5	NA
Decreased		No Effect		Increased	

Comments:_____

7. Improved personal job motivation:

1	2	3	4	5	NA
Decreased		No Effect		Increased	

Comments:_____

8. Improved willingness to cope with changes:

1	2	3	4	5	NA
Decreased		No Effect		Increased	

Comments:_____

9. Helped in keeping assembly line running:

1	2	3	4	5	NA
Decreased		No Effect		Increased	

Comments:_____

10. Overall improved work habits:

1	2	3	4	5	NA
Decreased		No Effect		Increased	

Comments:_____

The data from a supervisor's survey is often subjective. You will also need his or her cooperation to complete these reports. Other intervening business factors can affect the report's results and, if possible, should be clearly identified. Finally, make sure that the participant has had the opportunity to use what was learned on the job, before conducting the initial survey (Phillips, 1991).

Training's Return-On-Investment

The most difficult form of measurement, at the top of the Training Evaluation Pyramid, compares the financial benefits of a program against its cost (see Figure 8.1). The call for cost effectiveness is becoming louder and more persistent throughout every business. Too often training is undervalued because some accountants and economists may argue that it is not possible to measure the long-term, quantitative effects of training and educational programs. However, we beg to differ. The authors have considerable evidence documenting that both American and foreign businesses invest considerable training funds on the basis of their relationship to operating profits. If this measurement is possible, then we must quantify and compare both training's financial costs and its financial benefits (Mosier, 1990; Patrick, 1992; Phillips, 1991; Schneider et al., 1992).

Many systems exist to determine training's return on investment (ROI). Some soft data areas include using existing data or historical costs, expert opinion, participant estimation, and management estimation. Hard data methods include calculating payback periods, discounted cash flow, internal rate of return, cost-benefit ratio, utility analysis, and performance evaluation (Phillips, 1991; Swanson & Gradous, 1988). The authors have attempted to apply the performance evaluation model to various field-based training applications. Let us review the training issues that need to be addressed to conduct a meaningful financial analysis, and how to apply the performance evaluation model.

R. A. Swanson and D. B. Gradous (1988) argue that training needs to develop economic forecasting data to help choose between human resources development (HRD) program options and between HRD and non-HRD options. The performance value forecasting method helps to make decisions before investing in a program, rather than waiting to evaluate after completing the program.

We have found one distinct advantage to a forecasting approach is the organizational thinking process that must occur to gain acceptance of any potential training results. How can any financial training analysis ever gain top management's acceptance unless a financial officer has helped determine some of the fiscal issues addressed by the program?

You begin quantifying hard data during the training program's needs assessment. In interviews with department managers or staff, you help them determine how their operating issues may translate into specific quantifiable training results. Phillips (1991) established four basic business factors around which to organize potential financial evaluation:

1. Quality
2. Time
3. Costs
4. Output.

Quality is currently a major business concern due to competitive necessity and the need to control cost. Manufacturing, service, and professional organizations can consider many of the following quality issues that will produce hard financial data:

- Percent of tasks completed correctly
- Revisions, reworking
- Deviation from performance standards
- Error rates
- Scrap
- Shortages
- Product defects
- Waste
- Product failures
- Rejects
- Number of accidents
- Inventory shortages/buildup
- Time card corrections.

Time-related problems are costly for almost every business. They are often at least partially sensitive to training-based solutions. Some of these issues include

- Processing time
- Supervisory time
- Training time
- On-the-job training time
- Lost time (days)
- Late reporting
- Work stoppages
- Waiting for directions
- Equipment downtime
- Overtime
- Project completion time
- Meeting schedules

▪Order response time
▪On-time ordering
▪Repair time
▪Job efficiency.

Cost control has many variables that can be addressed by training. These areas include the following:

▪Operating costs
▪Cost by account
▪Project cost
▪Sales expenses
▪Program costs
▪Fixed costs
▪Variable costs
▪Cost per unit
▪Potential cost reduction
▪Cost of accidents
▪Budget variances
▪Project overrun costs.

The final hard-data category is output measurement. We need to express a word of caution. In the majority of work environments, the employees will not be motivated to support a productivity improvement program based solely on the concept of increasing output. Most of our clients may have experienced some output-related issues. However, they are often linked to diversifying types of reports prepared, units produced, customers serviced, and other quality-related issues. This reduces potential negative attitudes that employees are being asked to do more, at the same rate of pay. Output related issues include the following:

▪Forms processed
▪Reports completed
▪Applications processed
▪Tasks completed
▪Units produced
▪Tons manufactured
▪Items acceptable
▪Inventory turnover rate
▪Shipments made
▪Money collected
▪Projects sold
▪Products sold
▪Loans approved
▪Guest rooms occupied.

There are many other potential operational issues that your business can address by carefully studying the four basic business factors of quality, time, cost, and output. The training department needs to involve management in setting acceptable targets within the organization. If you can gain agreement on realistic and not too politically sensitive issues for improving your business, you are halfway to gaining acceptance for the results of your program's financial analysis (Phillips, 1991).

Measuring Performance Value

The mathematical method used to calculate performance value is orderly, is not very complex, and has been used often by trainers for program financial analysis. The key to success is gathering from within your organization four essential pieces of information (see Figure 8.5).

The Unit of Work Performance. After conducting the training needs assessment and reviewing the four basic business factors, what clearly definable work issue does your business wish to address that is part of a job role or task for a particular audience? If you cannot agree on this issue, maybe you should not be doing the training.

Performance Levels. What are the existing and desired levels of performance that can be reached during the training and evaluation time periods? As a trainer you need to know what performance changes a training program is capable of producing for an "average" group of trainees. You clearly cannot agree to post performance goals unless you have some historical information on the quality of a training program's typical results.

Value Assigned to Each Performance Unit. This is a key business consideration. Do not be surprised if very few business units know how much it costs to produce a good or a service, or how much profit is derived from the production or sale of the unit they wish to measure. In some instances it may take considerable time to arrive at this dollar value and have it accepted by the finance people in your company. This time is well spent, since a nonjustified amount will undermine your final performance value results.

Performance Value. The first three information pieces must be negotiated with other people in your organization. This final calculation is obtained by multiplying the value of one unit of work performance by the total number of units that can be attributed to the training program (Swanson & Gradous, 1988).

Case Study I

Let us first apply the performance value worksheet to the XYZ Accounting firm (see Figure 8.6). This accounting firm had invested considerable funds in state-of-the-art personal computers, software, and secretarial training. Unfortunately, as business increased, the productivity of the secretaries in completing audit reports remained constant. Basic business writing, grammar,

Figure 8.5
Performance Value Worksheet

Note that performance units and time units for all options <u>must remain consistent</u> throughout the forecast.

PROGRAM: _____

Training Option Name	1._____	2._____
Data required for calculations:		
a. What unit of work performance are you measuring?	‾‾‾‾‾‾‾ unit name	‾‾‾‾‾‾‾ unit name
b. What is the performance goal per worker/work group at the end of the training program?	___/___ no. units/time	___/___ no. units/time
c. What is the performance per worker/work group at the beginning of the training program?	___/___ no. units/time	___/___ no. units/time
d. What dollar value is assigned to each performance unit?	$_____ /unit	$_____ /unit
e. What is the training time required to reach the expected performance level?	___ ___ no. time	___ ___ no. time
f. What is the training evaluation period? (Enter the longest time (e) of all options being considered.)	___ ___ no. time	___ ___ no. time
g. How many workers/work groups will participate in the training program?	_____ no. workers/groups	_____ no. workers/groups
Calculations to determine net performance value:		
h. Will worker/work group produce usable units during the training program? If no, enter-0-. If yes, enter known performance rate to calculate average performance rate. [(b + c)/2]	___ ___ no. units	___ ___ no. units
i. How many total units per worker/work group will be produced during the training time? (h x e)	___ ___ no. units	_____ no. of units
j. How many units will be produced per worker/work group during the training evaluation period? {[(f - e) x b] + i}	___ ___ no. units	_____ no. of units
k. What will be the value of the worker's/work group's performance during the training evaluation period? (j x d)	$_____	$_____
l. What is the training value gain per worker/work group? [k - (c x d x f)]	$_____	$_____
m. What is the total training value gain for all workers/work groups? (l x g)	$_____ (Option 1)	$_____ (Option 2)

Figure 8.5 continued
Performance Value Worksheet

Option	1._____	2._____
Performance Value	$_____	$_____
Minus Cost	_____	_____
Benefit	$_____	$_____

Note: Circle your choice of option.

Source: Swanson & Gradous, 1988.

and proofreading problems were identified as the training needs to improve the production time per audit report. The tutorial training for writing skills was a ten-week program conducted twice a week, two hours per class, for a total of forty hours.

The accounting firm worked with our trainers to pinpoint the audit report as a unit of work performance measurable in time and dollar value (see item a). The firm established that 3.33 audit reports were currently being performed per worker each week. We mutually agreed to the goal of five audit reports per secretary by the end of ten weeks of training. This was based on our prior experience with similar training populations' experiences, spelling, grammar, punctuation, and business numeracy problems (see items b and c).

The dollar value assigned was the current salary cost of the secretary to complete a typical audit report. The accounting firm carefully calculated this value (see item d). The training time (see item e) and the training evaluation period (see item f) in this case were the same — ten weeks. In some instances, if the training is not to be used on the job immediately, the training evaluation would extend beyond the training program period to measure training effect. The number of workers (see item g) in the training program was fifteen, three tutorial groups of five secretaries each.

Items h throught m involve the calculations to determine net performance value. The benefit analysis worksheet subtracts the writing skills program's costs from the performance value. Make sure you include all potential costs (see Patrick, 1991):

Program cost (if vendor-provided)
Internal development costs (if designed by the business)

Figure 8.6
Performance Value Worksheet: Case Study I

Note that performance units and time units for all options **must remain consistent** throughout the forecast.
PROGRAM: XYZ Accounting Firm/Writing Skills

Training Option Name	1st 50 days	2nd 50 days
Data required for calculations:		
a. What unit of work performance are you measuring?	**Audit Report** unit name	_____ unit name
b. What is the performance goal per worker/work group at the end of the training program?	**5 AR/Day** no. units/time	_____/_____ no. units/time
c. What is the performance per worker/work group at the beginning of the training program?	**3.33 AR/Day** no. units/time	_____/_____ no. units/time
d. What dollar value is assigned to each performance unit?	**$ 144/AR/Unit**	$_____/unit
e. What is the training time required to reach the expected performance level?	**10 Weeks** no. time	___ ___ no. time
f. What is the training evaluation period? (Enter the longest time (e) of all options being considered.)	**10 Weeks** no. time	___ ___ no. time
g. How many workers/work groups will participate in the training program?	**15** no. workers/groups	_____ no. workers/groups
Calculations to determine net performance value:		
h. Will worker/work group produce usable units during the training program? If no, enter-0-. If yes, enter known performance rate to calculate average performance rate. [(b + c)/2]	**8.33/2 = 4.165** no. AR units	___ ___ no. units
i. How many total units per worker/work group will be produced during the training time? (h x e)	4.165 x 10 = **41.65 units**	_____ no. of units
j. How many units will be produced per worker/work group during the training evaluation period? {[(f - e) x b] + i}	**41.65** no. of units	_____ no. of units
k. What will be the value of the worker's/work group's performance during the training evaluation period? (j x d)	$41.65 x $144 = **$5,997.60**	$_____
l. What is the training value gain per worker/work group? [k - (c x d x f)]	$5,997.60 - 4,795.20 = **$1,202.40**	$_____
m. What is the total training value gain for all workers/work groups? (l x g)	$1,202.40 x 15 = $18,036.00 **(Option 1)**	$_____ **(Option 2)**

Figure 8.6 continued

Option	1st 50 days	2nd 50 days
Performance Value	$18,036	$_____
Minus Cost	Program & Release Time $12,790 $ 5,246	_____
Benefit	5,246 12,790 = 41.01% ROI	$_____

Note: Circle your choice of option.

Source: Swanson & Gradous, 1988.

Employee release time + taxes, benefits (if done on company time)
Materials (books, tests, equipment, software, etc.)
Travel/housing (if employees are coming from another location).

The final dollar benefit can then be calculated as an ROI measure.

Case Study II

Our second application of the performance value worksheet is for Acme Home Products, a small manufacturing business (see Figure 8.7). This particular plant annually produced 10 million bottles of four different cleaning products. Increasing computerization of the assembly line to better diversify product runs and batch orders allowed the plant to project production of ten different products with an ultimate target of 12 million produced items. The training issue was the reading of computer software manuals by the workers in order to be able to operate a much more varied assembly process. Increasingly complex math calculations and tracking results with written reports were required to make this new production system work. This needed to be accomplished fairly quickly by reeducating the existing highly motivated worker population (see Figure 8.7).

The unit of work performance measured was cleaning products (see item a). The performance goal per week was to rise from 700 bottles per day to 840 (see items b and c) during 50 days (10 weeks) of training (see items e and f). The dollar value assigned was the average profit made by the business on each cleaning product unit (see item d). Fifteen workers were trained, five per tutorial group, two classes per week, two hours per class, over a period of ten weeks (see item g).

The calculations to determine the net performance value are shown in items

Figure 8.7
Performance Value Worksheet: Case Study II

Note that performance units and time units for all options <u>must remain consistent</u> throughout the forecast.

PROGRAM: ACME HOME PRODUCTS/Reading, Writing, Math Program

Training Option Name	1st 50 days	2nd 50 days
Data required for calculations:		
a. What unit of work performance are you measuring?	Cleaning Products unit name	_____ unit name
b. What is the performance goal per worker/work group at the end of the training program?	840 Bottles/Day no. units/time	___/___ no. units/time
c. What is the performance per worker/work group at the beginning of the training program?	700 Bottles/Day no. units/time	___/___ no. units/time
d. What dollar value is assigned to each performance unit?	$ .20 /Unit	$_____ /unit
e. What is the training time required to reach the expected performance level?	50 Days no. time	___ ___ no. time
f. What is the training evaluation period? (Enter the longest time (e) of all options being considered.)	50 Days no. time	___ ___ no. time
g. How many workers/work groups will participate in the training program?	15 no. workers/groups	_____ no. workers/groups
Calculations to determine net performance value:		
h. Will worker/work group produce usable units during the training program? If no, enter -0-. If yes, enter known performance rate to calculate average performance rate. [(b + c)/2]	700 ___ no. units	840 ___ no. units
i. How many total units per worker/work group will be produced during the training time? (h x e)	38,500 no of units	_____ no. of units
j. How many units will be produced per worker/work group during the training evaluation period? {[(f - e) x b] + i}	38,500 no. of units	_____ no. of units
k. What will be the value of the worker's/work group's performance during the training evaluation period? (j x d)	$7,700.00	$_____
l. What is the training value gain per worker/work group? [k - (c x d x f)]	$700.00	$_____
m. What is the total training value gain for all workers/work groups? (l x g)	$10,500 (Option 1)	$21,000 (Option 2)

Figure 8.7 continued

Option	1st 50 days	2nd 50 days
Performance Value	$10,500	$21,000
Minus Cost	$10,500	$10,500
Benefit	$_____0	$\dfrac{10,500}{21,000} = 50\%$

Note: Circle your choice of option.

Source: Swanson & Gradous, 1988.

h through m. The benefit analysis worksheet shows that during the first ten weeks, a fifty-day training module, the benefit ROI was zero. However, during the second fifty-day, ten-week training module the ROI rose to 50 percent.

THE PRACTICAL ASPECT OF USING ROI ANALYSIS

Training professionals must be careful not to oversell using performance value measures or other financial analysis formulas in justifying program results. Whenever a financial model is used, make sure that senior management personnel approve the model and an acceptable return. They need to be involved in determining how a return is calculated and measured in the solution of an operational need. Make sure your training program is capable of producing the desired results before agreeing to any financial targets. Achieving a good, feasible return in senior management's eyes is the reason for making this entire effort. The more experience you have in using a specific training program application, the better your results will be when using an ROI training evaluation model (Phillips, 1991).

Total Quality Management (TQM) and other quality team efforts are contemporary areas where ROI for training is gaining widespread interest. Poor quality in products or services may often cost tens of percent of value added. High potential training payoffs will only be reached if the specific education programs precisely uncover local TQM employee needs. The Japanese, members of the European Union (EU) and other TQM practitioners clearly have demonstrated in recent years how productivity gains can be achieved that might once have been regarded as preposterous (Crawford et al., 1992).

PROVING IT WORKS

We believe that you can make full use of the Training Evaluation Pyramid to measure audience reaction, learning, behavior changes, and return on investment. You can prove that most training programs really work, are worth your company's investment, and probably deserve greater budgetary resources as part of any future competitive strategic plan. These evaluation components are mutually self-supporting and deserve all the time you can practically allow for their implementation. By not relying too heavily on only one evaluation method, you will have the opportunity to demonstrate that the training department understands how the entire business operates, what different audiences need to do a better job, and that investment in people can be as important as that in capital or other investment strategies.

If training programs can be accurately measured, how can we improve design to achieve these better results? In the next chapter we tackle how to use cognitive learning concepts specifically to design training that will be better retained and used more effectively by people on the job.

REFERENCES

Anderson, J. 1983. *The Architecture of Cognition.* Cambridge, MA: Harvard University Press.

___. 1982. Acquisition of cognitive skills. *Psychological Review* 89:369–406.

Bean, R. M.; Byra, A.; Johnson, R.; & Lane, S. 1988. *Using Curriculum Based Measures to Identify and Monitor Progress in an Adult Basic Education Program.* Pittsburgh, PA: University of Pittsburgh, Institute for Practice and Research in Education.

Bean, R. M., & Lane, S. 1990. Implementing curriculum-based measures of reading in an adult literacy program. *Remedial and Special Education* 11 (5):39–46.

Bloom, B. S. 1976. *Human Characteristics and School Learning.* New York: McGraw-Hill.

Brown, R. G. 1991. *Schools of Thought: How the Politics of Literacy Shape Thinking in the Classroom.* San Francisco: Jossey-Bass.

Bruner, J. S. 1966. *Toward a Theory of Instruction.* New York: W. W. Norton.

Cancelli, A. A., & Kratchowill, T. R. 1981. Advances in criterion-referenced assessment. In T. R. Kratchowill, ed., *Advances in School Psychology*, vol. 1. Hillsdale, NJ: Erlbaum.

Crawford, F. W., & Webley, S. 1992. *Continuing Education and Training of the Workforce.* London: British-North American Research Association.

Elkins, A. 1977. Some views on management training. *Personnel Journal* 42 (June):305–11.

Fry, E. 1968. A readability formula that saves time. *Journal of Reading* 11:513–16, 575–78.

Glaser, R. 1988. Cognitive and environmental perspectives on assessing achievement. In *Assessment in the Service of Learning: Proceedings of the 1987 ETS Invitational*

Conference. Princeton, NJ: Educational Testing Service.

___. 1982. Instructional psychology: Past, present, and future. *American Psychologist* 37:292–305.

Gordon, E. E. (1993a). *Audience Reaction Questionnaire*. Oak Lawn, IL: Imperial Corporate Training & Development.

___. 1993b. *Work Force Education Skills Training Program, Post-Six Month Evaluation by Supervisory Personnel*. Oak Lawn, IL: Imperial Corporate Training & Development.

___. 1993c. *Work Force Education Skills Training Program, Supervisor's Post-Education Evaluation*. Oak Lawn, Illinois: Imperial Corporate Training & Development.

Gordon, E. E.; Ponticell, J. A.; & Morgan, R. R. 1991. *Closing the Literacy Gap in American Business: A Guide for Trainers and Human Resource Specialists*. New York: Quorum Books.

Haney, W., & Madaus, G. 1989. Searching for alternatives to standardized tests: Whys, whats, and whithers. *Phi Delta Kappan* 70 (9):683–87.

Harte, S. 1990. Results, not good feelings, are seminar's test. *Chicago Tribune*, 1 April, sec. 7, 4.

Hassett, J. 1992. Simplifying ROI. *Training* 29 (9):53–57.

Jacques, E. 1985. Development of intellectual capability. In F. R. Link, ed., *Essays on the Intellect*. Alexandria, VA: Association for Supervision and Curriculum Development.

Jeleniewski, L. 1993. Evaluating training programs. Presentation at Loyola University, Chicago, Graduate Adult Corporate Industrial Management Program, 16 April.

Kubiszyn, T., & Borich, G. 1987. *Educational Testing and Measurement*. Glenview, IL: Scott, Foresman.

Kuhn, T. S. 1970. *The Structure of Scientific Revolutions*. Chicago: University of Chicago Press.

McCombs, B. 1984. Processes and skills underlying intrinsic motivation to learn: Toward a definition of motivational skills training interventions. *Educational Psychologist*, 19 (4):199–218.

Marzano, R. J., & Kendall, J. S. 1991. *A Model Continuum of Authentic Tasks and Their Assessment*. Aurora, CO: Midcontinent Regional Educational Laboratory.

Mikulecky, L., & D'Adamo-Weinstein, L. 1991. *How Effective Are Workplace Literacy Programs?* U.S. Education Resources Information Center, ERIC Document ED 330 891.

Mosier, N. R. 1990. Financial analysis: The methods and their application to employee training. *Human Resource Quarterly* 1 (1):45–63.

Patrick, J. 1991. *Training Research and Practice*. New York: Academic Press.

Phillips, J. J. 1991. *Handbook of Training Evaluation and Measurement Methods*. Houston: Gulf.

Resnick, L. 1987. *Education and Learning to Think*. Washington, DC: National Academy Press.

Schneider, H.; Monetta, D. J.; & Wright, C. C. 1992. Training function accountability: How to really measure return on investment. *Performance & Instruction* 31 (3):12–17.

Shepard, L. A. 1989. Why we need better assessments. *Educational Leadership* 46 (7):4–9.

___. 1988. Should instruction be measurement-driven? A debate. Paper presented to the annual meeting of the American Educational Research Association, New Orleans.

Spady, W. B., & Marshall, K. J. 1991. Beyond traditional outcome based education. *Educational Leadership* 49 (2):67–72.

Swanson, R. A., & Gradous, D. B. 1988. *Forecasting Financial Benefits of Human Resource Development.* San Francisco: Jossey-Bass.

U.S. Department of Education and U.S. Department of Labor. 1988. *The Bottom Line: Basic Skills in the Workplace.* Washington, DC: Office of Public Information, Employment and Training Administration.

Wang, M. C.; Haertel, G. D.; & Walberg, H. J. 1990. What influences learning? A content analysis of review literature. *Journal of Educational Research*, 84 (1):30–43.

Webster, L. P. 1986. *A National Survey of Evaluation Procedures in Adult Basic Education.* Paper presented at the thirty-first annual conference of the International Reading Association, Philadelphia.

Wiggins, G. 1989. Teaching to the (authentic) test. *Educational Leadership*, 46 (7):41–47.

___. (1989). A true test: Toward more authentic and equitable assessment. *Phi Delta Kappan*, 70 (9):703–13.

Worthen, B. R., & Spandel, V. 1991. Putting the standardized test debate in perspective. *Educational Leadership* 48 (5):65–69.

Chapter 9

Designing Effective Cognitively Based Training and Development

BOTTOM-LINE QUESTIONS

In the past chapters we have explored many aspects of the contemporary "business learning game." Our principal focus has been how cognitively based training and development can advance the adult learning process beyond the limits of behaviorally based instruction.

Training must address the issue of what can be done to make a business better. The authors have attempted to illustrate this broad-based concept through our case studies of ongoing field-based IIP and MIDP business training models. We have presented related anecdotal (qualitative) (see chapters 3, 4, and 6) and quantitative research (see appendixes II and III) results. Throughout this book we have offered examples to describe the use of cognitive "best practices" for practical training classroom applications.

However, two related, unanswered bottom-line questions remain for many trainers/educators/managers reading this book:

How can I easily translate your ideas into practical design and improved instructional methods?

Where are the blueprints to newer, clearer, more creative thinking techniques that I can use to better train almost any employee?

In this chapter we will attempt to outline additional useful design and instructional methods for enhanced thinking, problem-solving, and creativity training for the workplace.

THE FACILITATOR AS CHANGE AGENT

Before we can design a more open, creative business learning model, we must reconsider the role of our primary change agent, the trainer. We need to move most business-related teachers, instructors, and trainers from their current presentation mode toward a facilitator/mentoring role model (see Figure 9.1). Unless we train the trainer to become a cognitive facilitator, our newly designed models will fail. Here is why.

Traditional classroom teachers, instructors (technical training), and the company management trainer view their students or trainees as passive learning agents (see Figure 9.1). They present or demonstrate new information. In their expert role they seek to shape effective learner behaviors. They focus on learning concepts, new skills, or practical how-to knowledge. The traditional educator makes the learning process meaningful and helps the learner achieve a new level of understanding, adopt a new technique, or acquire the desired effective behavior by using rewards. These developmental educational roles can be compared with the previously reviewed characteristics of the behaviorally based learning models. (See Chapter 5 and Figure 5.1.)

The desirable alternative is a facilitator/mentor, cognitive change agent model (see Figure 9.1). The focus shifts to the adult learner as an active participant rather than a passive attendee. The facilitator becomes a helper in the discovery process. This role supersedes, but does not completely eliminate, aspects of the behaviorally based models. Content is mastered through discovery learning that gives added personal meaning to each adult, rather than filling the mind with facts, skills, or behaviors. The learning process has meaning because it is built around the individual adult's work/life instead of the educator's interpretations. The bottom-line outcomes are the personally learned discoveries that the adult can apply on the job today and adapt tomorrow to changed work assignments. This facilitator/mentor role is the central determinant of success supporting a new thinking and problem-solving training design. It supports the characteristics we have established for successful cognitively based business learning models. (See Chapter 6 and Figure 6.1.)

To use this change agent model, several specific design elements must be addressed in a training program (Altizer, 1993):

To accept new material, adult learners have a need to know "what's in it for me."

Most adult learners have personal experiences that will give meaning to their learning of new ideas.

It is far easier for participants to accept a new concept if they are involved in its development during the training process.

If the facilitator can state something, why not have the facilitator ask the participants to help develop the same information from their own perspectives, by

Figure 9.1
Developmental Education Role Models

	ROLE / DIMENSION	TRAINEE	ROLE VIS-À-VIS "HELPEES"	CONTENT EMPHASIS	LOCUS OF MEANING	DESIRED OUTCOMES
CHANGE AGENT	FACILITATOR/ MENTOR	Participants	Helper in a Discovery Process	Inductive Learning	Individual "Explorers"	Discovery and Application
	TRAINER	Trainees	Shaper of Effective Behavior	Skill Acquisition	In the Trainer	Effective Behavior
TRADI-TIONAL	INSTRUCTOR (TECHNICAL TRAINING)	Students	Expert and Demonstrator	'How to…'	In Definition of Effectiveness	Strategy, Tactics, and Technique
	TEACHER	Students	Imparter of Information and Meaning	Conceptual Understanding	In the Teacher's Interpretation	Awareness and Understanding

Source: Adapted from Jones & Woodcock, 1985, p. 113.

asking open-ended questions?

The facilitator builds the participants into subject-matter experts and does not remain the sole source of knowledge.

Participants' responses are never completely wrong. Some piece of their idea may be linked to the desired training application or principle, or the facilitator can extend the participant's thinking and build upon it.

The primary task of any facilitator is to develop maximum learner participation and understanding.

To implement what has been learned, a primary task for all participants and their managers is to formulate a personal action plan for the workplace.

LEARNER-CENTERED LEARNING

What we have described above is hardly new. Early in the twentieth century, John Dewey espoused the merits of experience-based, self-directed learning. Closer to our own time, Malcolm Knowles became a proponent of a humanistic, learner-centered approach to the process of teaching adults (andragogy). His seven basic design principles for a self-directed learning experience include the following ideas (Feuer & Geber, 1988):

Climate: Facilitators need to create a physical and psychological climate that encourages small-group interaction and generally promotes cheerfulness. This means cultivating respect and trust through an atmosphere of openness, support, and collaboration. Learning may not become fun, but why not make the experience pleasurable?

Mutual Planning: Before the training course, involve the future participants in design committees or focus groups to voice their preferences regarding content and learning activities.

Diagnosing Needs: What does the business need? What are the participants' needs? Use a model of competencies that presents an individual diagnosis of the gap between the skills employees possess and the new knowledge they need to learn.

Formulating Learning Objectives: Establish a learning contract that translates learning needs into learning objectives. What internal/external resources will help meet individual objectives? What certifies objective attainment? How will that evidence be used in a personal development review?

Design Learning Plans: Each employee establishes a learning contract to attain personal learning objectives.

Implement Learning Plans: Learning contracts are reviewed as objectives are realized.

Evaluate Learning: How well did the employees achieve the learning objectives? What is the quality of the training programs used by the company?

FOOLS RUSH IN

Knowles admits that "Some people develop these characteristics earlier than others. We need to know where learners are in terms of these evolving characteristics" (Feuer & Geber, 1988). The important limitation to self-directed learning seems to be that, "if the adult is ready to learn, it works like this." This is a major training obstacle because not every adult is thrilled to learn something new.

In recent years there have been too many instances where a joint decision by management and unions to begin a major training program met employee resistance. Some people do not want to change: "We have been doing it one way for years, and we feel you're demanding too much." Some employees are frightened of the new responsibility. "Tell me what to do, and I'll do it" suddenly changes to "Decide for yourself what needs doing, and do it."

Other workers are more personally distressed than resistant. With learner-centered training, employees may be afraid to try learning so many different things, perhaps to fail, and then to look "dumb" to their peers or customers. Change is not easy for anyone (Kaeter, 1993).

TRAINING PARADIGM SHIFT

A major strategic paradigm shift for human resources that is now emerging requires trainers to attempt to empower all employees with higher-level thinking/problem-solving skills that until recently were the purview only of top management. Enhancing everybody's leadership now means meeting a new set of strategic training objectives (Berry, 1990):

Providing a global perspective

Increasing creative employee strategies tailored to local work environments

Preparing key leadership for the year 2000 and beginning to look at changes out to 2015

Continuing to anticipate major competitive changes that will accelerate with further technology and increased world trade

Building the organization to maintain ongoing capacity for renewal and transformation.

Figure 9.2 compares the design of the traditional model for management development (1950–1990) with the emerging twenty-first century model.

ASSESSING THE NEED

The majority of workers have rarely been called upon to use the thinking skills now demanded for successful teams, quality programs, or leadership training.   Many resist this training because of previous negative school experiences.   Others, who lack formal postsecondary education, feel at a comparative disadvantage.

We believe that training designs need to evaluate these reluctant employees' learning needs individually, as part of an outcome-based education (OBE) strategy.   This may well prove to be the most successful educational mobilization plan for the entire American work force.   The IIP and MIDP are both OBE models. They are mastery learning models for training, as previously shown (see chapters 3, 4, 6, 8).   As OBE models they set criterion-based or curriculum-based performance standards identically for all employees.   They allow the training time needed to reach those standards to vary.

Training designers using OBE for new management development programming assess the interpersonal dynamics of the workers, supervisors, and managers. Pilot programs are provided in which these dynamics (team building, decision making, interpersonal communication, etc.) are assessed and openly discussed by the participants. Based on these focus groups' results, revised company wide programs are prepared and implemented year to year throughout the organization for *all* employees.

TASK ANALYSIS

The first step by the training designer in implementing this OBE strategy is to analyze the cognitive tasks to be trained in a specific program. This means addressing three significant problems (Patrick, 1992):

Identifying the types of knowledge involved

Determining how to present the knowledge content in alternative ways

Assembling this knowledge and its presentations into a complete and coherent model of expert performance.

Let us discuss each of these areas.

Figure 9.2
Management Education Model: Strategic Design Comparison

Model Characteristics	Traditional Management Behavioral Model (1950-1990)	Emerging Management Cognitive Model (1990-2015)
Training Objectives	Mainly educational. Companies wanted well-educated, experienced managers.	Collaborative, consultative. Managers still need to be well educated but must be better able to deal with strategic or tactical issues.
Strategic Outcomes	Individual effectiveness	Organizational and unit effectiveness
Business Skills Required	Individual job competencies	Competencies required for a business to compete
Groups Targeted for Management Development	Top, middle and some entry-level managers	All members of the team. Lines between manager and worker become meaningless.

Identifying Knowledge Types

Many types of knowledge support the performance of a complex management task. To complete an analysis for the design of an effective training program, we must distinguish between declarative knowledge and procedural knowledge (Anderson, 1982, 1983, 1987).

Declarative knowledge is essentially factual knowledge that can be stated explicitly. A typical insurance company's customer-service program may be composed of six essential business activities:

1. New business inquiry
2. Commercial underwriting
3. Retail underwriting
4. Customer inquiries
5. Claims adjustment
6. Accounts receivable/collection

All of these elements combine to produce the customer services for this insurance company.

In contrast, procedural knowledge determines how to do something. This is often implicit and more difficult to describe, such as how to sell commercial insurance, or how to answer customer inquiries. Procedural knowledge is the cognitive basis for management performance. Declarative knowledge is equivalent to knowing that something is true. Procedural knowledge is related to knowing how to do something (Patrick, 1992).

Trainers can learn some valuable ideas for the design of cognitive management-development programs from J. R. Anderson's procedures (1982, 1983, 1987). He shows how procedural knowledge is developed from declarative knowledge, and then turned into fast, accurate, and flexible skills for training. Simply put, factual knowledge in a specific area of management is gradually assembled into a set of procedural rules of an "if... then" type. This rule training supports skilled management performance (Patrick, 1992).

A design system can be composed of a set of production rules:

If condition X is met,
THEN execute Y.
or
IF the customer indicates a willingness to buy,
THEN offer a contract.
or
IF the team reaches a consensus,
THEN make a final group decision.
or
IF the course goal is to train for better listening skills, and the management trainees have had little prior experience, and the pre-test shows their weak knowledge,

THEN demonstrate with them the ideas and skills to become better listeners.

IF the trainees through simulations show they now have mastered many listening skills,

THEN have the trainees formulate action plans to use these new listening skills in their daily work.

Based on prior knowledge and experience, each training audience determines how detailed and accurate the rules to guide them toward skilled management performance will be. These rules are particularly useful in explaining the nature of problem solving in a specific management area. For example, a more experienced marketing manager already has a larger repertoire of these rules, which enables him or her to diagnose faster than a marketing trainee why a customer refuses to buy a product.

The goal of the training designer is to identify through careful analysis, and pass on to the trainees, a general rule structure underlying skilled performance that can be applied broadly to new task-specific procedures. In the initial training stages the key is to mobilize whatever facts the trainees already know about the new task in conjunction with general problem-solving procedures. Sometimes analogies and advanced organizers are useful in working out how to help adults master new material (see Chapter 2).

Too often management training fails because the adult learners are not adequately instructed on how the task should be performed. Good task analysis may eliminate many discrepancies between classroom training and what is actually needed on the job. However, adult learners still need experience to develop the right management procedures by doing the task in the classroom through simulations, role-playing, personal presentations, or other application exercises (Patrick, 1992).

At some point during a training program the adult trainee has developed new knowledge into task-specific procedures. This means the individual does not always have to recall information in order to execute the rule. For example, if a marketer has mastered a ten-rule consultative selling process, and the tenth rule's conditions are met by the client who wants to buy, the marketer may jump from rule 1 to rule 10.

Cognitive skill acquisition helps develop and refine these rules (Anderson, 1982, 1983, 1987). Learning is accomplished by doing the skill during training. The better the training material, the more likely that the adult learners will respond well to the acquisition of new material. They will compile the new information into meaningful rules for doing the skill during training simulations and modifying them on the job. Training must provide numerous opportunities for performing new tasks if they are to be transferred successfully to daily work.

Presenting Knowledge Differently

There are not only different types of knowledge but also different ways to describe the same knowledge. In a good cognitive training system, the same subject matter can be represented in different ways and from different perspectives for the adult learner (Ohlsson, 1986). The authors believe that alternative representations (such as the IIP or MIDP) are likely to be more successful for training. They are better able to meet the different levels of trainee competencies assessed by the mastery learning, personal system of instruction, and tutorial approaches (see chapters 3, 4, and 6).

One of the authors enrolled in an advanced college-level physics course taught by an articulate, knowledgeable instructor. The course used a very theoretical, abstract approach to physics. It attempted to have the students apply scientific laws creatively from their course work. During the instructor's lectures, two blackboards were generally filled with equations and formulas. However, if a student asked a question, the instructor's only response was to start again at the beginning and repeat what he had just taught. He failed to develop alternative representations of the same knowledge to meet different levels of understanding by his students.

We have all had similar frustrating learning experiences as students in school or the corporate classroom. Different presentations of the same knowledge in a training class may only be approximately equivalent in content. However, such presentation alternatives will improve instruction by better accommodating the individual differences of adult learners.

Expert Training Models

The training designer's task analysis of a management skill will have three results:

1. A model of how an expert performs the task

2. The types of knowledge used to perform the task

3. Alternative presentations of the same knowledge used to perform the task.

The expert moves between different types of knowledge and their representations while performing the task. Complex cognitive tasks involve knowledge of goals, strategies, rules, and facts. It is difficult to perform a comprehensive task analysis of a complex management task. It also is difficult to construct a model of expert performance for a training course. But we believe that the enhanced long-term knowledge gains by the adult learner are worth the extra effort. In the rest of this chapter we will demonstrate how to apply the principles of cognitive design to management training.

FRAMEWORK FOR TRAINING DESIGN

Once some form of training-needs analysis has been completed (see Chapter 8 and Appendix IV), the information can be translated into the design of a specific training program. This often has led to the purchase of a generic training package that comes close to covering the desired content areas.

Another approach is to mass the content and present the material to the trainees using almost indoctrination-like courses from one to five days in length. Here the trainees are "indoctrinated" to accept a certain point of view as best for certain on-the-job policies. Until recently many senior executives believed that this type of intensive, short-term training was the best means to funnel the company's business practices and philosophy into the trainees' minds. As we have seen, the development of the science of management behavior was largely an issue of determining appropriate controlling behavior from the top down.

Times have changed. What is now sought is a training design that centers on developing the higher-level thinking skills needed for FutureWork organizational excellence (quality issues, teams, empowerment, increased comprehension ability, etc.). Three areas of training design merit our detailed analysis:

1. Content
2. The adult learner
3. Methods.

Content

The content of training for adult learners needs to be sequenced and broken into manageable learning components. This training needs to be spread over time and practiced on the job between training classes. The simple rule of thumb is usually that spaced practice of management training concepts is far better than short-term massed practice.

The integration of new knowledge and skills with old information requires this transition time as well as focused efforts on the job. Work applications help transfer this new knowledge as do training action plans and follow-up training sessions (Zemke & Zemke, 1988).

The authors' ongoing field research provides some additional guidelines on how best to sequence different training content:

1. In order to successfully introduce new management content areas, several consecutive full-day or half-day classes seem to be necessary. A later follow-up class can be useful to allow a team to self-monitor and make a progress report to an impartial outside source (the trainer).
2. Training content areas need to be learned by building skills one upon the other in as realistic a manner as possible. Ideally, this will be determined by trainee focus groups, surveys, or other acceptable alternatives. As much latitude as possible should

be given to the trainees to determine for themselves what comes next. By their choosing these additional management skills, they become much more vested in each training component as it is introduced. This will take more trainer designer time to facilitate. However, we have found that overall improved final training results are worth this effort.

3. Teaching new skills for individual proficiency takes time. This is true for a wide range of activities from continuing professional education to basic skills. However, our research has found that small-group or one-to-one tutorials organized around cognitive instructional principles are capable of shortening overall classroom time and improving long-term trainee retention (Gordon et al., 1991). (For more detailed information see chapters 3 and 4.)

The Adult Learner

From a cognitive perspective, the adult learner uses prior knowledge and skills to search out and construct personal meaning from what is being taught. The design of the training program also dictates how much new information is understood, assimilated, and transferred to daily work uses. We believe that using various learning strategies will improve this process.

The Nine Events of Training

Gagne and Briggs (1974, 1979, 1985) developed a list of general training design concepts that link specific training events to how well an adult will learn new material. Their nine training events are:

1. Gaining the adult's attention
2. Informing the adult of the training objective(s)
3. Stimulating individual recall of prior training
4. Presenting the new information
5. Providing guidance to the trainee
6. Giving time to practice with new information
7. Providing feedback
8. Assessing learning mastery
9. Enhancing retention and transfer to the job.

Figure 9.3 offers a detailed explanation of how to design each of these instructional events around the adult's learning abilities. The authors' IIP and MIDP training programs attempt to deal with each of these cognitive information-processing issues.

The Child Versus the Adult Learner

What important training design characteristics clearly separate the child from the adult learner? Many children seem to have the insatiable ability to acquire

Figure 9.3
The Nine Events of Training

	Type of Capability				
Training	Intellectual Skill	Cognitive Strategy	Information	Attitude	Performance
			Training Program: Stimulate Personal Interest		
1. Gain attention					
2. Inform of training objective	Provide description and example of the training to be learned and applied	Clarify the general nature of the training expected	Indicate the kind of questions to be answered by the training	Provide examples of the kind of personal actions aimed for by the course	Provide a demonstration of the training results expected
3. Stimulate individual recall of prior training	Stimulate recall of supporting concepts and rules	Stimulate recall of job task strategies and associated intellectual skills	Stimulate recall of prior organized information	Stimulate recall of relevant information, skills, and job/personal model identifications	Stimulate recall of job applications
4. Present the new information	Present training examples	Present novel problems	Present information as a proposed solution	Present job/people models demonstrating choice of personal action	Provide external reasons for performance, including tools or implements
5. Provide trainees guidance	Provide verbal hints to combine information	Provide hints to novel situations	Provide verbal links to larger work context	Trainer choice of action and reinforcement to be given trainee	Provide trainee with practice giving feedback on performance
6. Give practice time with new information	Ask learner to apply information to new examples	Ask for problem solutions	Ask for information in paraphrase, or in adult's own words	Ask adult to indicate choices of action in real or simulated situations	Ask adult to apply on the job
7. Provide feedback	Confirm correctness of training application	Confirm originality of problem solution	Confirm correctness of statement of information	Provide direct or indirect reinforcement of training choices	Provide feedback on degree of accuracy and timing of performance on the job
8. Assess learning mastery	Adult demonstrates application of training	Adult originates a novel training solution	Adult restates training in paraphrased form	Adult makes desired choice of personal action in real or simulated training situation	Adult executes performance of total trained skill(s)
9. Enhance retention and transfer to the job	Provide spaced follow-up training, including a variety of examples	Provide occasions for a variety of novel problem solutions	Provide verbal links to additional sources of new information	Provide additional varied situations for selected choice of action	Adult continues skill practice on the job

Source: Adapted from Gagne and Briggs, 1979.

new information for their undefined, long-term future use. In contrast, adults have a greater capacity to pick and choose from many facts and wisely apply the right information. How quickly and well we can assist an adult in developing this wisdom is the point of this entire book. R. Zemke and S. Zemke (1988) offer several useful curriculum design implications, on which we will elaborate, that help improve training results.

1. Adult learners prefer a single-concept course that offers specific applications to relevant personal work problems.
2. Personal information processing is slowed when the trainer presents new ideas that conflict sharply with prior beliefs. A cognitive conflict occurs, forcing adults to reevaluate the old material. Give adults time to complete this process.
3. Adult learning slows if a training course presents material to which a trainee has not been exposed either through experience or education. Because of this lack of conceptual overlap, the trainee must be given the time to build up a new mental concept before reaching an acceptable level of understanding.
4. Unlike children, adults need training designed to offer explanations from more than one viewpoint. Training content must appeal to more than one developmental life stage.
5. Adult learners prefer multimedia training presentations. These include peer-group team learning, video instruction, audiovisual-assisted presentations, simulations, expert guest speakers, on-site visits as part of the training course, and the use of computer-based/ programmed instruction.
6. Training is not teaching. Teaching centers on offering facts and theory. Training centers on a how-to content. The majority of adults have a great need for training applications and how-to information to successfully motivate personal learning. (The authors' greatest challenge for this book has been how to offer trainers and other adult educators learning theory facts, applied to credible training applications and the how-to of training design.)
7. Adults may learn a great deal from a lecture or a seminar. However, the presenter must be a true expert and have something important to offer each individual in the audience. One way to plan more effective formal lecture presentations is to involve any potential employee audience in planning the seminar's content and even in selecting the expert speaker.

Methods

Two important strategic manpower questions need to be answered when training adults in the workplace:

Under what circumstances will adults learn as rapidly as children?

Is there a deterioration in basic cognitive capabilities of thinking, problem solving, and creativity with increasing age? If so, can training methods be designed to circumvent these problems?

The authors' own field-based training programs repeatedly had to address these questions in specific business applications. The cognitive information-processing approach in the IIP (see chapters 3 and 4) and the MIDP (see Chapter 6) have proven very effective both in shortening overall training time and in improving adult long-term thinking, problem-solving and creative job application abilities.

We offer the following suggested training methods for the design of more effective adult learning:

Memory Development

1. Training must avoid as much as possible the heavy use of rote memorization. When memorization needs to be employed, consider using cognitive learning strategies such as the following to increase adult comprehension (Newsham, 1969).

    a. Mnemonics are techniques to build associations between facts so that we are better able to learn and remember new information. A simple mnemonic is to associate a new fact with something familiar that you will never forget. It can even be quite absurd, such as a mnemonic used to spell "arithmetic": "a rat in the house might eat the ice cream."

    Below, the first letter of each key word forms an acronym that produced a meaningful word to the trainee.

    Stop the main motor.
    Turn off the main isolator.
    Ensure mold is fully closed.
    Purge the machine if necessary.

    STEP becomes a mnemonic cue to the steps of a machine shutdown procedure for a trainee technician.
    Simple rhymes are also mnemonic devices that can improve memory. "Thirty days has September..." is the memory aid most of us have used from early childhood to remember the number of days in each month. In England practically every schoolchild remembers the fate of the six wives of King Henry VIII by the rhyme

    Divorced
    Beheaded
    Died
    Pensioned
    Beheaded
    Survived

Peg words or peg list mnemonic systems can also aid memory building:

Keep
It
Simple
Salesperson

The KISS formula can be used in sales training programs for new hires. They are constantly reminded to keep the selling situation with the customer as simple as possible.

Task
Others
You, the supervisor

TOY can be used for supervisor training programs. What are the consequences of an employee's nonperformance? Supervisors are taught to handle this situation by discussing each consequence in order—, task-others-you—, stopping when they reach compliance.

Mnemonic imagery gives the trainee a mental photograph or diagram to help memory recall. Sometimes using this approach, which is unusual or interesting, is an aid in itself to memory (Patrick, 1992).

2. Analogies often help adults learn new information by relating it to well-understood, familiar ideas. In Chapter 2 we discussed the usefulness of the "team car" analogy as part of a team-building training program (see figures 2.3 and 2.4).
3. Notetaking
4. Paraphrasing
5. Categorizing
6. Summarizing
7. Underlining
8. Using advance organizers such as questioning students at the beginning of training to mobilize prior knowledge related to the new training topic. We discussed the effective use of advance organizers in Chapter 2 (see figures 2.5 and 2.6).

All of these various individual learning strategies strive to improve how adults learn and to reduce the memory load on the learner. In some instances these strategies can be designed into a training program. Other aids are more related to personal learning skills that can be applied by the trainees to many future learning situations. Their chief limitation is that they are useful mainly for learning from text materials (Campione & Armbruster, 1985). However, there are also many other design ideas that will improve training effectiveness for the adult learner.

Content and Attention

Our research shows that it is important to limit the range of training content used in a typical program. Less is often better than more. To maintain individual interest and attention, use a variety of training methods rather than expanding the content of the course. Too many changes in subject material may lead to confusion between the topic content areas (Newsham, 1969; Patrick, 1992).

Longer class sessions sometimes are needed to allow adults to think more about the information while free from daily work interference. Adults generally have longer attention spans than children. Overall course time may not be longer, but individual class periods may be lengthened to induce better learning.

Training Aids and Content

Role-playing exercises, team simulations, training games, computer-based training, and interactive video training are valuable training aids. However, they must be designed to model learning that can be related to the adult's daily job practices, problems, or procedures. If the training content is not designed around these issues, it will soon be forgotten by the employee on the job (Newsham, 1969; Patrick, 1992).

Abstract Learning

If abstract information must be learned, relate this new knowledge to a concrete example, issue, or problem clearly understood by the adult. We have attempted to use this strategy with the reader throughout this book. Try always to relate the abstract to a concrete example, a new abstract concept to a known idea (Newsham, 1969; Patrick, 1992).

Pacing and Training

It is far more productive to allow adults to pace themselves throughout a course than to rush through a program and not achieve individual mastery of the training materials. As we previously discussed, the use of curriculum-based measures (CBMs) will allow the trainer to check on the pacing for each section of the program. The trainer needs to ensure consolidation of personal learning before passing to the next task. CBM allows both trainee and trainer to use a self-testing checking strategy to pace learning within certain overall defined course limitations. Its aim is to allow the adult to meet his or her own learning/pacing targets rather than those imposed by the entire class or the trainer (Newsham, 1969; Patrick, 1992).

Building Trainee Self-Esteem

Many adults have experienced demeaning classroom learning programs in school or at work. They possess low learning self-confidence and may feel very threatened at the beginning of a new training program. For this high-risk audience, use written training instructions as much as possible. Avoid formal testing. (The use of CBMs will be very helpful; see Chapter 8.)

In the course's new-information presentation phase, the trainer will probably have to introduce new job applications very gradually to avoid trainee rejection. Social learning will help relieve personal stress over accepting the changes presented by the trainer. Peer acceptance of course proposals may be very important. Recruit groups of workers as the trainees. Allow this peer group to feel comfortable about new course ideas. Peer tutoring and cross-training procedures may also be used during the training. This will help workers question each other informally and "translate" course information from a fellow worker's point of view.

As far as possible, the time limits for the training program must be determined by individual trainee mastery rather than formal time limits. This reduces fear of personal failure, and shifts the training's primary goal to learning how to learn the new information for use on the job.

Since so many adults "hated" school, avoid using a blackboard or typical classroom learning conditions. The authors have found the use of one-to-one or one-to-five tutorials of maximum learning utility for a wide variety of training programs (see Chapter 4) (Newsham, 1969; Patrick, 1992; Gordon et al., 1991).

Case-Study Approach

Business, law, and medical schools have established the design and use of the case-study method to bridge the gap between theory and practice (Graff, 1991). The authors have utilized case studies both for the corporate classroom and in graduate/undergraduate university courses. If properly designed, the case-study method is a highly efficient and manageable process, and can include authentic tasks (see Chapter 8). It allows the introduction of information-rich materials to trainees for the practice of multiple tasks related to a specific training program. Adult learners experience a wide range of contexts. They gain multifaceted perspectives on the case study's related business problems and solutions.

Simulations

The authors have long recognized the value of simulations in adult learning.

We have given examples of useful simulations related to specific training issues. In general terms, the design of this training tool encompasses the following features:

1. A simulation attempts to represent a real situation in which specific business skills are used by the trainees.
2. The simulations offer the trainees choices of how to manipulate the situation.
3. Though basically realistic, the design omits certain parts of a real business operational situation so that the trainees can arrive at a definitive conclusion to the exercise. In the real world, business projects are seldom if ever "completed"; they usually lead into a new set of operational problems.
4. The simulation content is designed to teach the adult learner both textbook knowledge and "tacit"/heuristic (rule-of-thumb) knowledge. Experienced managers often make unconscious use of this type of knowledge. This is information that schools fail to tell you, and yet lack of it will trip up the novice manager. Simulations as authentic tasks (see Chapter 8) are designed to uncover, demystify, and explicitly train this type of knowledge.
5. The simulation must teach knowledge and skills through a concrete situation that reflects how the knowledge will be applied in real life. This eases the transfer of new learning from the classroom to real job conditions.
6. The simulation gives adults both explanations and role models. It shows the trainees both how a process unfolds and why it happens in a specific way.
7. Trainers act as coaches, giving feedback before, during, and after the simulation. This one-to-one training feature allows the trainer to pinpoint learner performance problems and give personalized counseling to prevent failure, or the development of erroneous concepts or habits. However, as the simulation proceeds, these supports tend to fade as more and more control of the training task shifts to the learner.
8. Simulations are designed to give adult learners the opportunity to reflect and articulate the reasons behind their decisions and actions. This activity makes tacit knowledge more explicit. Discussing problem-solving procedures helps adults develop more appropriate thinking skills for future on-the-job use.
9. Simulations are designed to allow experimentation with different strategies in order to enable trainees to see their effects. There is no one correct answer. Mistakes are useful because they offer the opportunity to confront trainees with anomalies and counterexamples.

Training that uses simulations encompasses the core stages of training development: targeting training objectives, job analysis, and design of a training course. Simulations help maximize a positive transfer of training content to the job because of its hands-on proactive approach. The simulation represents real-world tasks but omits certain complicating features in order to maximize transfer to daily work (Brown et al., 1989; Brown & Van Lehn, 1980; Burton & Brown, 1979; Burton et al., 1984; Collins & Stevens, 1983; Gagne, 1962; Leplat, 1989; Patrick, 1992).

General Creative Methods

1. The trainer's teaching style must encourage trainee cooperation, personal risk taking, and personal intellectual growth. A major course goal will always include attaining early learner buy-in and commitment to formulating personal course goals in writing, with an action plan prepared by each participant at the course's conclusion.
2. Course design must be based on authentic business problems and job contexts. In this way the learning task requirements will draw upon significant job tasks to be used in the workplace.
3. Every course participant can in some way share expert knowledge. Adult learners can draw on their own experiences during the training. This encourages active learning by attaching personal meaning to new information. Adults listen to and learn a great deal from information offered by their peers.
4. The trainer needs to orchestrate a conclusive learning environment by constantly fine-tuning details: adjusting equipment, learning tasks, heat, light, noise levels, seating, interpersonal frictions. These nuances go a long way to increase participants' physical and psychological comfort levels.
5. Too many trainers have a tendency to hold forth (lecture) rather than to facilitate new learning. This natural human tendency can be reduced by designing open-ended questions that are placed throughout the leader's guide to elicit personal trainee knowledge and experience, and the sharing of relevant trainee "war stories."
6. We need to ask "How are you doing?" throughout the learning experience. CBM will help, but trainers must ask trainees for constant feedback on curriculum content and provide opportunities for adults to think about their own learning and how well they are learning.
7. In training there are no wrong answers. The words, "No," "That is wrong," "I don't think so," "That is stupid," or any variations must not escape the trainer's lips. If we wish to encourage class participation and build up each learner's self-esteem, we must recognize that answers may be partially right or wrong. Never completely reject an adult learner's attempt at a problem solution. This does not mean lowering training standards or losing control over the presentation of new material. No two training courses are ever the same. The learners' degree of experience and openness, induced through thoughtful trainer facilitation, may consolidate, rearrange or eliminate some of the required steps listed in the leader's guide. A key role for trainers is facilitating learners' understanding of and belief in their ability to be successful at a task.
8. Transfer to the job requires transition time and focused efforts on the part of the adult learner and the company. Personal action plans for specific on-the-job problems will be of little use if the trainee's supervisor or team members are not in some way involved in pre- and post-course activities. One of the principal reasons that so little training is retained and used on the job is the disregard of these knowledge transfer requirements (Resnick, 1983; Zemke & Zemke, 1988).

CHANGING THE MIND-SET VERSUS BUSINESS REALITY

A recent graduate of Duke University lamented, "My lasting regret is that I spent $40,000 to learn useless tools from academicians who never worked for a real business. I can crunch numbers to death, but I didn't learn anything about managing, motivating, and leading people" (Boyett & Conn, 1991).

Can good management skills be taught? Probably. Is management an art or a science? It is a little bit of both. No business can seriously address this quality issue without empowering all of its employees. You cannot offer education that empowers unless your people have a solid base of skills and training.

This chapter has offered many concrete suggestions for using cognitive learning principles to design enhanced training and development programs (see Figure 9.4). These include: active learning, developing understanding, building mental structures, "learning how to learn" (metacognition), time on task, alignment, feedback, and efficacy.

We are attempting to reach beyond training management behavior, toward teaching management thinking. Our goal is an 80 percent retention rate of new information. This coincides with the benchmarks for effective training established by Boyett and Conn (1991). They point to Harley-Davidson, Motorola, Sara Lee, Wal-Mart, and other companies where this has been achieved over the past ten years. We can point to many other companies that participate in our field-based case studies as evidence that cognitively based learning through the Work Force Education Triad will indeed maximize human potential!

In our last chapter we look to the future of training and development. What will be America's leadership development needs to the year 2001 and beyond?

Figure 9.4
Applying Cognitive Science Variables to Enhance Learning

	Curriculum	Instruction	Assessment
Active Learning	Problem solving; single concept focus	Facilitation through creative role-playing and simulations; discussion of multiple view points; generation of work applications; games; computer-based training; interactive video	Authentic tasks; action planning for workplace transfer of skills
Development of Understanding	Linkages to existing knowledge; outcomes-based, small content units	Recall and reconstruction of personal experience and knowledge; analogies; advance organizers; follow-up on-the-job tasks	Criterion-referenced tests; authentic tasks; curriculum-based measurements
Building Mental Structures (Schemata)	Themes integrated across content and tasks; classification of new information	Multiple-mode tasks around single theme; generation of rules and principles from experience; concrete models; summarizing, outlining, and graphing	Case study; authentic tasks
"Learning how to learn" (Metacognition)	Attention to learning processes; how one learns how to learn	Rehearsals of solutions; planning, self-evaluation, and monitoring of decisions; reciprocal training	Self-critique; process evaluation prediction; analysis of problems; summary of work strategies; application of decisions; monitoring of results; evaluation of success
Time on Task	Small content units conceptually linked	Gradual introduction of content with transfers to job tasks; individually paced progress	Multiple, criterion-referenced tests; curriculum-based measurements
Alignment	Content- and context-specific knowledge; outcomes-based focus	Specific acquired skills applied to realistic work tasks	Criterion-referenced tests; authentic tasks; curriculum-based measurements
Feedback	Linkage of performance outcomes to instruction; focus on success attribution to build self-esteem	Frequent taking stock of progress; positive, accurate, specific critique; generation of alternative solutions	Criterion-referenced tests; authentic tasks; curriculum-based measurements
Efficacy	Job-role application reflected in content; attention to cognitive styles	Goal profiles; job role application tasks	Goal setting; success attribution inventory; criterion-referenced tests; authentic tasks; curriculum-based measurements

REFERENCES

Altizer, C. 1993. It's better to ask than to tell: Adults learn best when they're involved in the process. *Performance and Instruction* 32 (1):25–28.

Anderson, J. R. 1987. Skill acquisition: Compilation of weak-method problem solutions. *Psychological Review* 94 (2):192–210.

___. 1983. *The Architecture of Cognition.* Cambridge, MA: Harvard University Press.

___. 1982. Acquisition of cognitive skills. *Psychological Review* 89:369–406.

Berry, J. 1990. Linking management development to business strategies. *Training and Development Journal* 44 (8):20–22.

Boyett, J. H., & Conn, H. P. 1991. *Workplace 2000.* New York: Penguin Books.

Brown, J. S.; Collins, A.; & Duguid, P. 1989. Situated cognition and the culture of learning. *Educational Researcher* 18 (1):32–42.

Brown, J. S., & Van Lehn, K. 1980. Repair theory: A generative theory of bugs in procedural skills. *Cognitive Science* 4 (4):379–426.

Burton, R. R. & Brown, J. S. 1979. An investigation of computer coaching for information learning activities. *International Journal of Man-Machine Studies* 11:5–21.

Burton, R. R.; Brown, J. S.; & Fischer, G. 1984. Skiing as a model of instruction. In B. Rogoff & J. Lane, eds., *Everyday Cognition: Its Development in Social Content.* Cambridge, MA: Harvard University Press.

Campione, J. C., & Armbruster, B. B. 1985. Acquiring information from texts: An analysis of four approaches. In J. W. Segal, S. F. Chipman, & R. Glaser, eds., *Thinking and Learning Skills,* vol. 1 *Relating Instruction to Research.* Hillsdale, NJ: Erlbaum.

Collins, A., & Stevens, A. L. 1983. A cognitive theory of inquiry teaching. In C. M. Reigeluth, ed., *Instructional-Design Theories and Models: An Overview of Their Current Status.* Hillsdale, NJ: Erlbaum.

Feuer, D., & Geber, B. 1988. Uh-oh...Second thoughts about adult learning theory. *Training* 25 (12):31–39.

Gagne, R. M. 1962. Simulators. In R. Glaser, ed., *Training Research and Education.* Pittsburgh, PA: University of Pittsburgh Press, Reprint. New York: Wiley, 1965.

Gagne, R. M., & Briggs, L. J. 1985. *The Conditions of Learning and Theory of Instruction.* New York: CBS College Publishing.

___. 1979. *Principles of Instructional Design,* 2nd ed. New York: Holt, Rinehart and Winston.

___. 1974. *Principles of Instructional Design.* New York: Holt, Rinehart and Winston.

Gordon, E. E.; Ponticell, J. A.; & Morgan, R. R. 1991. *Closing the Literacy Gap in American Business: A Guide For Trainers and Human Resource Specialists.* New York: Quorum Books.

Graff, D. 1991. A model for instructional design case materials. *Educational Technology Research and Development* 39 (2):81–88.

Jones, J. E., & Woodcock, M. 1985. *Manual of Management Development.* Aldershot, UK: Gower.

Kaeter, M. 1993. Cross-training: The tactical view. *Training* 30 (3):35–39.

Lee, C. 1993. Industry report. *Training* 29 (10):25–65.

Leplat, J. 1989. Simulation and simulators in training: Some comments. In L. Bainbridge, S. A. R. Quintanilla, eds., *Developing Skills and Information Technology.*

Chichester, UK: Wiley.

Newsham, D. B. 1969. *The Challenge of Change to the Adult Trainee.* Training Information Paper 3. London: Her Majesty's Stationery Office.

Ohlsson, S. 1986. Some principles of intelligent tutoring. *Instructional Science* 14:293–326.

Patrick, J. 1992. *Training: Research and Practice.* London: Academic Press.

Resnick, L. 1983. Toward a cognitive theory of instruction. In S. G. Paris, G. M. Olson, and H.W. Stevenson, eds., *Learning and Motivation in the Classroom.* Hillsdale, NJ: Erlbaum.

Spady, W. G., & Marshall, K. J. 1991. Beyond traditional outcome-based education. *Educational Leadership* 49 (2):67–72.

Zemke, R.. & Zemke, S. 1988. Thirty things we know for sure about adult learning. *Training* 25 (7):57–61.

Chapter 10

FutureWork: The Revolution
Reshaping American Business

REVIVING THE AMERICAN DREAM

Today's changing business conditions often puzzle the American worker. The history of the twentieth century provides some valuable clues to global economic riddles. Lawrence H. Summers, chief economist of the World Bank, sees today's business events from the perspective of this century's three great struggles: World War I, World War II, and the Cold War. The allies at the end of World War I sought to humiliate Germany rather than to rebuild Europe's economy. They adopted protectionistic trade policies, stinted credit, and torpedoed any sort of international economic cooperation. The result was the Great Depression, Adolf Hitler, and World War II.

At the conclusion of World War II, according to Summers, the victors took an opposite course. America, through the Marshall Plan, rebuilt Europe and Japan. The International Monetary Fund, the World Bank, the General Agreement on Tariffs and Trade (GATT), NATO and the United Nations all helped establish international free trade and security (Warsh, 1992).

From 1945 to 1990 the world in general, and the United States in particular enjoyed the best years of economic growth in recorded history. This is the legacy of economic opportunity created largely by U.S. business. The world today is more pluralistic, not because America has declined but because it has succeeded. Think of how the postwar period might have been different. When ancient Rome destroyed Carthage, it sowed salt into the earth. Carthage never rose again. If America had destroyed Germany and Japan totally after World War II, would the world today be as prosperous or as safe? A world of competitors is much healthier than an economic empire of subjects (Gordon et al., 1993).

The abrupt ending of the Cold War and the continuing rise of new technologies has brought about a new international economic order. The glue of the common Soviet threat has been replaced by a transitional economy that is compelling American business to redefine its idea of itself. The fact that the United States is now interdependent with the rest of the world is not a pleasant subject for many business leaders. Many sense that the fundamental and continuing shift of the marketplace's economic realities is leaving American business far behind (Farney, 1992).

IBM, GM, Sears, and Pan Am, to name but a few of the American business icons in difficulty or oblivion, seem to prove that something is terribly wrong with the U.S. economy. We are at a socioeconomic watershed, a second industrial/technology revolution ushering in massive, fundamental world change for the twenty-first century. Some of these changes are of America's own doing: our narrow, short-term view of the future; our general indifference to research and planning; our lack of a national social contract between business, unions, schools, and government for the education of our youth; and our lack of investment in human capital (Franklin, 1992).

THE BUSINESS GURUS SPEAK

If we care to listen, there is a startling sense of agreement among America's top business gurus regarding work force education:

Peter Drucker, *Managing for the Future* (1992)

For the first time in human history it really matters whether or not people learn...the most urgent learning and training must reach out to the adults. Thus, the focus of learning will shift from schools to employers. Every employing institution will have to become a teacher.

Lester Thurow, Dean, Sloan School of Management, MIT, *Head to Head* (1992)

Competition revolves around the following questions: Who can make the best products?...Who has the best-educated and best-skilled work force in the world?...Better schools are only the beginning. American firms do not invest as much in training their work forces as firms abroad, and what they do invest is much more heavily concentrated on professional and managerial workers. The oft-cited reason is turnover. If turnover is the real reason, then firms need to take actions such as deferred compensation to reduce turnover. Without a much better trained work force, they will not be competitive.

Tom Peters, Journalist and coauthor of *In Search of Excellence* (1993)

The new economy, based on brains rather than brawn, a true global village, is catching us all unprepared.... We need to provide significant human investment tax credits for corporations and individuals to support perpetual education for all, from remedial reading to advanced engineering.

John Naisbitt, Author of *Megatrends*, *Reinventing the Corporation*, and *Megatrends 2000* (1992)

Today, capital is a global commodity. That leaves human resources. Whether a company or a country, human resources is the competitive edge. That means our number one economic priority has to be education and training.

Michael E. Porter, Economist, Harvard Business School, *The Competitive Advantage of Nations* (1990)

There is little doubt from our research that education and training are decisive in national competitive advantage....What is even more telling is that in every nation, those industries that were the most competitive were often those whose specialized investment in education and training had been unusually great.... Education and training constitute perhaps the single greatest long-term leverage point available. . .to upgrading industry. . .[and] setting policies that link the educational system to industry and encourage industry's own efforts at training.

Ray Marshall, former Secretary of Labor, and March Tucker, President, National Center on Education and the Economy *Thinking For a Living*, *Education and the Wealth of Nations* (1992)

Total quality and high performance work organizations require very large corporate investments in continuing education and training....The successful firm is the firm that organizes itself as a learning system in which every part is designed to promote and accelerate both individual learning and collective learning — and to put that learning to productive use.

Peter M. Senge, *The Fifth Discipline* (1990)

An organization's commitment to and capacity for learning can be no greater than that of its members....But surprisingly few organizations encourage the growth of their people in this manner. This results in vast untapped resources....For an innovation in human behavior, the components need to be seen as disciplines....A discipline is a development path for acquiring certain skills or competencies....To practice a discipline is to be lifelong learner....Thus, a corporation cannot be "excellent" in the sense of having arrived at a permanent excellent; it is always in the state of practicing the disciplines of learning, of becoming better or worse.

Joseph H. Boyett and Henry P. Conn, A. T. Kearney, *Workplace 2000* (1991)

Why is education so important now? Obviously, one of the reasons is the change in workplace practice...particularly the move to turn over more operational and problem solving responsibilities to American workers. Such changes are not driven by desire — in fact, as we have noted, there has been a lot of opposition from managers and supervisors. These changes have been driven by competitive necessity. It isn't something American business necessarily wants to do. It's something American business has to do to compete. The alternative to changing is an economic disaster.

Thomas R. Horton, President, American Management Association, *The CEO Paradox* (1992)

Effective management does not hinge on a restricted field of knowledge, no matter how expert you are in it. The higher you rise in the corporation the more encompassing becomes your view.

The business gurus have spoken in near unanimity. Have America's senior managers comprehended the message? It seems that some have. The U.S. Labor Department's *Monthly Labor Review* in late 1993 reported, "the trend toward a more-skilled work force." Between 1983 and 1991 the number of workers who received company training surged 39 percent, while total employment climbed only by 19 percent. In January 1991, 47 million workers, 41 percent of all employees, received work force education skills training, up from 35 percent in 1990. "The workplace has been reorganized, and more jobs now require reading, mathematics, and communication skills," conclude economist Alan Eck (Conte, 1993; Eck, 1993).

THE WORKER DROUGHT

The Current Work Force

We must not blindly cling to the old myths of "doing business by the numbers" using a military command and control system of multitiered layers of management. Competitiveness means doing more with fewer resources. Total Quality Management (TQM), self-empowered work teams, and participatory management are organizational models that offer industry competitive advantages. However, they all hinge on creating the most educated work force in American's history.

The recession of the early 1990s has partially masked the dire shortage of educated workers for many jobs. Overwhelming research points to the sobering fact that today only 20 percent of all American workers fit into the new international high-tech workplace. Eighty percent never developed the necessary personal thinking skills! They will not be able to find any work, anywhere, at any time, in the future unless given additional education. We are now employing over 80 million Americans in management, support, service, or production who are in danger of becoming the "new peasants of the information age" (Gordon et al., 1991, 1992; Gordon, 1993; Boyett & Conn, 1991; Chall et al., 1987; Costa, 1988).

The flexible, customer-oriented delivery of products and services, rather than mass production, is the new baseline for the global economy. However, only highly skilled, well-educated employees with advanced thinking and problem-solving skills can quickly master these challenging new processes. Approximately 35 million Americans (30 percent of the work force) hold managerial and professional jobs. Although they are college educated, they need continuing professional educational programs to keep their management, communication, and technical skills up to date. It is estimated that 11 percent of these employees lack the educational abilities to do their job competently.

Skilled workers, such as secretaries, police, fire fighters, computer and other technicians, and skilled trade workers comprise approximately 36 percent of all American workers (42 million). These workers' jobs require additional technical/professional education beyond high school but not a four-year college diploma. Many companies now have difficulty in finding more highly skilled workers to fill these jobs. At least 29 percent of these workers will need more education to keep up with changes on the job.

According to the *Wall Street Journal* during the next decade, such employers as Westinghouse and USAir, believe that 70 percent of jobs will require training other than college. Louis Dimasi, Director of the Penn Technical Institute agrees. "Four years of college may not qualify a student for the kinds of jobs projected to become available in the coming years" (Conte, 1993).

Forty million semiskilled workers (about 34 percent of all workers) hold jobs requiring less than a high school education. These are mainly service, manufacturing, and construction occupations. Technology is replacing these individuals with a better-educated worker or, more commonly, these low-skill jobs are being exported overseas. At least 30 percent of these individuals need reeducation to keep or find a job in the high-tech workplace. By the year 2000 only one in ten of these jobs will remain for the low-skilled worker.

The U.S. Department of Labor estimates that before the end of the 1990s, 75 percent of job classifications will require some postsecondary training for entry-level positions. This is a 25 percent increase over current job standards. It is an educational increase that American society is now ill equipped to handle (National Center on Education and the Economy, 1990).

Future Workers

By 1990 U.S. labor force growth had fallen from 3 percent to 1 percent per year. A significant demographic shift is accelerating as more women, minorities and recent immigrants comprise a larger percentage of the labor force. Only 9 percent of the 1990s labor force growth will be white males. Fifty-six percent will be minorities. Much of this labor pool traditionally has been poorly educated or uneducated (Odiorne, 1990).

How do America's high school graduates, ages eighteen to thirty-five, perform in relation to twelfth-grade educational levels? Eighty percent read at or above the level of the average eighth grader. About 60 percent read at or above the eleventh-grade level. However, numerous reports shows a disturbing inability among young adults to reason above a literal, concrete level. Only a small percentage have the ability to synthesize the main argument from a newspaper article, compute the cost of a restaurant meal, or determine exact change. Only about 40 percent of white students, 20 percent of Hispanic students and 10 percent of black students were successful at these activities (Costa, 1988).

The aptitude picture is even bleaker for those who fail to complete high school. The International Association for Evaluation and Education Achievement estimates that in 1990 29 percent of America's youth dropped out before completing the twelfth grade. Of these 20 percent were considered functionally illiterate. This means that about one in five lacked the skills to read, write, or compute at a level appropriate to accomplish the kinds of basic, everyday tasks found at home or on the job (Gordon et al., 1991).

How will these young adults be able to work in TQM environments that require them to diagnose, estimate, obtain/organize information, identify alternatives, analyze, plan, coordinate, work collaboratively, implement, and monitor for continuous change? (Cohen, 1988).

MANAGEMENT DEVELOPMENT TRENDS 1960–2020

Over the past thirty years and into the next millennium, American business has undergone, and will undergo, a fundamental change in the concept of the manager (see Figure 10.1). In the 1960s industry used traditional behavioral methods to teach skills to managers. Training was seen as a "technique, packages of behavioral techniques, gimmicks." Far too often complex management skills were reduced to a "ten-step process." Senior management "vision" was conferred downward and throughout the organization. Rewards were based upon how well individual managers followed this corporate culture driven from the top. No mavericks or creative types were encouraged or tolerated.

The introduction of computers began to shift the emphasis to training groups of managers (department heads) in a systems approach that broadened their business knowledge. Organizational development for senior management was seen as a strategic tool to further this process at the top levels of business.

By the 1980s the new technologies were beginning to bypass middle-management and place daily decisions into the hands of first-line supervisors and even shop foreman or service supervisors. Often middle management became redundant leading to much corporate "downsizing". International competition was beginning to offer consumers far more product and service choices. Shorter, more diverse product runs and innovative service solutions began requiring, for the first time, that supervisors be trained to develop new approaches. Quality circles began to involve employees in the management development process. These programs were an additional response to the high-tech business pressures.

Figure 10.1
Management Development Trends (1960–2020)

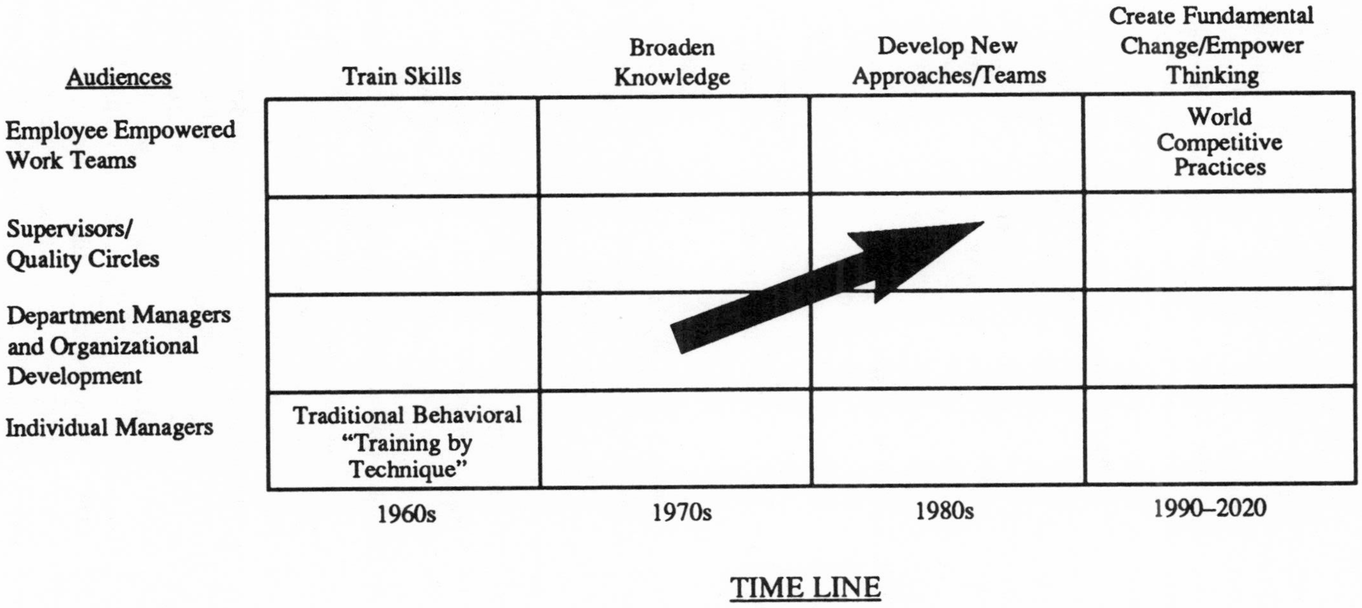

Audiences	Train Skills	Broaden Knowledge	Develop New Approaches/Teams	Create Fundamental Change/Empower Thinking
Employee Empowered Work Teams				World Competitive Practices
Supervisors/ Quality Circles				
Department Managers and Organizational Development				
Individual Managers	Traditional Behavioral "Training by Technique"			
	1960s	1970s	1980s	1990–2020

TIME LINE

In the 1990s and well into the twenty-first century, world competitive business practices will require all organizations to do more with less. American business is fundamentally changing in the way it manages itself in order to survive and prosper. Employee empowered work teams are being trained across America to solve problems, think, and create new ideas. We predict that the artificial divisions between management and employees will continue to blur. Team leaders are needed to give direction, to monitor, and to challenge, but not to wield iron control.

The new organizational structure is flatter, with cooperation replacing fiefdoms and day-to-day business responsibility pushed down and throughout the organization. Traditional methods of evaluation and promotion are being replaced by compensation based on supporting the team's performance. For a company to gain a true competitive edge in the future, business decisions to develop the team's work abilities must come ahead of the quarterly bottom line (Boyett & Conn, 1991).

This raises a large number of training issues as more and more managers, professionals, and technicians begin discovering their rapid technical obsolescence, even if they have had very advanced training. Estimates are that the engineer's education has a half-life of five years, meaning that half of what is learned in school is obsolete five years after graduation (Goldstein & Gilliam, 1990).

Other issues are driving American business toward far better employee education programs. The linkage between school and work needs to be established by direct business collaboration with colleges and secondary schools to prepare youth for new, emerging occupations. Severe shortages of skilled technical workers have begun, and will increase unless American business adapts education models pioneered by European industry.

We need to better inform the public that high-skilled, high-tech jobs are highly paid jobs. When will American society begin to realize that FutureWork means fewer and fewer managers and more and more skilled technicians?

At present too many college marketing, finance, and communications graduates are selling neckties in department stores. Our society has done a terrible job of disseminating high-tech career information to students and parents. We fail to offer America's youth a wider variety of successful adult role models other than those requiring a four-year college degree. Business must lead the charge to change society's attitudes regarding job models and success, or continue to experience significant skilled technical job shortages.

Globalization of the economy is encouraging more organizations to compete internationally. In 1991 the United States was the world's largest exporter, selling a record $422 billion in goods and $145 billion in services abroad. Each billion dollars of exported merchandise generates 20,000 jobs. One-third of America's economic growth in the past five years flowed from this surge in foreign sales (Gordon, 1993). About 100,000 U.S. companies do business overseas, including 25,000 with foreign affiliates and 3,500 major multinational companies. One-third of U.S. corporate profits is derived from international business, along with one-sixth of America's jobs (Cascio, 1986). A survey by Ernst & Young in 1993 saw a further globalization of American companies. Most indicated that their most significant market growth will take place outside the United States, in developing countries (Yates, 1993).

From a corporate education standpoint this means that managers must learn to effectively select, train, and motivate a multicultural workforce. They must be able to communicate in different languages, "read" different cultures accurately, work and manage multicultural teams. There is no quicker, better road for internationalizing American managers than education.

LEADERSHIP THINKING AND CHANGE

The daunting array of business trends means developing leadership abilities for many more employees. Educating for these leadership abilities, now more than ever, means empowerment of people at work. All employees must sense that they are important to the business and be enthusiastic about their work. Learning and improving must become personal goals. Training for leadership motivates personal excellence in performance (Reiner & Morris, 1987). Unbelievable and unpredictable world events of the late 1980s and 1990s have placed all employees on this learning curve. "If you think you can be successful in the future as you were in the past, using the same strategies, you are out of your mind," says Roberto Goizueta, Coca-Cola's CEO (Mason, 1992).

Many of America's top business leaders see that the major business "stem-winders" — technology, globalization, and demographic diversity — have placed the world in such a state of flux that business must educate all people to realign their thinking and be open to change. "Every great leader has something in common with other great leaders: Great leaders never tell people how to do the job," said General Norman Schwarzkopf. Instead, they tell them what needs to be done, establish a level playing field, and get out of the way so employees can achieve their own success.

Leaders make waves because they have a mission and a vision; they do not defend the status quo. Warren Bennis, a professor of management at UCLA, sees five characteristics that turn managers into leaders: technical competence, people skills, conceptual skills, judgment, and character. The consensus of America's top business leaders is that the best way to impart these leadership attributes is through better business educational programs that change thinking rather than just behaviors (Mason, 1992).

In an American Management Association leadership poll taken in January 1993, leaders in business, academia, economics, and public policy were asked how to prepare the United States for the next millennium. The prevailing conviction was that America's most crucial resource is its people and the development of their thinking abilities.

Helping people fulfill their leadership potential is not just part of the American way of life, it is also good business. Learning, striving people are happy people and good workers. But learning to be a leader requires change. Unfortunately, this journey is not neat and orderly, like a well-detailed strategic and tactical business plan.

Ralph Staver, CEO of Johnsonville Foods Inc. of Sheboygan, Wisconsin, established work teams as part of his quality program. The team leaders, chosen by team members, were supposed to function as communication links. Instead they began to act as supervisors. Why? Because they fell back upon the familiar management role they had always seen. Their thinking had not changed: "We had neglected to give them and the plant managers adequate training in the new team model. The structure changed, but mind-sets didn't. It was harder to alter people's expectation than I had realized" (Staver, 1990). Work force education for every person is the number-one business tool to support changing mind-sets throughout American industry.

Managing change through FutureWork is developing into the number-one business strategy for 1990s competitiveness. In the next ten years changing technologies will affect larger and more diverse businesses faster than ever before. Personal expectations of the organization are being replaced by fear of unknown change. As Peter Senge (1990) put it, "People don't resist change. They resist being changed." Most adults have been educated to work toward direct results, from point A to point B. Because of massive changes coming from so many different directions, these old patterns of linear thinking no longer produce the dynamic results needed in today's business environment.

A nonlinear, indirect, creative thinking approach to business problems is now being enshrined as part of TQM. This means teaching employees to look at issues from different perspectives. People must again learn to trust each other so that no one will be punished for breaking the old business culture rules, for doing things differently. We may speak of organizational change, but this really means changes in individuals (Steinburg, 1992).

RETRAIN WHOM? TO DO WHAT?

While American business is trying to empower teams of people to improve quality, learn new technologies, and compete globally, the employees' response may only be a shrug. Our exhortations may be falling on deaf ears because of the workplace schizophrenia caused by the early 1990s recession, from which America is just emerging. However, the fundamental restructuring of not only the U.S. but also the world economy will continue to see white-collar employees and managers who need massive reeducation for new jobs with new businesses or in emerging, yet-to-be discovered technologies.

According to the Conference Board, in 1991, 25 million people, 20 percent of the work force, were unemployed at some time. Future job cuts were being announced at the average rate of 2,600 per day. It is not surprising that a Northwestern National Life Insurance study conducted in 1992 showed that nearly half of all workers are concerned about holding onto their jobs.

The other alternative for business reorganization is employee retraining rather than termination. FutureWork for the twenty-first century will be supported by a dramatic increase in the technical training done by industry on an ongoing basis. American utilities present good examples of an industry that offers its people ongoing technical education, since technology changes rapidly, rather than constantly turning over their work force in the hope of finding better-prepared workers.

Train Whom?   We must reinvest in our tech-craft-vocational education programs to reeducate current members of the work force who are out of work, or whose knowledge is rapidly becoming obsolescent. We also must prepare the next generation of young people for the high-tech workplace realities of the twenty-first century.

To do what? Most of the modern consumer goods used by every American — the automobile, television, video cassette recorder, compact disk player, tape deck, and so on — were invented in the United States. Yet almost all of these products are now manufactured overseas because America lacks the technically qualified, educated personnel to make the product in a high-tech, controlled-cost, quality environment. Who will make the next generation of high-tech products: high-definition television (HDTV); hypersonic air craft; battery-driven cars; smaller, faster, more powerful computers? Will those products be invented in America only to be manufactured in Korea, Singapore, or Germany?

Prior to its unification struggles, the (West) German economy was very productive because of its highly skilled labor force. Sixty-six percent of all employees are certified graduates of the German youth training system. About 596,000 (as of 1992) German teenagers between 15 to 19 participate in this program. Overall, 1.6 million apprentices (6.5 percent of the labor force) undertake a two-to-three-year job preparation program in any one of some 380 occupations. The cost to German industry in 1991 was about $10,500 per apprentice. Does the system benefit business? One indicator is that businesses offer 22 percent more apprenticeship slots than there are applicants.

One reason for this broad support is that the apprentice system is so well established throughout Germany that companies are not afraid of having workers stolen. German unions do not severely limit student apprenticeships in order to create artificial shortages of skilled workers. Senior German management recognizes that profits and productivity are a direct result of a strategic long-term investment in continuing, lifelong employee education. Five hundred thousand mostly small businesses invest $40 billion in the German youth apprenticeship program. An additional $40 billion is allocated by these companies to train their current adult workers (Prevo, 1993).

U.S. efforts to replicate the German system in some way have already begun. In Virginia Beach, Virginia, Stihl, the German-owned maker of chain saws, lawn trimmers, and blowers, began an intensive four-year apprentice program in the 1970s. It tripled worker productivity. Instead of being short of skilled workers, it has blossomed into Virginia Beach's biggest manufacturer. It has 498 workers, 40 more than in 1974 (Salwen, 1993).

In 1992 Sears established, near Chicago, an apprenticeship program with the DuPage (County) Area Occupational Education System. It links Sears appliance service centers with innovative high school academic/technology classes. Sears has invested $3 million to establish the program and is collaborating with educators in developing the classroom and work site curriculum. This means the apprenticeship program content remains up to date and on target. On graduating from the program, a student may or may not be hired by Sears (Gordon, 1993).

These efforts are representative of the scores of new apprenticeship efforts under way throughout the United States. Some 20 million young adults, aged sixteen to twenty-four who do not attend college, are available for company-sponsored work force education. A mountain of business-economic studies leaves no doubt that American business must begin to seriously retrain our nation's youth to meet present and future job needs (Porter, 1990; Thurow, 1992; Marshall & Tucker, 1992; Gordon, 1993).

A NEW SOCIAL CONTRACT FOR AMERICAN BUSINESS

Until recently such companies as IBM, AT&T, Sears, Xerox, and United Airlines implicitly guaranteed their workers a job for life. In exchange, people gave a company their complete loyalty, often placing it ahead of family or personal needs (Reynolds, 1992).

Worldwide economic, competitive, technological, political, and social changes have introduced a new era in which to survive and prosper, all businesses must become small, lean, and highly focused. Bureaucracy is being eliminated. Middle management is shrinking.

Many business planners now see 250 to 500 people as the optimal work unit. Beyond that size people lose interest in the important touchstone — the customer, who has become the only source of business security. Customer loyalty must be constantly earned through outstanding performance. Business interest in TQM is a quest for a workable strategy that requires consistently better performance from every employee (Boyett & Conn, 1991).

America now stands at an economic crossroads. One path leads to a continued decline in the standard of living and sees the United States eclipsed as the world's leading economic power. The other road leads toward FutureWork — a fundamental restructuring of American business for 2001 and beyond.

The Cold War is over, but an international competitive war has begun. America has proven it can resist invading armies; but will business and political leaders recognize the new economic course charted by the world's industrial community? In the late twentieth century, international business investment in human capital has emerged as the single most important business strategy to attain and retain a significant competitive economic advantage (Gordon et al., 1993).

The authors believe that better educating all adults with the Work Force Education Triad is an attainable goal for every business, large or small. Aging may slow people down somewhat. However, our research, and that of many others, indicates that if adults can control the pace of learning, and if hearing and visual problems are corrected, people have the same ability to learn in their fifties as they had in their twenties. This continues to be true until old age, sometimes even after the age of seventy (Sonnenfeld & Ingols, 1986; Gordon et al., 1991, 1992, 1993).

Everywhere the new global marketplace is undermining the nation-state as the fundamental socially integrating force. This new international economy now benefits only 20 percent of American workers. The other 80 percent are economically standing still or falling behind. The well-educated people in America typically work in office buildings. These "glass-tower people" are linked to their counterparts in Germany and Japan. Their economy is upward bound. Unfortunately, too many of their undereducated fellow Americans are not heading in the same direction (Farney, 1992).

Unless this basic socioeconomic condition is corrected, the United States will become a two-tier economic society. A well-educated, economically mobile upper class will be dwarfed in numbers by a large, poorly educated economic underclass that lacks the educational ability to function in a high-tech, glass-tower business environment. This means the end of the American economic system as we have known it, and perhaps a severe disruption of our society as the universal standard of living sinks out of sight. This is too high a price to pay for our lack of agreement on a new social agenda for the reform of American education.

America is pretty much in the same position as it was at the beginning of the nineteenth century (Drucker, 1992). At that time, there was a gradual realization by business, union, and government leaders that a fundamental change was required in America's basic business agenda. The United States sensed it could not compete with a rapidly industrializing Europe unless the average American worker was literate and had vocational skills. Between 1890 and 1920, American society embarked on the difficult task of introducing sweeping educational reforms.

There was tremendous opposition by some in business to mandatory public education. Child labor was cheap; schooling would drive up business costs. However, the new technology of the early twentieth century demanded a realistic partnership between business and labor that enacted into law America's first educational revolution. The time has now dawned for a second effort. The demands of the marketplace have far outpaced the schoolhouse's ability to educate the majority of our children for life beyond 2001.

A widespread national consensus is being mobilized for significant change both in the schoolhouse and in the corporate classroom. Diverse groups across America are demanding basic educational reform for all people, young and old. A second American education revolution may unfold (see Figure 10.2).

No matter what the eventual scenario of the second American education revolution, it will not reach completion overnight. Even drastically improved public education is incapable by itself of supporting America's industrial competitiveness. Of equal importance is quickly establishing a corporate policy that expands the role of employee education within all businesses, both large and small.

Senior managers must understand that planning includes investing in employee work force education through expanded company training and development programs. The realization of these twin strategic objectives — national education reform and local company work force education programs — will help America regain lost productivity and international competitive advantage in almost every business sector. Let us consider each element of this second American education revolution and the role of business.

Business/Education Alliance

An alliance is being welded between education and business so that all entry-level employees will leave the twelfth grade with strong educational skills. Businesses will invest in specific job education programs that are a part of the total schooling process. They will also begin offering lifelong education for all their people, not just managers, to keep their work force up to date on technological and managerial innovations. This means investing more funds in training and development on the same world-class business level as western Europe and Japan.

Schooling Innovations

If we expect the schools to produce better overall students in the humanities, math, and science, we must link quality and wages. The schools once featured a captive female labor supply; first-rate teachers were not paid high wages. Can the United States honestly hope to be the world's scientific leader when at least one-third of those teaching high school physics never took a formal college physics course?

Higher teaching salaries must be linked to increased time in the classroom. In 1992 a thirty-five-year-old teacher in Germany earned an annual salary of $51,000. However, he or she worked a full eight-hour day and a 220-to-240-day school year. The 180-day school year needs to be consigned to the nostalgia of its nineteenth century agrarian harvest-schedule origins. More time is needed in school if U.S. students are to learn what a modern society requires to support widespread prosperity for all its members.

Figure 10.2
Scenario for the Second American Education Revolution
(1983–2020)

Phase One (1983–1984)
A Nation at Risk begins a period of criticism and general dissatisfaction
with America's schools.

Phase Two (1985–1988)
The Carnegie Commission and other think tanks issue reforms centered
on more of the same, ideas that only tinker with the system: spend more
money, reform curriculum, change teacher training, establish local school
councils, etc.

Phase Three (1989–1990)
Individual states, cities, or civic groups initiate radically different
educational programs that depart from past contemporary schools: the
state of Minnesota's Choice Program, Wisconsin's voucher system for
Milwaukee's disadvantaged children, Chicago's "Corporate Community
School," etc.

Phase Four (1991–1995)
Revisionist educators, and business leaders research and apply selected
new educational models and publish their successful results. Public
awareness and support increase for adopting broad systemic change
(*America 2000*, The Scans Report, etc.).

Phase Five (1995–2000?)
Political, business, union, and educational leaders begin backing new
education models that have earned popular acceptance with local
communities. New state/federal legislation establishes significant new
school model programs.

Phase Six (2000–2010?)
Professional educators begin supporting these new school initiatives.

Phase Seven (2010–2020?)
Local, radically changed school programs are available across the United
States.

Placing the schools on a competitive wage and attendance calendar means that Americans must spend more on elementary/secondary education. Though we are the world's leader in higher education expenditures, the United States now spends 4.1 percent of GNP on elementary and secondary education; Germany spends 4.6 percent and Japan 4.8 percent.

Increasing our financial commitment to education in business or the schoolroom will have little impact unless America adopts objective quality standards for everyone. Nationally recognized educational mandates must be based on minimum world education standards. Some communities or schools may wish to surpass these standards. However, the current watered-down "educational mandates" in many states assure that only 40 percent of our high school students graduate with twelfth-grade skill levels (Chall, 1990).

We need to double the number of students attaining acceptable high school graduation standards before the year 2000. By that date, according to a 1991 prediction by the U.S. Commerce Department, at least 80 percent of all jobs in America will require twelfth-grade skill levels or above.

Business Commitment To Work Force Education

A schooling revolution fueled by new curricula, business collaboration, and more funds is insufficient by itself to guarantee our competitiveness. Most companies, regardless of size, remain reluctant to deal with the skill and educational deficiencies of their workers. They need information on practical workplace educational programs that have proven to be effective. Most businesses have not yet heard, understood, and acted on this message. Many CEOs still blame schools and employees for poor skills.

The availability of qualified, well-educated, entry-level workers continues to wane across the United States. In 1991 the American Human Resource Association cited a $6,000 average cost to recruit and train a new entry-level worker. In 1992, the average manufacturer rejected five out of six applicants because they were undereducated.

In order to support the needs of a competitive American economy, U.S. business must seriously reconsider the meager 2 percent it annually invests in training and development. By comparison western European and Japanese businesses allocate 5 to 6 percent of their annual budgets to training and development. If we are to compete successfully on an international scale by the year 2000, the National Association of Manufacturers and the American Society for Training and Development predict that U.S. business must increase its formal annual training budget from $40 billion in 1992 to $88 billion by 2000. Even now, many of our competitors are moving ahead with well-educated national work forces.

AMERICA'S RESPONSE TO FOREIGN COMPETITION

The Netherlands Foreign Investment Agency gives compelling reasons why America's CEOs must pay attention to this message. A recent advertisement states:

> Holland's work force is one of its strongest business assets, embodying an extraordinary combination of language and technical skills, know-how, discipline, work ethic and "can do" attitude. We have about the highest productivity as measured by relative unit labor costs in manufacturing in the EC. The Dutch people are seen as the most outwardly oriented and multi-lingual of Europeans. English is virtually a second language. Government policy and spending forge strong links between education and industry. Thirteen universities and more than 100 technical institutes train the management and staff you need in Computer Implemented Manufacturing, telecom, biotech, med-tech, information processing, office automation, software and micro-electronics.

This compelling work force portrayal by a smaller member of the European Union (EU) must be recognized as a direct, legitimate challenge to the future profitability of American business. This competitive message is being echoed again and again by other nations in Europe and Asia (see Figure 10.3). These trends will only increase. American business must meet the international work force education challenge or face a grim future of declining market share, lower profits, and a substantial decline in our overall standard of living.

During the 1992 election campaign, Bill Clinton proposed a 1.5 percent "training tax" to reeducate America's work force. Every company with over fifty employees would be taxed 1.5 percent of revenue, unless it already budgets an equivalent amount for worker training. Many union, business, and government leaders accept the basic premise behind Clinton's proposal — too many American workers don't have the educational skills demanded by the emerging high-tech, competitive world marketplace. Other countries, most notably France, already levy a business training tax to help keep their workers competitive.

Whether or not such a training tax is enacted, American business needs to carefully consider several basic issues at the heart of this idea. Who will receive training? What will be defined as training? How will training programs be offered?

If we wish to better educate more Americans, it is apparent that any new training funded by a training tax must be targeted at production workers and office support personnel. Many current managers also need retraining for new jobs that did not exist when they attended school. However, America will be better served by having business allocate this retraining from the $40 billion already targeted for management development. President Clinton must consider using this new training tax revenue to reeducate the majority of workers who now receive little, if any, training in the workplace.

Figure 10.3
Scotland's Competitive Message

WE'D LIKE TO TELL YOU WHY THE SCOTS ARE SO ADEPT AT TECHNOLOGY. DO YOU HAVE 500 YEARS?

Some 500 years ago, Christopher Columbus discovered an entirely new land. America. That very same year, in 1492, the people of Scotland discovered a new idea as well.

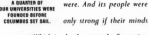

TODAY, SOME OF THE GREATEST BREAKTHROUGHS IN SEMICONDUCTOR TECHNOLOGY HAPPEN RIGHT HERE.

Compulsory public education.

You see, the Scots truly believed that a society was only as strong as its people were. And its people were only strong if their minds

A QUARTER OF OUR UNIVERSITIES WERE FOUNDED BEFORE COLUMBUS SET SAIL.

were strong. Which is why they were the first society in history to make education mandatory for all.

Not surprisingly, the Scots, to this day, place a high priority on education. To the age of 14, all students pursue a broad curriculum, with a par-

ALEXANDER GRAHAM BELL, THE INVENTOR OF THE TELEPHONE, WAS BORN HERE.

ticular focus on science and mathematics. And instead of learning how to memorize, they learn how to think.

In later years, these students specialize, many of them pursuing technical careers. Currently, you'll find some 90,000 Scots studying for degrees in chemistry, physics, mechan-

THE NEXT TIME YOU DRIVE DOWN ANY ROAD, THANK MR. MACADAM.

ical engineering, electrical and electronic engineering, or computer sciences. Upon graduation, they're ready to put these skills to work.

No wonder so many companies think Scotland's a very intelligent place to locate their business. For more information, call 1-800-THE-SCOT.

JOHN LOGIE BAIRD INVENTED TELEVISION.

LOCATE IN SCOTLAND
INNOVATION RUNS IN OUR BLOOD

LOCATE IN SCOTLAND, 4 LANDMARK SQUARE, SUITE 500, STAMFORD, CT. 06901, US OFFICES ALSO IN HOUSTON, CHICAGO AND SAN MATEO. LOCATE IN SCOTLAND IS THE JOINT INWARD INVESTMENT ORGANIZATION OF SCOTTISH ENTERPRISE (FORMERLY THE SCOTTISH DEVELOPMENT AGENCY) AND THE U.K. GOVERNMENT.
This material is prepared by ClarkGowardFitzMattison, 535 Boylston Street, Boston, MA 02116 which is registered with the Department of Justice, Washington, D.C. under the Foreign Agents Registration Act as an agent of Locate In Scotland, Glasgow, Scotland. This material is filed with the Department of Justice where the required registration statement is available for public inspection. Registration does not indicate approval of the contents of the material by the United States Government.

Scottish Enterprise

JUST A FEW
OF THE INNOVATIVE
U.S. COMPANIES
WHO'VE LOCATED
IN SCOTLAND

ALDUS
BURR BROWN
CAMPBELL FOODS
COMPAQ
CONNER PERIPHERALS
DIGITAL
W.L. GORE
HEWLETT PACKARD
HONEYWELL
HOOVER
HUGHES
HYSTER
INMAC
IBM
JOHNSON & JOHNSON
LEVI STRAUSS
MOTOROLA
NATIONAL SEMICONDUCTOR
NCR
PENNWALT
PLANTEX
POLAROID
ROHM AND HAAS
SCI
SEAGATE
SUN MICROSYSTEMS
TANDY
TEREX EQUIPMENT
WRANGLER
WYKO PRECISION

What will be defined as training? Training is more than just specific job preparation. Modern workplace training requires higher-level thinking skills for all workers. What this really means can be seen from the complaints of overseas suppliers that cannot sell their latest high-tech innovations in the U.S. market. They often find their equipment is being poorly operated. American employees cannot perform math calculations using fractions, decimals, or ratios. Others cannot apply these skills to specific problem-solving tasks. Still other workers fail to comprehend computer software manuals.

Our competitors in western Europe and Japan are committed to the norm of lifelong learning for all employees. They don't see training as narrow skill applications or just on-the-job experiences. Instead, they invest 4 to 5 percent of their budgets on employee learning, supporting world-class quality standards like ISO 9000 or the "6th sigma" approach of a 99.99 percent defect-free production rate. Unless America raises its training standards for all workers to these levels, how can we expect to compete successfully against the increasing pace of technological change in the world workplace?

How will we offer these training programs? The worst scenario is the establishment of a new federal training bureaucracy that will siphon off training funds at national, state, county, and local levels. Instead, let the training tax be levied and collected by the IRS. Every business will set up a training-tax account at its local bank and make deposits each month as it now does for payroll taxes. Nationally recognized training and development professionals can assist the IRS in formulating specific regulations on how funds in this training account are to be spent for worker training programs. Each year, every business will report in its tax return on the exact expenditures from the training-tax account. Failure to comply with IRS regulations will result in stiff penalties. This method will place an emphasis on spending the training tax on training, not on bureaucracy. It also gives businesses a broader role in matching employee training to local job conditions.

In addition to a training tax, President Clinton may wish to consider several other useful alternatives for worker reeducation. Instead of levying a comprehensive business training tax, he might offer small employers a human resource tax credit. This option allows businesses with under 300 employees to provide the types of employee training and education targeted by the training tax, but instead receive a tax credit. This strategy will help foster small business growth. It offers a monetary incentive for worker education tied to an immediate return on investment.

Another training option is to expand a federal program that already works — the Job Corps. Since the 1960s this residential training program has prepared unemployed youth for a lengthening list of career opportunities. Each year 108 Job Corps centers around the country prepare 42,000 youths, 16 to 21 years old, for entry-level jobs. Many of the Job Corps centers are partially privatized through local business partnerships.

It is also a good investment of taxpayer dollars. Each dollar spent returned

$1.46 over a lifetime of paying income taxes, and non-reliance on welfare, unemployment compensation, Medicaid or other programs. This happens because more than eight in ten Job Corps graduates are placed in jobs. Why not plan to double or even triple the size of the Job Corps over the next five to ten years as local sites and sponsoring business partners are identified? Many metropolitan areas like Chicago do not have even one site located in or near to the city.

The Clinton administration seeks a variety of answers to the question of how best to reeducate the American worker. These proposed options will allow the government to reach out quickly to a great number of American workers. They will encourage job growth at the community level. By empowering the average employee through better education on the job, the concept of a training tax might become a flexible human resource development plan that will rebuild the U.S. economy for generations to come.

FUTUREWORK TODAY

The future is now. Companies both large and small across America have begun to adopt the training, skills, and education components of the Work Force Education Triad (see Figure 10.4). These include Nucor Steel, Lincoln Electric, Wal-Mart, Motorola, Sara Lee, Harley-Davidson, and GM Electro-Motive (Boyett & Conn, 1991; Moberg, 1993; Ziemba, 1993).

At the biennial (Autumn 1993) meeting of the American Management Association Executive Council, business leaders addressed the issue as to why too many employee, self-managed work groups are not working. The solution discussed was having all employees complete company training in basic management, problem-solving techniques and decision-making skills similar to training for managers. As one council member put it, "When the workers get the picture, they are better prepared to solve the problem. And without teaching them the fundamentals of business management and decision making, don't expect them to understand what you are doing" (Peak, 1993).

We offer any organization the following policy recommendation on how to make the Work Force Education Triad a driving force within a successful strategic business plan:

Recommendation One   The CEO and senior managers will make a strategic training plan an essential part of the business' overall strategic plan. This includes both a long-term and short-term training plan.

Recommendation Two   The vice president responsible for training and education will have an active role in formulating these business strategies.

Recommendation Three   These business strategies will embrace the three essential elements of the Work Force Education Triad:
1. Skills
2. Training

Figure 10.4
FutureWork: The Work Force Education Triad

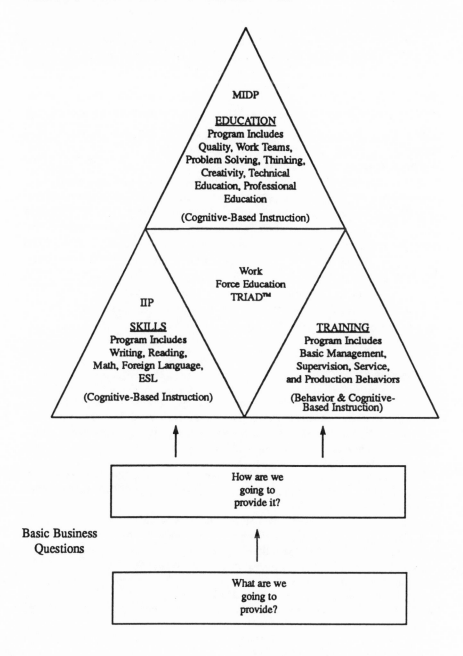

MIDP

<u>EDUCATION</u>
Program Includes
Quality, Work Teams,
Problem Solving, Thinking,
Creativity, Technical
Education, Professional
Education

(Cognitive-Based Instruction)

Work
Force Education
TRIAD™

IIP

<u>SKILLS</u>
Program Includes
Writing, Reading,
Math, Foreign Language,
ESL

(Cognitive-Based Instruction)

<u>TRAINING</u>
Program Includes
Basic Management,
Supervision, Service,
and Production Behaviors

(Behavior & Cognitive-
Based Instruction)

How are we
going to
provide it?

Basic Business
Questions

What are we
going to
provide?

	3. Education.
Recommendation Four	The CEO will monitor the results of these strategic training plans to ascertain:

a. that *all* employees are involved

b. that *real* business and people problems are being addressed

c. that a *realistic return on investment measurement system* is ultimately developed that tracks bottom line results (Rosow & Zager, 1985).

To demonstrate these points we have prepared a case-study model based on an alternative scenario for the closing of U.S. Steel, Chicago South Works, (see Appendix V). This case study will help trainers apply the FutureWork model to their company's training needs.

Our message to the education and business community is simply this: America's future prosperity rests upon the education of all our citizens. We no longer have "disposable" students or workers. Neither Japan nor Western Europe has any inherent technological advantage or production system that cannot be duplicated or improved in the United States. However, they earned their global competitive edge by making sustained and significant investments in the education and training of *all* their people.

A growing cry for help can be heard from within companies across the land. Can America afford to ignore this call to prepare all our people for the competitive twenty-first century world of FutureWork?

REFERENCES

Boyett, J. H., & Conn, H. P. 1991. *Workplace 2000*. New York: Penguin Books.

Cascio, W. F. 1986. *Managing Human Resources*. New York: McGraw-Hill.

Chall, J. S.; Heron, E.; & Hilferty, A. 1987. Adult literacy: New and enduring problems. *Phi Delta Kappan*, 69 (3):190–96.

Chall, J. S. 1990. Policy implications of literacy definition. In R. L. Venezky, ed., *Toward Defining Literacy*. Newark, Delaware: International Reading Association.

Cohen, M. 1988. *Restructuring the Educational System: Agenda for the 1990s*. New York: Carnegie Corporation.

Conte, C. 1993. Labor Letter. *Wall Street Journal*, 9 November, A1.

Costa, M. 1988. *Adult Literacy/Illiteracy in the United States: A Handbook for Reference and Research*. Santa Barbara, Calif.: ABC-Clio.

Drucker, P. F. 1992. *Managing for the Future*. New York: Dutton.

Eastburn, R. A. 1987. Management development. In R. L. Craig, ed., *Training and Development Handbook*. New York: McGraw-Hill.

Eck, A. 1993. Job-related education and training: Their impact on earnings. *Monthly Labor Review* 116 (10):21–38.

Farney, D. 1992. Even U.S. politics are being reshaped by a global economy. *Wall Street Journal*, 28 October, A1, A10.

Franklin, S. 1992. Expectations grow dimmer as American dream fades. *Chicago*

Tribune, 13 December, sec. 6, 3.

Goldstein, I. L., & Gilliam, P. 1990.   Training systems issues in the year 2000. *American Psychologist* 45 (2):134–43.

Gordon, E. E. 1993. *The Need for Work Force Education*. Bloomington, Ind. Phi Delta Kappa Educational Foundation.

Gordon, E. E.; Ponticell, J. A.; & Morgan, R. R. 1993. Training in crisis. *Workforce* 2 (1):14–24.

___. 1992. *Closing the Literacy Gap in American Business*. New York: Quorum.

Horton, T. R. 1992. *The CEO Paradox*. New York: Amacom.

Hunt, V. D. 1992. *Quality in America*. Homewood, IL: Business One, Irwin.

Marshall, R., & Tucker, M. 1992. *Thinking for a Living, Education and the Wealth of Nations*. New York: Basic Books.

Masland, T. 1990. Work it out: Employers are seeking to bridge the "trust gap." *Chicago Tribune*, 11 February, sec. 4, 4.

Mason, J. C. 1992. Leading the way into the 21st century. *Management Review* 81 (10):16–19.

Moberg, D. 1993. Last train out. *Chicago Tribune*, 24 January, sec. 5, 1, 6.

National Center on Education and the Economy. 1990. *America's Choice: High Skills or Low Wages*. Rochester, NY: The Center.

Odiorne, G. S. 1990. Beating the 1990s labor shortage. *Training* 27 (7):32–35.

Peak, M. H. 1993. Conversation in the boardroom. *Management Review* 82 (11):22.

Peters, T. 1993. To get ahead, don't be lax about your homework. *Chicago Tribune*, 11 January, sec. 4, 6.

Porter, M. E. 1990. *The Competitive Advantage of Nations*. New York: Free Press.

Prevo, W. 1993. The sorcery of apprenticeship. *Wall Street Journal*, 12 February, A16.

Reiner, C. A., & Morris, H. 1987. Leadership development. In R.L. Craig, ed., *Training and Development Handbook*. New York: McGraw-Hill.

Reynolds, L. 1992. America's work ethic: Lost in turbulent times? *Management Review* 81 (10):20–25.

Salwen, K. G. 1993. The cutting edge. *Wall Street Journal*, 19 April, A1.

Senge, P. M. 1990. *The Fifth Discipline*. New York: Doubleday.

Sonnenfeld, J. A., & Ingols, C. A. 1986. Working knowledge: Charting a new course for training. *Organizational Dynamics* 15 (2):63–79.

Staver, R. 1990. How I learn to let my workers lead. *Harvard Business Review* 63 (November–December), 66–83.

Steinburg, C. 1992. Making choices about change. *Training & Development* 46 (3):24–32.

Thurow, L. 1992. *Head to Head*. New York: William Morrow.

Warsh, D. 1992. 20th century history provides clues for solving global economic riddles. *Chicago Tribune*, 4 October, sec. 7, 5.

Yates, R. E. 1993. Home ties weakening at many firms. *Chicago Tribune*, 19 April, sec. 4, 1-2.

Ziemba, S. 1993. Electro-Motive firmly on track with new order. *Chicago Tribune*, 16 April, sec. 3, 3.

Appendix I

A Description of the IIP Research Program

In order to enhance the ability of American businesses to compete successfully both at home and abroad, there has been a push to improve worker productivity by retooling older industrial plants with more sophisticated machinery. Much of this new computer-driven equipment requires more sophisticated basic literacy skills (particularly reading and math) than are normally possessed by the majority of the available labor force.

For the most part, the prevailing view has been that the schools were designed to produce a manufacturing "grunt" labor force. That is, large numbers of public school students were never expected to become more than functionally literate (i.e., able to read and compute at about the fourth-grade level). Since 1900, about 20 percent of the American population has remained at this level of literacy. In sum, the present work force is composed of many inadequately skilled and poorly educated workers.

For the past twenty-five years tutoring/training curricula have been operated by Imperial Corporate Training & Development, and Imperial Tutoring, an educational/business training consulting firm. To date, the population served has included 7,000 individuals tutored and 14,000 individuals trained. These individuals have been tutored/trained by over 300 trainers or teacher consultants utilizing a specially designed curriculum to facilitate either training or tutoring. Eight managers have been involved in the selection and training of this staff, student intake evaluations, and general program supervision. Program offerings have included adult academic and vocational skills programs and management development.

Many businesses have contracted with the investigators to improve skills, training, or educational levels in the shortest possible time. During the course of these programs, skilled or semiskilled workers or managers have attended classes at work or at home. Individualized instructional programs (IIP) have been specially designed for use by a trainer/administrative team to bring about rapid, verifiable skills or training. With their associated written methods and reporting materials, these programs were designed to help the trainer follow a thoughtful, sequentially arranged, systematic presentation with each individual or small group of no more than five students. Particular attention has been given to the inclusion of administrative quality control, student learning awareness, and the provision of constant feedback to the company management during the training process.

EVALUATION OF PROGRAM OFFERINGS

To facilitate better individualized tutoring across types of subjects, a number of specially crafted IIP curriculum scripts were designed to teach adults competencies at the introductory, maintenance, and/or mastery levels. Over 300 learning descriptors were systematically developed and used to document academic achievement, social-emotional outcomes, and selected job-related skills. These learning descriptors were assessed by means of tutor observations, and criterion- and norm-referenced achievement and personality tests.

An informal evaluation of the program offerings indicated that there were differences in tutoring outcomes across time blocks (0–10 hours, 10–20 hours, 20–30 hours). The assumption was made that these differences occurred because time was needed (1) to assess how the tutee approached the learning situation; (2) to discover what specific sequential subject-matter skills the tutee lacked; (3) to reorganize and improve tutee achievement/study habits; (4) to assess and improve tutee motivators that supported learning (i.e., improving workplace employer motivators).

Given the findings from the informal evaluation of the program offerings, two research questions were of special interest to the developers of the literacy training tutoring program: What specific effect(s) did the tutoring program have on student outcome measures of achievement and/or social-emotional functioning? Did the number of hours a student was tutored in the program relate significantly to both short- and long-term achievement and job performance? Exploratory pilot studies were conducted in an attempt to determine the effectiveness of a number of existing programs where tutoring was blocked into naturally occurring time segments. The results of these pilot studies were reported at the 1988 annual meeting of the American Educational Research Association.

Consistent performance differences over time (0–10 hours, 10–20 hours, 20–30 hours) were found. Maximum grade-level improvement appears to occur at around the thirtieth hour of instruction. It is of special importance to note that at least a six-month to one-year gain in skill improvement resulted from each module for every participant receiving instruction.

In addition to the rather promising quantitative results from this series of increasing-scale pilot studies, qualitative pilot data evaluations (i.e., tutee, tutor, and employer evaluations) indicated significant growth in student academic skills, and study skills, and numerous positive motivational changes related to learning in general, academic learning, and work performance. Two key motivational factors appeared to be the close proximity to a supporting workplace environment and individual perseverance. Long-term qualitative follow-up studies indicated that the majority of students retained what they learned while being tutored. Tutee attitudes toward study, personal motivational levels, and individual achievement showed consistent improvement after enrollment in the tutoring programs of study.

DESCRIPTION OF THE RESEARCH PROGRAM

In light of the data from the pilot studies, the developers of the IIP skills program decided to continue to collect data as part of an ongoing action research project (see Figure AI.1). In addition to an expanded sample of students receiving individualized literacy tutoring, an adult peer tutoring group and a classroom control group were added to the original data set. Adult peer tutoring group subjects used the IIP curriculum materials, but the curriculum was modified for use by adults acting as nonspecialized peer tutors. These adult peer tutors were carefully trained to use the IIP diagnostic/remedial methods and were supervised in their daily work by a learning disabilities specialist. It should be noted that all adult peer tutoring was done on an individualized basis (one-to-one). The classroom control groups consisted of traditional classrooms of adults (15–20 students) instructed by a certified teacher. The IIP model was not used in the classroom control group instructional program, but these students were administered the same pre-/post-test measures used with the other two groups.

In addition to compiling pre- and post-test outcome results for all participants, employee, employer, and peer quantitative and qualitative evaluations of training outcomes are being systematically compiled. In addition, comparisons of the quantitative and qualitative evaluations across tutees, tutors, and employers are being made. Comparison of pre- and post-tutoring outcome results are being made across treatment conditions (individualized literacy training, adult peer tutoring, classroom control training), across time blocks (10–19 hours, 20–29 hours, 30–45 hours), and across types of tutoring interventions (academic, job-related, social-emotional) for all participants in the adult literacy tutoring programs.

At present, a quantitative and qualitative analysis of the existing data base is under way. Attention is being given to coding of the type of intervention (e.g., behavioral, cognitive) along with multiple outcome findings across treatment conditions and time blocks. A special attempt is being made to compare tutoring outcomes for adult subjects assigned to individual, adult peer tutoring group, and classroom control group training conditions. Finally, a careful examination of the results is being made, comparing the outcome results for tutees whose employer cooperated in the training treatment versus situations where the employer did not cooperate.

Figure AI.1
Overall Analytic Paradigm

	TREATMENT CONDITIONS					
	Xa1 Individualized Skills Tutoring Group		Xa2 Adult Peer Tutoring Group		Xa3 Classroom Control Group	
Ab1 Academic Xc1 Social-Emotional Xc2 Job-Related Xc3	Yb	Ya	Yb	Ya	Yb	Ya
Xb2 Academic Xc1 Social-Emotional Xc2 Job-Related Xc3	Yb	Ya	Yb	Ya	Yb	Ya
Xb3 Academic Xc1 Social-Emotional Xc2 Job-Related Xc3	Yb	Ya	Yb	Ya	Yb	Ya

Where: Independent variables:
— Treatment conditions Xa1, Xa2, Xa3.
— Time blocks Xb1, Xb2, Xb3.
— Type of intervention Xc1, Xc2, Xc3.

Dependent variables:
— Academic, social-emotional, and job-related pre- and post-test outcome measures.
— Triangulation of quantitative and qualitative tutee, tutor, employer, and peer evaluations of tutoring outcomes.

REFERENCES

Coleman, J. S.; Campbell, E. Q.; Hobson, C. J.; McPartland, J.; Mood, A. M.; Winfeid, F. D.; & York, R. L. 1966. *Equality of Educational Opportunity*. Washington, DC: U. S. Government Printing Office.

Spady, W. G.; & Marshall, K. J. 1991. Beyond traditional outcome-based education. *Educational Leadership* 49 (2):67–72.

Walberg, H. J. 1984. Improving the productivity of America's schools. *Educational Leadership* 41 (8):19–30.

Appendix II

Use of Pre- and Post-Test Data in the IIP

Of what use are pre- and post-test data? As noted in Chapter 8, both norm-referenced and criterion-referenced tests have their places in learner assessment. It is important to know how training programs can use test data to inform instructional decision making and program design.

In this appendix, we will share three examples of how we have used both norm-referenced and criterion-referenced test data in the IIP. We will look at (1) the use of criterion-referenced data and task analysis reporting, and (2) the use of norm-referenced test data and statistical analysis.

USING CRITERION-REFERENCED DATA AND TASK ANALYSIS REPORTING

Because criterion-referenced tests cover specific skills, test data retrieved from such tests are most useful when reported with regard to what increased performance in specific skills means. For example, a common way of reporting increased reading skills is through grade-level equivalents. But what does it mean to "gain a year" in reading skills?

In a forty-hour basic reading skills improvement program at Clorox Company, participants ranged in pre-test performance from a nonreader to early fourth-grade reading skills. Pre- and post-test raw score distribution on a twenty-eight-item test of reading comprehension illustrates this initial range of performance (see Figure AII.1).

Raw-score distribution, listed in rank order of initial performance, provides a convenient way of seeing increases in performance in a simple, straightforward reporting format. The reporting of mean (M) performance allows us to see how much better or worse participants did in relation to the mean (or average) performance of a sample group. In this case, six of the eight participants ranked better than the mean in post-test performance. In general, participants were

Figure AII.1
Raw Score Distribution

Pre-test		Post-test	
22		23	
22		22	
19		27	
18		25	
13		24	
12		15	
11		24	
0	M=14.6	10	M=21.5

learning reading comprehension skills. Still, such raw-score, or even percentile-score, distributions do not tell us much more than general trends.

If we look at grade-equivalent distribution around mastery of a specific skill, in this case comprehension of factual detail, we get more information (see Figure AII.2).

Figure AII.2
Grade-Equivalent Distribution

Pre-test	Post-test
4.1	5.1
4.1	5.1
4.1	5.1
4.1	5.1
3.1	4.1
2.1	3.1
3.1	4.1
nonreader	1.5

What these grade equivalents tell us is that all participants gained at least one year in reading performance with forty hours of IIP instruction in comprehending factual details. What does this gain mean? (See Figure AII.3) Most technical training manuals are written for at least a sixth-grade reading level; 73 million people today cannot read at this level. Gaining a year's reading performance means significant changes in reading skills. If we look

Figure AII.3
IIP Critical Skills Needed for Mastery of Fifth-Grade Reading Performance

<u>1st Grade</u>

In one-syllable words:
    Recognizes initial and ending consonants
    Decodes by single letters and whole-word meanings
    Implies meaning
    Classifies information through comparison and contrast with
      what is known

<u>2nd Grade</u>

Recognizes final consonant
Recognizes long and short vowels
Recognizes two-letter blends (e.g., bl, cl)
Comprehends through single word meaning
Uses context clues

<u>3rd Grade</u>

Recognizes 3-letter consonant blends (e.g., thr) and digraphs (e.g., sh, th)
Recognizes vowel controllers (e.g., awe, fur), digraphs (e.g., ai,
    ea), and diphthongs (e.g., oi, ou)
Recognizes silent letters
Recognizes accent and syllable patterns
Comprehends cause- and effect-relationships
Recalls details
Recalls character traits
Reinforces new vocabulary
Locates information

<u>4th Grade</u>

Decodes words by prefix, suffix, and syllable patterns
Recognizes main idea
Predicts outcomes
Infers sequence of events
Comprehends through sentence meaning

<u>5th Grade</u>

Decodes words by root-word patterns
Recognizes pronouns
Recognizes verb variations
Recognizes main idea and supporting details
Recognizes description
Recognizes misplaced events in sequence
Recognizes fact and fiction
Interprets simple summaries and follows directions

closely at Figure AII.3, we can see several specific skills emerging with increased performance:

1. Increased capacity to see and understand patterns and differences in words and sentences

2. Increased capacity to make inferences from facts and to recognize differences in literal versus implied meanings

3. Greater ability to process multiple sources of information

4. Greater capacity to sort, sequence, and define steps in a process or event

5. Greater capacity to decode independently what printed text means

6. Greater capacity to determine what the meaning of printed text implies for tasks or decision making (i.e., translating what printed text requires one to do).

As we look at the increased IIP critical-skill performance from grade to grade, it becomes clearer what we mean by gaining a year in reading performance. In addition, attention to the specific skills yet to be mastered if our standard of performance is mastery of fifth-grade reading skills, provides important information regarding where an individual learner needs more or less work on a specific skill or set of skills. With this kind of information, we can make program or instructional changes to best address learner needs.

USING NORM-REFERENCED TEST DATA AND DISTRIBUTION OF MEANS

As noted in Chapter 8, what norm-referenced tests tell us is what any given group of learners knows in general. Looking at the distribution of individual performances around a group mean lets us see how well individual learners are doing in general in relation to a group's average performance. If a norm-referenced test is used pre- and post-training or instruction, the data tell us if our program has made a difference in the most general sense. Unlike criterion-referenced test data, norm-referenced data do not inform decision making for specific learner remediation or challenge.

Let us look at a distribution of percentile scores for a group of thirteen secretarial students taking an IIP basic skills program in reading comprehension at Fox College (see Figure AII.4). Percentage distributions, like raw-score distributions, provide a simple way of seeing gains in performance. Again, the

Figure AII.4
Percentage Distribution

Pre-test		Post-test	
88		90	
86		91	
86		87	
86		86	
80		90	
76		82	
72		95	
72		86	
72		86	
64		72	
62		64	
57		64	
51	M=75.2	68	M=80.8

reporting of means allows us to see how much better or worse participants did in relation to the group's mean (or average) performance. In this case 9 of 13 participants performed better than the mean on post-test performance. In general, these participants are learning reading comprehension.

Again, unlike criterion-referenced tests, which enable us to diagnose individual needs in skills performance, norm-referenced data only enable us to gain a general picture of what learners know in an area such as reading comprehension. Such data let us see if our training group "learned" reading comprehension, but it does not let us make specific program or instructional decisions for individual learners.

USING STATISTICAL ANALYSIS OF NORM-REFERENCED DATA

We can use several statistical methods with norm-referenced data to determine whether students are learning what we intend them to learn. Let us look at a sample of forty-five adult learners in an IIP basic skills reading program. We can use standard deviation to indicate the amount of variance around a sample mean; this allows us to determine, for example, if any one subgroup of learners is realizing greater results than another.

Let us say we have designed an IIP basic skills tutoring program in reading, and we have varied the amount of time spent in tutoring within the sample because the employer is trying to find out how much time is most effective for maximum gain. Some learners in the program will receive ten to nineteen hours of tutoring;

others twenty to twenty-nine hours; and yet others thirty to forty-five hours. Does the amount of time in tutoring make a difference?

A simple pre- and post-test table of means and standard deviations suggests that the amount of time does make a difference (see Figure AII.5). An examination of the data indicates that the greatest variance around the population mean is in Group 2 (20–29 hours of tutoring). The post-test means Group 1 (51.6) and Group 3 (51.8) were below the population mean (52.6), while the post-test mean for Group 2 (53.8) was above the population mean.

Regression analysis allows us to examine separate effects, if any, on post-test performance across number of hours of tutoring. Because of the small sample size (N=45), we interpret the results of a regression analysis conservatively. A summary of the regression results (see Figure AII.6) shows that the significance of the variables in the regression equation (Beta weights) indicates Group 3 (30–45 hours of tutoring) is significant at the .04 level. It would appear that extended hours of IIP tutoring influence post-test performance.

Why is this of interest? P. A. Cohen et al. (1982) meta-analysis of studies related to the effects of tutoring indicated an initially high rate of success in a relatively short time. These initial gains appeared to diminish over time. However, the IIP data tend to demonstrate smaller initial gains, with increased post-test performance over increased number of hours of tutoring. Maximum grade-level improvement appears to occur from the thirtieth to the fortieth hour of instruction. This information enables us to recommend forty-hour time blocks of instruction to this employer.

SUMMARY

Generally, we tend too often in training and educational programs to be data rich and information poor. In other words, we often collect data in helter-skelter ways and do not take, or make, the time to interpret what we collect. It is important for sound program and instructional decision making that we know what we can learn from various types of data, how to interpret the figures we gather, and how to use such data for specific kinds of decision making. It is also important that data be collected systematically over time, so that we are making decisions not on one-shot events but rather on accumulated measurements of group and individual performance that capture growth throughout a training or educational program. In Appendix III we will examine another kind of data, curriculum-based measurements associated with the MIDP.

Figure AII.5
Means and Standard Deviations

	Pre-test		Post-test	
	Mean	S.D.	Mean	S.D.
Group 1 (10–19 hours)	44.7	11.4	51.6	16.8
Group 2 (20–29 hours)	48.9	24.3	53.8	23.9
Group 3 (30–45 hours)	48.6	27.7	51.8	22.8
Total population	47.6	21.9	52.6	21.3

Figure AII.6
Regression Results

Variable	Beta	Significant F
10–19 hours	.095969	.7497
20–29 hours	.243559	.3409
30–45 hours	.495769	.0410

REFERENCE

Cohen, P. A.; Kulik, J. A.; & Kulik, C. C. 1982. Educational outcomes of tutoring: A meta-analysis of findings. *American Educational Research Journal* 19 (2):237–48.

Appendix III

Use of Curriculum-Based Measurements in the MIDP

Because of the concerns educators and trainers have with the mismatch between the content of norm-referenced, and sometimes criterion-referenced, tests and the curricula of training or instructional programs, attention is being directed toward curriculum-based measurements (CBMs). CBMs use the actual curriculum provided in an educational or training setting as the basis for tracking learner performance.

In this appendix, we will share a CBM sequence used in an MIDP for effective commmunications with a work team. We will examine (1) designing a CBM, (2) scoring CBMs and establishing goal lines, and (3) engaging learners in self-assessment.

DESIGNING A CBM

Before designing a CBM task, we have to know what outcomes we expect of a learner as a result of a specific training or educational program. In the effective communication with a work team MIDP, participants were expected to master seven key skills:

1. Opening a meeting with warmth and a statement of mutual support
2. Stating one's view of the situation, based upon specific, descriptive behaviors
3. Getting the team members' point of view
4. Asking for feedback on solutions
5. Agreeing upon a solution with team members
6. Agreeing upon a plan of action with team members
7. Agreeing on follow-up.

We then created a task or a series of tasks that represents the outcomes the learner is expected to demonstrate. We keep the task simple and focused enough to take about five minutes to do. For example,

> You have a claim representative who was actively recruited because of his expertise and "can-do" attitude. It has been six months, and you are preparing your first coaching session. Some of the other reps have commented on some difficulties working with this person. A few even questions his ability to handle some critical files he's been assigned to. He's been cooperative and pleasant with you. How and what would you prepare for this meeting? How would you conduct this session?

We give participants five minutes to design a written plan for the meeting, including content (what would be discussed and what materials would be used in the meeting) and process (how the meeting would actually be conducted). On each day of the training we would give a similar assessment. Each assessment would be a variation on the same key skills we would expect participants to master during training. The assessment would be part of the training activities, so that it didn't have the feel of a "test," but rather appeared to be just another training exercise. We would keep a portolio of completed assessment on each participant.

SCORING CBMS AND ESTABLISHING A GOAL LINE

Scoring CBMs is relatively easy. In this case, each of the skills we expect to see learners demonstrate is worth one point; the top score would 7; the lowest score a 1, or 0 for nonresponse. A performance scale that can guide a learner's assessment of strengths or weaknesses is then created. In this case,

7   Learner has superior feedback/communication skills
5-6 Learner has strong feedback/communication skills
3-4 Learner has moderate feedback/communication skills
2-1 Learner has weak feedback/communication skills
0   Learner did not respond to the scenario.

A goal line, or optimal performance target, can be determined by using the average of participants' performances on two baseline scenarios and extending the score as a target for improvement. For example, consider the following baseline performances of ten participants in the effective communications with a work team MIDP. A target for improvement might be the accumulation of the means (average scores) of the two baseline scores (i.e., 4):

	Baseline 1	Baseline 2
Learner A	0	1
Learner B	1	2
Learner C	1	2.5

Learner D	1	2.5
Learner E	2	2.5
Learner F	2	3
Learner G	2.5	3
Learner H	2.5	3
Learner I	2.5	3
Learner J	3	3

Mean = 1.75   Mean = 2.5   Target = 4

Scores on individual CBMs can be graphed across measurements to visually demonstrate a learner's progress toward mastery. With a goal line of 4, the ten participants in this MIDP program can be "measured" against this goal line.

	CBM1	CBM2	CBM3
Learner A	1.0	1.0	2.0
Learner B	3.0	4.5	6.0
Learner C	3.0	3.0	5.0
Learner D	2.0	3.0	6.0
Learner E	4.0	4.0	7.0
Learner F	2.0	3.0	5.0
Learner G	3.0	3.0	6.0
Learner H	4.0	5.0	7.0
Learner I	2.5	3.0	5.0
Learner J	4.0	6.0	7.0

Individual participants' progress toward a goal line is more easily seen in the bar graph representations of their CBM scores (see Figure AIII.1) If later training were to be provided to refine skills, a new goal line might be established based upon the average performance on CBM3 (in this case 5.6). The increase in goal line from the first to second training session is a good indicator of the anticipated effects of training. Participants' performance in the second training session around the new goal line would establish the long-term effects of a training program.

Figure AIII.1
Graphed Progress of MIDP Participants

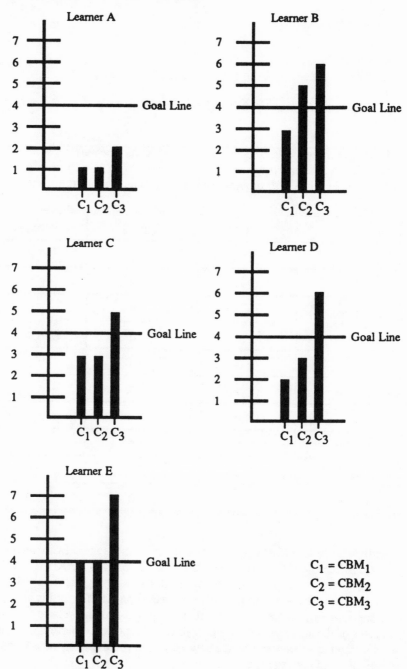

$C_1 = CBM_1$
$C_2 = CBM_2$
$C_3 = CBM_3$

Figure AIII.1 Continued
Graphed Progress of MIDP Participants

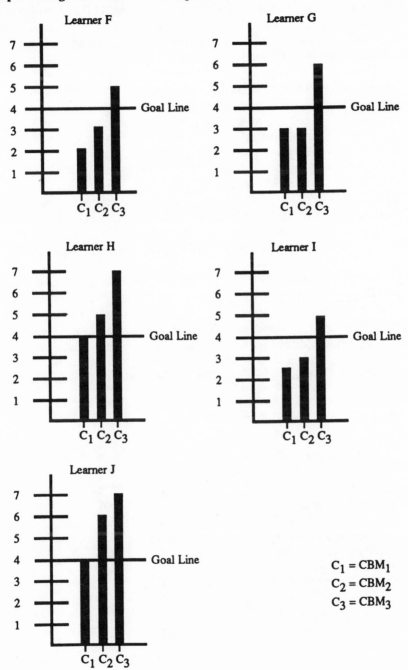

$C_1 = CBM_1$
$C_2 = CBM_2$
$C_3 = CBM_3$

ENGAGING LEARNERS IN SELF-ASSESSMENT

Accompanying the CBMs, we like to use both a goal-setting exercise and an effectiveness profile. Both of these activities enable trainers and participants to look at progress toward self-imposed goals. For example, let us look at the goals set by the ten participants in this MIDP:

Learner A — To be more patient with people and their problems
Learner B — To deal better with difficult situations
Learner C — To be more effective in communicating with upper management
Learner D — To provide more specific feedback to my group
Learner E — To provide clearer communication to my group
Learner F — To provide clearer communication to my group
Learner G — To be more patient with people and their problems
Learner H — To deal effectively with negative employees
Learner I — To provide more specific feedback to my group
Learner J — To increase my self-confidence in communication situations.

If we take these learner-identified goals, together with the outcomes to be mastered for the program, we can design an efficacy measure (see Figure AIII.2) specifically for this MIDP. A pre- and post-training efficacy measure enables us to monitor changes in learners' beliefs that they can, with the skills they have, communicate effectively. We can look at the same data in a number of ways. First, we can look at an individual learner's responses on each item to measure pre- and post-training growth. For example, let us look at a profile of Learner E.

Item	Pre-	Post-
1. Warmth and mutual support	2.8	4.0
2. Specific goals	3.8	4.5
3. Participation solicited	3.0	3.8
4. Active listening practiced	3.6	4.6
5. Two-way communication	2.8	3.6
6. Problem mutually defined	3.4	4.0
7. Flexibility in generating solutions	2.8	3.8
8. Solutions mutually defined	3.0	3.8
9. Positive attitudes toward difference	3.0	4.6
10. Commitment to specific action plan	3.6	4.5
11. Mutual control over outcomes	3.4	4.8
12. Agreed-upon follow-up	3.6	5.0

1.3

Curriculum-Based Measurements

actors must be taken into consideration to assure useful performance-
urements:

t tasks for the measurements that will represent tasks the adult
er is expected to perform in class training sessions. Such tasks can
ken directly from sample curriculum materials being used in the
'training sessions.

rmance-based measures are timed. Keep the measurement short —
ourpose of curriculum-based measurements is to track learner
rmance in multiple tasks over time. Five minutes would be a
mum measurement time.

rmance-based measurements are most useful when they are given
ently (e.g., every other day, every week, or every two weeks,
iding upon the length of the class/training sessions). Useful
urement occurs when the measurement task looks and functions like
other class/training session task. In other words, learners should not
hey are taking a test.

rmance-based measurements should be normed. Give the same
urement to a sample of five–ten learners identified by teacher or
oyer as average peers of the learner or as top-rated performers if the
er or employer wants to compare the learner's performance with
ially desired performance. The performance of this sample of
ten average or optimal learners sets the baseline for comparison of
earner's performance against the "norm."

most effective way to represent learner growth is to do so
iically. On a sheet of graph paper, record the "norm" in one color.
plot the learner's performance over time in another color.

"performance-based measurement" sounds more complicated than
iothing more than a task taken from the curriculum, except that the
ormed frequently, learner performance is tracked systematically, and
formance is compared with a "norm" of average or optimal
e on the same task.

Figure AIII.2
Effective Communication Competency Measure

<u>Directions:</u> Indicate your level of comfort on each item by circling the
appropriate response (5=high; 1=low).

1. Meeting was opened with warmth   1   2   3   4   5
   and a statement of mutual support.

2. Specific, descriptive meeting goals   1   2   3   4   5
   and objectives were defined.

3. Participation of group members was   1   2   3   4   5
   solicited.

4. Active listening was practical.   1   2   3   4   5

5. Two-way communcation was practiced.   1   2   3   4   5

6. The problem was mutually defined.   1   2   3   4   5

7. Flexibility was practiced in generating   1   2   3   4   5
   solutions.

8. Problem solutions were mutually   1   2   3   4   5
   agreed upon.

9. Positive attitudes toward differences   1   2   3   4   5
   of ideas were demonstrated.

10. Commitment to a specific plan of   1   2   3   4   5
    action was established.

11. Mutual control over outcomes was   1   2   3   4   5
    established.

12. Follow-up was agreed upon.   1   2   3   4   5

We might also place the individuals into artificial work teams to complete authentic problem-solving tasks. We can compare comfort-level measures across teams for each item on the inventory. For example, we assigned learners A, D, and G to Team A; learners B, E, and H to Team B; and learner C, F, I and J to Team C. Pre- and post-test team responses to the efficacy measure are shown below.

Item		Team A		Team B		Team C	
		PRE	POST	PRE	POST	PRE	POST
1.	Warmth/support	2.8	4.0	3.8	4.0	4.4	5.0
2.	Defined goals	3.8	4.2	3.6	4.0	3.4	4.3
3.	Participation	3.0	3.6	4.2	4.2	3.8	4.8
4.	Active listening	3.6	3.6	4.0	4.0	4.0	4.8
5.	Two-way communication	2.8	3.6	4.0	4.3	4.2	4.8
6.	Mutually defined problem	3.0	3.6	3.4	4.0	3.6	3.5
7.	Flexible solutions	2.8	3.6	3.8	4.0	3.8	4.5
8.	Mutual solutions	3.0	3.6	3.4	4.0	3.6	3.5
9.	Positive attitude	3.0	3.6	4.2	4.5	3.8	4.5
10.	Action plan	3.6	4.0	3.8	4.5	4.4	4.8
11.	Mutual control	3.4	3.4	3.8	4.2	2.6	3.3
12.	Follow-up	3.8	3.6	4.4	4.2	3.2	3.0

We can also look for the mean (or average) efficacy level for each learner with regard to the items on the inventory taken as a whole.

	PRE	POST
Learner A	3.2	3.2
Learner B	3.2	4.1
Learner C	3.0	4.1
Learner D	3.5	4.3
Learner E	3.7	4.4
Learner F	3.7	4.1
Learner G	4.2	4.8
Learner H	4.4	5.0
Learner I	4.2	4.8
Learner J	3.9	5.0

All of these ways of looking at the perfo indicate that learners appear to be learning the training program.

SUMMARY

CBMs use the general curriculum provid as the basis for tracking learner performa measurement procedures that can be used

Trainers need to seriously consider u produce a more credible and accurate pictu because they are based on your local train CBM test has great content validity. Sinc employees, you will be able to facilitate employees. For example, in future effec another ten or more employees can be m comparing this peer data of current and pas trainer a general estimate of "typical" lear communication training classes.

A final strength of the CBM is instead post- test results, CBMs compare a traine i.e., during each phase of the training cou advantage of seeing if each person underst course of training and to modify instructi individual employee's understanding of a

The primary advantage of CBMs is tha behaviors they are expected to perform or that employee performance can be graphic

Trainers need to consider the five CB Figure AIII.3 when preparing a training p

Figure A
Designing

Several
based mea

1. Sele
   lear
   be
   clas

2. Per
   the
   per
   max

3. Per
   freq
   dep
   mea
   any
   feel

4. Per
   mea
   emp
   teac
   opti
   five
   the

5. The
   gra
   The

The ter
it is. It is
task is pe
learner p
performa

Appendix IV

Survey of Training Needs Assessment for Business

I. <u>Macro Training Assessment</u>

- What do employees need?
- What do they want?
- Where are they having problems?
- Where can we get the most impact for our development dollar?
- What are management priorities for employee growth and development?
- What are employee priorities? Why?
- Of all the possible areas toward which we might direct resources, which one holds the most promise for the organization and for individuals?

II. <u>Micro Training Assessment</u>

- What do employees need to know in order to make the sandwich or to operate the computer system?
- Of all the skills and knowledge that one might acquire regarding computers or the new appraisal system, which are essential to doing the job?
- Why is the "magical money-market account" not selling? Will training help?
- What other interventions might solve the problem or support the introduction of the new system?
- How do employees feel about the situation?
- They've already been trained on the topic. Why can't we see it in the field?

III. Work Force Education Task Force Assessment Method

Phase I: Target Productivity, Quality, or Production Problems to Work Force Skills

The task force must identify these programs at all job levels and operating sections. How are these issues driven by a need for improved basic skills?

1. Can you document these employee deficiencies?
2. What is the present cost to the business?
3. What is the future cost to the business?
4. Who composes the populations needing work force education?
5. How large is each group?
6. What are the skill levels required for each targeted job?
7. How will you gain union and employee participation in the new program?

Phase II: Prepare Work Force Education Program Alternatives

1. Select appropriate training-educational programs for each targeted group.
2. What specific skills are needed?
3. At what grade level are the skills needed?
4. Determine the appropriateness and efficiency of each program, beginning with the most remedial instructional services and ranging upward to self-based or computer-based training.
5. When appropriate, prepare a task analysis for selected jobs to complete the above planning.
6. Determine an evaluation system for each instructional program and a recordkeeping system.
7. Prepare a budget detailing typical alternatives at different company locations.

Phase III: Present Work Force Education Task Force Report to Senior Management

The report will point out specific operational problems and their related costs. You must present a clear, concise picture of past problems, present needs, and future workplace consequences. Your documentation must demonstrate how a work force education program will enhance corporate competitiveness and decrease operating costs. The plan presented must show broad participation of employees at all levels of the organization and probable costs. The report should include items such as the following:

1. Management: writing skills, foreign languages
2. Support staff: grammar training, shorthand, typing, word processing/ office software
3. Industrial shop: reading, math, ESL, grammar training, blueprint reading.

Phase IV: Gain Worker-Union Support for Work Force Education Program

In some instances, formal negotiations will be conducted with union representatives. Even if this is not necessary, informational sessions must be scheduled throughout the company to acquaint all employees with the work force education program. Participation should be voluntary in the initial implementation phase. At first, expect some employees to be reluctant to enroll. However, as fellow workers succeed in the program, others will begin to see this as a personal opportunity to ready themselves for the office or shop of the twenty-first century. Initial emphasis must be placed on the confidentiality of all programs. Job evaluations or promotions will not be tied to program test results. Less threatening evaluation procedures that are part of this program are available to accurately measure training results.

Phase V: Prepare the Work Force Education Curriculum

In preparing the curriculum, you should address the following questions:

1. What specific programs are to be offered at each company location?
2. Who will staff these programs?
3. Use in-house staff?
4. Use part-time staff?
5. Use external consultants?
6. Use local educational programs?
7. Where and when will the training be given?
8. Will it be offered on company or employee time?
9. What materials or equipment is required for each program?
10. A complete recordkeeping system and testing/evaluation procedures should be in place for each phase of the program.

Phase VI: Initiate Work Force Education Program

Attention must be directed to the following components:

1. Conduct train-the-trainer programs for company training staff.
2. Determine local program management.
3. Orient part-time or outside consultants to organization and program responsibilities.
4. A voluntary, trial program is a reasonable approach that will lessen employee stress and resistance, and acknowledge personal needs.

Phase VII: Ongoing Evaluation and Implementation

1. How do supervisors rate participating employees' job performance before, during, and six months after their enrollment in the program?
2. What local program modifications will be made, based on instructors' and supervisors' evaluations?

Twelve months after the program has begun, a company can begin to consider the permanent incorporation of the work force education program into the training and development department. A key factor in making this decision will be a report to senior management on how the program has begun to reduce the organizational problems documented earlier by the task force. Discounting outside economic factors, operational costs will begin decreasing as quality improves and productivity increases.

IV. Management Training Assessment Agenda

Step One — Decide to plan by using data from a needs assessment.

Step Two — Select the needs assessment and planning level: middle, comprehensive, or strategic.

- **Middle**. At this level there is a concern for organizational resources, the procedures and methods to be employed in organizational activities, and the immediate results accomplished. An example might be improving competence of bank tellers or drug abuse intake specialists.

- **Comprehensive**. This level combines the middle-level concerns with the products or services an organization can or does deliver to its clients. An example of this level in action is bank teller competence combined with a new client oriented savings plan, estate planning materials, and competent bank sales personnel.

- **Strategic**. This level combines the concerns of the comprehensive level with a consideration of how useful the organization's contributions (or outcomes) are to its clients and to the world in which its contributions must function. The combination of this training and an attractive bonus plan should increase the number of new clients, retain the existing ones, and help clients become self-sufficient.

Step Three — Identify the needs assessment and planning partners

- Those who will be affected by the results
- Those who will implement the plan
- Clients or society that will receive the results.

Step Four — Obtain the planning partners' participation.

Step Five — Obtain acceptance of the needs assessment and planning level.

Step Six — Collect both internal and external needs data.

Step Seven — List identified and documented needs.

Step Eight — Place needs in priority order.

Step Nine — Reconcile disagreements.

Step Ten — List problems to be resolved and obtain agreement of partners.

V. Cost Justification/Improving the Bottom Line

Cost justification issues that will indicate the success of a company's education/training programs include the following applications.

1. Decreased hiring costs. Before the program, how many interviews were conducted to fill a vacant job? How much did this personnel process cost your company? What are the current hiring standards (i.e., interviews to hires)?

2. Decreased training costs. Even if your company offered a new employee little, if any, new formal job training, information on the job (OJT) had to be given to every new hire. Since the work force education program initiated, can you document:

    a. A reduction in the turnover of new hires?

    b. A decrease in OJT time spent with a new hire?

3. Employee accidents on the job can result from a failure to read or understand work rules or equipment operations. How many accidents have been reported over the twelve months since the work force education program began? Does this represent a decline compared with the previous year? How much cost was reduced because of fewer sick days? Lower workers' insurance claims?

4. Incremental employee costs versus services or products sold is a key company indicator. By your normal measures of employee productivity, the work force education program should document increased operational efficiencies, such as:

    a. Fewer employee work errors

    b. Less time spent by supervisors answering basic questions

    c. Higher production levels

    d. Better employee troubleshooting abilities

    e. Overall, more employee interest in job advancement

    f. More employee suggestions of practical, new solutions to job-related production concerns.

All of these factors add up to increased competitiveness, small operating margins, and profitability. They are the realistic bottom line for work force education.

5. What new equipment or work procedures have been introduced because of the employees' increased educational abilities? Does this increase production or reduce operating costs?

All of the above cost justification questions will accurately measure the success of work force education. To document many of these issues, you will need to survey shop stewards, first-line supervisors, or employee managers about short-term or long-term employee work changes they have observed. These surveys should be conducted immediately after the employee's training ends, six months later, or up to twelve months after class attendance. Human resource managers can feel comfortable conducting these potential cost-reduction surveys since industry has long purchased labor-saving equipment based on some of the same assumptions.

REFERENCES

Gordon, E. E.; Ponticell, J.; & Morgan, R. 1991. *Closing the Literacy Gap in American Business*. New York: Quorum Books.

Kaufman, R. 1987. A needs assessment primer. *Training and Development Journal* 41 (10):78–83.

Rossett, A. 1989. Assess for Success. *Training & Development Journal* 43 (5):55–59.

Appendix V

FutureWork Case Study

This FutureWork case study presents an alternative scenario to the closing of U.S. Steel's Chicago South Works in the early 1990s. The situation is reversed by the U.S. Steel board of directors and a major capital commitment is made to modernize the plant's equipment and the human capital of its work force.

What follows is a strategic plan that encompasses FutureWork's Work Force Education Triad of training, skills, and education. This plan is part of an overall effort to make this plant a profitable operation within five years. The authors wish to acknowledge the work of Anne Zimmerman, an employee of Xerox and a graduate student in the Adult Corporate Instructional Management program at Loyola University, Chicago, for her work in preparing this model case study.

CURRENT SITUATION

U.S. Steel South Works has been in existence since 1881. The complex became a major part of the surrounding community, providing jobs, stores, and hospitals. It even had its own telephone and postal services. For people in the community, U.S. Steel meant prosperity. They worked in the mill and lived near it. U.S. Steel was the heart of the neighborhood.

However, since the late 1970s, the steel industry has undergone some major economic changes. Foreign competition has eroded America's steel production market share and has forced many mills into bankruptcy. The South Works complex must either modernize to keep up with competition or close.

The old South Works complex has ceased to function as it did in it's prime. From a high of 20,000 employees to a factory on the brink of ruin, the complex has lost out to modernization, new supervisory practices, and a much less powerful labor union.

The board of directors has made a major commitment to modernize and refurbish the South Works plant with the clear understanding that if it is not profitable by the end of 1997, the plant will close. The company is about to begin a new strategy for manufacturing steel.

With the infusion of a large capital expenditure for state-of-the-art steel production equipment and other required resources to support this endeavor, the board has requested a proposal from Training and Development that will outline a strategic plan for the organization's work force training and education.

Currently, there are some issues that need to be recognized as influential factors in the overall view of the organization.

Inputs

Environmental
- Competition
- Installation of high-technology manufacturing equipment
- Capital investment for redesign of the organization
- Pressure to change organizational culture and update technology

Resources
- Semiskilled work force
- Long tenure, loyal, and committed work force
- Low employee morale
- Top management commitment to change program
- Complex has five years to become profitable

History
- Union pressure
- South Works complex *is* the community
- Union created nonunion competition
- Management reneged on proposal to build new rail mill after long negotiations with union, city, and state governments
- Employee buyout plan failed
- U.S. Steel was once the leader in steel industry
- Faces intense global competition
- Factory outdated and in need of modernization

Training
- OJT on as-needed basis
- Management development optional
- No generalized training

Informal Organization
- Poor communication between management and workers
- Poor morale
- Improved involvement between union and management
- Supervisors had "tough" attitude

- Culture was company, now company image is fading
- Noncognitive and noncreative

Task
- Assembly line
- No crosstraining/functioning
- Management nonparticipatory
- No teamwork

Formal Organization
- Overall management style directive/autocratic
- Functional areas work separately
- No teams
- No work groups
- Hierarchical

Individual
- Low- to semiskilled work force
- Poor attitude: "It's not my job"
- Rewards for individual effort
- No development of new skills

PROPOSAL

In order to make an educated recommendation, Training and Development needs to conduct an in-depth analysis of the entire organization. We will also need to examine the organizational environment to make sure that all elements of the organization are taken into consideration. This proposal will be a recommendation for a systematic transformation from the current way of performing to a plan that prepares the work force to operate and manage in a high-technology environment that fosters an environment for lifelong learning.

Therefore, there will be several steps necessary in order to know what to recommend and how to design a strategic plan for Training and Development over the next five years. This proposal will present a short-term and a long-term plan for implementation, and include the following steps as a basis for the evaluation. This plan will be based on the assumption that the board of directors has given complete approval and has allotted the time needed for a full investigation of the organization. An additional assumption is that the South Works complex has space available to be used as a training center and that a redesign of the space is under way. In addition, the assumption is being made that the company is aware of current management trends and would like to implement many of them as part of its overall strategy.

The recommendation will encompass the following categories:

- Needs Assessment — a systematic survey, questionnaire, and interview process designed to compare the current needs with the future needs of the company
- Organization Development — examining the whole organization, both the informal and the formal structures
- Management Development — a process for developing the skills of existing and future managers
- Assessment Issues — developing a process for evaluating training
- Work Force Education — education designed to increase the basic skills of the work force
- Quality — process that leads to greater communication and problem solving by the worker, increases productivity and decreases waste
- Other training/education needs.

Currently, there are no training programs in place. The available training is on the job, on an as-needed basis. The goals and objectives of Training & Development are to ignite the motivation and interest in learning. The outcome will be a new generation of ideas that will foster change. The thinking of the management must shift from controlling to monitoring and facilitating. Therefore, Training and Development first needs to determine what is needed and by whom.

Employee development is a collaboration among employees, managers/ supervisors, and the training department. The purpose of employee development is to encourage learning and individual growth. The end result will be employees who continue to operate at a high skill level and who have the opportunity for career development.

This represents an ideal world without interruptions. It is difficult to predict with accuracy the unexpected training needs that may occur. Therefore, this is a general plan for educating and developing the organization. A needs assessment is the most efficient method of determining the immediate needs of the individuals and will enable them to become productive and efficient as the company moves toward modernization.

NEEDS ASSESSMENT

An ongoing evaluation of skills and the effectiveness of training is critical to the success of this plan. With such a large project and a limited time frame, we will need to know how effective training is in relation to the organizational strategic plan. Key training and educational assessment interviews will be held throughout the plant with top-level and mid-level managers, supervisors, foremen, plant personnel, union representatives, office support workers, security guards, and others. Focus groups made up of these individuals will be used to supplement this information.

This evaluation will target productivity, quality, and production. These results, monitored by management, will be a useful tool for training. In addition, we will utilize surveys immediately following training sessions. For longer-term skills-transfer assessment, we will interview trainees and their bosses six months later.

The objective is to be able to distinguish training that works from training that does not. Through systematic, ongoing evaluation, we will be able to make that judgment.

In addition, we will want to assess the effectiveness of management training. One way is to use an employee satisfaction measurement that rates the manager on skills ranging from use of quality tools to listening and understanding employees.

Finally, a data base will be set up to maintain individual attendance records. This can also be used to establish an employee development system that has been agreed upon by the managers and will target specific classes for individuals.

IMMEDIATE TRAINING NEEDS

We are operating under a five-year maximum time frame, which is a very short time to train the entire organization on technical skills, and management philosophies, and to restructure the thinking of the South Works complex. Based on the needs analysis, we will prioritize the most important areas for immediate training.

The assumption is that the entire work force will need to be trained in the operation and maintenance of the new equipment. We will be able to get assistance from the manufacturer; this will be an ongoing program for retraining present workers and training new hires.

Instructional design is a critical element of any training and development department. In order to design curriculum well, there must be a realistic time frame. Instructional design is very time-consuming and requires a great deal of skill. Therefore, the instructional design, at least in the short term, will be performed by outside subject-area experts working with the training department.

Over the long term, the entire organization, starting with senior management, will be trained in applying the new technology and changing management concepts. That includes operating and maintaining the equipment, competency in using PCs and applying software, interpreting reports, and using computers for greater efficiency in all areas of the job. Therefore, technical training will need to be fully developed on software that is used every day, and curricula for new software programs need to be developed as they are introduced into the organization.

In the final analysis, the strategic plan for training and development will encompass the Work Force Triad of: skills (writing, reading, ESL, math, foreign languages); training (basic management, supervision, service, and production); education (quality, work teams, problem solving, thinking, technical training, and professional education) (see Figure 10.4).

Training

Organizational Development

The most effective way to change behavior is to put people into a new organizational context that imposes new roles, responsibilities, and relationships on them. It forces new attitudes and behavior. At the South Works complex, a climate of low morale and poor attitudes exists.

There are three components to changing and revitalizing an organization.

Coordination. When quality, costs, and product development are an issue, as they are at South Works, the emphasis needs to be on educating the work force in working together. Departments, individuals, labor, and management need to work as teams to limit the duplication of work and effort.

Teamwork. As with coordination, everyone needs to work toward a common goal that should be aligned with the organizational goals and objectives. Teams may be composed of work groups, task groups, natural work groups, integrated teams, and short-term and long-term teams. Teamwork allows the workers to feel empowered. They feel ownership of and responsibility for their work. Teamwork also provides a natural influence on the workers to conform to the norms and performance standards established by the group. The research on teams shows that individuals feel better about themselves, increase their productivity, feel better about work, and have a sense of pride and accomplishment. The organization benefits by having more satisfied employees and improved productivity, fewer errors and redos, and increased profits.

Commitment. This requires new competencies: knowledge of the business and industry as a whole, analytical skills, and interpersonal skills. The focus is on the identification and solution of problems.

It is critical that the organization begin viewing itself as a whole and not as a sum of its parts. Each area of the company needs to work together to streamline activities and to keep the focus on the business goals and objectives. Training needs to address the higher-order thinking skills that are required when working from a "big picture" perspective. They include problem-solving and interpersonal communication skills training, decision making, quality, and teams. Then we can concentrate on further analytical skills development.

This type of training should be an ongoing process. People cannot make the shift in thinking overnight. Over the course of the next five years, we should begin with top management, focusing on problem solving and communication. They will set the tone for the adoption of new skills. We can then begin phasing in team concepts and fine-tune team building and processes.

Management Development

Since there has been no formal management development program, one needs to be established. The emphasis will be on improving the skills necessary for present and future managers. Management development will be ongoing and carefully evaluated.

Managers and supervisors need skill development in interpersonal communication, problem solving, managing work force diversity, and team building. There is a great need for managers to learn how to coach workers and facilitate teamwork.

Today's business environment is characterized by intense competition and new technology that constantly changes. The attributes a manager must possess are flexibility, acting as a change agent, thinking abilities, and a desire for continuous learning.

Managers need to shift their focus to thinking instead of reacting. This is a major adjustment from their current behavioral management style. Cognitive skills include analyzing, decision making and problem solving. These skills require a higher order of skill and competence.

Skills

Work Force Education

Work force education is broad-based training that allows the worker to make decisions, leading to greater self-esteem and job satisfaction. The more a worker knows about technology, the business environment, and changing conditions, the greater the opportunity for advancement. Some of the high-technology areas are telecommunications, computer systems, and electronics.

Senior management has traditionally overlooked developing a strategy that addresses these issues. Today's pool of available workers is uneducated in the skill areas businesses need in order to function in a rapidly changing world. Because our educational system does not meet the needs of business, businesses must educate the work force in the skills that are required.

Illiteracy among all available workers is growing at an alarming rate. Illiteracy translates into higher operating costs for business, such as higher waste, increased accidents, lower productivity, and lower morale. When workers have difficulty reading instructions or communications from management, learning new technology, and performing basic math and other skills, they will have difficulty performing well. Not only individuals suffer, but the company has a work force that cannot keep up with changing technology.

Therefore, it is recommended that U.S. Steel begin a work force education program that will meet worker job needs through testing and skills education. The program will consist of math, English, English as a second language, reading, and writing. This program will need to be marketed as an opportunity for individual growth. The largest obstacle is employee fear and shame. These classes are designed to allow adults to build on their experience and knowledge in other areas.

Work force education is a large undertaking that should be ongoing and constantly reviewed for attendance and interest. This is a program that can take years to implement; therefore, the recommendation is to hire part-time trainers to perform the needs assessment, design, and implementation of these classes. The training department will be involved in monitoring these consultants' activities and tying in this program to overall employee development.

Initially, the recommendation would be to have a task force composed of workers, supervisors, managers, and union representatives work with these trainers in developing the U.S. Steel work force education program at South Works. This process will gain acceptance and involvement in the program by a cross section of stake holders that will help overcome some of the resistance by the people who most need the education.

Education

Quality

Finally, it is the recommendation that U.S. Steel South Works complex convert to participative management and teamwork. This is the core of quality programs. Teams are the management process of the most dynamic organizations. They react quickly to change, the individual is accountable to teammates as well as the manager, and they have proven to motivate workers and improve levels of employee satisfaction, which is a current problem.

When teams are part of an overall employee involvement program, each employee's goals are tied to the team's and each member is appraised according to his or her contribution to the team. Research has shown that when team workers possess the skills to perform any task in the production process, the company benefits from increased flexibility and adaptability to change, the potential for a flatter organization, higher-quality output, decreased absenteeism, lower error and redo rates, and greater long-term productivity.

Quality processes and teams require much training and time for implementation. Converting an organization that has been as static as the South Works complex, takes commitment, cooperation, and a shared vision. Each individual needs to be trained as soon as possible. However, the quality conversion is long-term in nature. People cannot convert their thinking to teamwork overnight. There are some training programs that will help facilitate the process.

- Gaining total organizational commitment

- Personal and company awareness
- Workers, managers, and supervisors sharing a common vision
- Encourage employee empowerment
- Individual self-awareness
- Consensus building
- Establishing a vision for each work team
- Interpersonal skills
- Coordinating efforts and fostering team commitment
- Sharing knowledge and information
- Implementing and inventing performance strategies.

The task of guiding an entire organization through this change process can be overwhelming. Training and Development will play a key role. Our primary goal is to educate the entire work force on what is happening, what they can expect, and how they will perform in their new roles. Faced with intense competition and the prospect of this operation closing in five years, a drastic change in the structure and operation of the organization must take place. Initially, Training and Development must be the change agents (see Figure AV.1).

For the long term our goals are the following:

1. Continuously evaluate and design new training.

2. Continue using design teams and task forces to assist training and to propose relevant training programs (cross-functional teams).

3. Design refresher programs so training will be reinforced and ongoing.

4. Teach managers/supervisors to function as coaches.

5. Teach the collaborative model for use by all teams within the plant.

6. Emphasize team building, problem solving, and critical thinking.

7. Have the entire organization trained in quality by the end of year 3.

8. Phase in additional management development courses in rewarding teams, linking performance to strategic plan, succession planning.

9. Test new hires and existing employees for basic skill levels.

10. Implement work force education program in cooperation with local community college.

Figure AV.1
FutureWork Short-Term/Long-Term
Work Force Education Strategy

	STEPS	TIME FRAME	METHOD
1.	Organizational Goals/Objectives	Immediate	1. Design mission & vision statement for Training and Development that corresponds to organization mission & vision
2.	Needs Analysis	Immediate	1. Training needs survey a. Ask workers what knowledge or skills are needed to perform their job b. Prioritize skills 2. Competency survey a. Ask key people what competencies are needed by workers to reach competency b. Determine knowledge & skills required to reach competency level c. Prioritize skills
		Immediate	3. Task analysis survey a. What are the required tasks needed to perform well? b. Determine knowledge & skills required to perform tasks
		Immediate	c. Prioritize tasks, skills, & knowledge
3.	Instructional Design	Immediate	1. Design general skills training for: a. production workers on new technology & equipment b. determine knowledge & skills required to perform tasks c. management on new technology & equipment
		Immediate	2. Supervisor training a. introduce new dynamic management concepts: monitoring & facilitating vs. directing
		Immediate	3. Implement skills training immediately
		Immediate - 6 Months	4. Select vendor to deliver PC software training 5. General business knowledge
4.	Management Development	Immediately begin interviewing consultants with prior knowledge of "managing for change"	1. Manager as coach 2. Interpersonal skills 3. Manager's role: clarification & view of work life
		Immediate	4. Decision-making skills
		Within 6 months to 1st year	5. Problem-solving skills 6. Team building

5. Organization Development	6 months to 1 year	1. Design & implement seminar for management. Purpose: define & select a management team to develop a program to introduce concepts, strategies & benefits to other management
	Within 1st year	2. Design mini-training courses for management emphasizing "thinking" vs. behavior skills
		3. Develop management skills training: utilization of human resources, facilitating change, managing conflict, improving organizational effectiveness & evaluating effectiveness of organization
	Begin immediately	4. Conduct Train-the-Trainer program for management
		5. OD training addressing work force diversity, strategic planning, decision-making and information systems, renewal systems and other external factors
6. Work Force Education	Assign task force with 1st 6 months	1. Facilitate task force to analyze productivity, quality, production, problems. Identify & prioritize areas of weakness
	Task force priorities	
		2. Begin development of Work Force Education program. Focus on inadequate skill & performance areas. Prioritize skill areas for training
	Objectives & interviews with vendors/ consultants	
		3. Have task force evaluate vendors that may provide work force education training: ESL, grammar, writing, reading.
	Test program on a department where results are easily measured (math test to accounting)	4. Select methodology for training
	1 year +	5. Begin implementing classes by 2nd quarter of year 2
7. Assessment Needs	Immediate	1. Immediate feedback: survey class attendees before they leave class
	Short-term & ongoing	2. Six-month follow-up by phone & survey trainees re: satisfaction with level of training classes
	Within 1st 6 months	3. Written open-ended questionnaire to trainee's manager or supervisor re: transfer of skills to job & satisfaction level with training
	6 months & ongoing	4. Follow up manager questionnaire with face-to-face interviews
	By end of year 1	5. Compile survey results & determine effectiveness of training
	Year 1 & ongoing	6. Eliminate programs that are irrelevant (inventory training programs)
a. Management Assessment	Short-term to long-term Ongoing	1. Conduct follow-up study on change in attitude & style of managers 6 months after training
		a. Change in organizational activities & immediate results
		b. Change in customer satisfaction level
		c. Strategic plan comprehension & results

	18 months & every year thereafter	2. Ratings of manager by employees
		3. Compile survey results to determine training programs that are successful
	Short-term & ongoing	4. One year to 3 years: measure management as team builder through team assessment
8. Quality	Immediate	1. Immediate: introduce concept & supporting data to upper management
	6 months to 1 year	2. Gain upper management's support
	6 months to 18 months	3. Use upper management as pilot training program
	Ongoing	4. Continuously monitor upper management feedback re: quality program
	18 months to 2 years	5. If upper management reacts favorably, present proposal for organizationwide quality program
		6. Recommend that upper management participate in quality program at Quality University
	2 years	7. Gain acceptance to become leaders & role models for quality
	2–3 years	8. Have management task force investigate quality training programs for purchase
	2½– 3½ years	9. Begin training middle managers & 1st-line supervisors
	3½ years +	10. After completing manager training, begin training remainder of work force
	Ongoing	11. Emphasize problem solving, team formation, working in teams, design of group tasks & norms, employee empowerment

Index

About the Authors

EDWARD E. GORDON is President of Imperial Corporate Training and Development and teaches at Loyola University in Chicago.

RONALD R. MORGAN is Associate Professor of Educational Psychology at Loyola University.

JUDITH A. PONTICELL is Assistant Professor at Texas Tech University.

They co-authored *Closing the Literacy Gap in the American Workplace* (Quorum Books, 1991).